A HISTORY OF FINLAND

T0333326

HENRIK MEINANDER

A History of Finland

Translated from the Swedish by
Tom Geddes

HURST & COMPANY, LONDON

First published in the United Kingdom in 2011 by
C. Hurst & Co. (Publishers) Ltd.,
41 Great Russell Street, London, WC1B 3PL
© Henrik Meinander, 2011
Revised and updated paperback edition published 2020.
Translation © Tom Geddes, 2011
First published as *Finlands historia* by Söderströms, Helsinki
All rights reserved
Printed in Great Britain by Bell and Bain Ltd, Glasgow

The right of Henrik Meinander to be identified as the author
of this publication is asserted by him in accordance with the
Copyright, Designs and Patents Act, 1988.

A Cataloguing-in-Publication data record for this book
is available from the British Library.

ISBN: 9781787380301

This book is printed using paper from registered sustainable
and managed sources.

www.hurstpublishers.com

TRANSLATOR'S NOTE

Finland has two official languages, Finnish and Swedish, the latter now spoken by about 5 per cent of the population. For historical reasons, in the first half of this book place names are given in their Swedish form, with the Finnish form in parenthesis on initial occurrence. In the latter half of the book, place names are usually rendered in their Finnish form. The exceptions here are Vyborg after 1721, a transliteration from the Russian of the former Viborg/Viipuri, and Helsinki, well established in English and internationally in its Finnish form and referred to thus throughout, but still called Helsingfors by Swedish-speakers.

For the sake of consistency, Swedish monarchs are named on the Swedish pattern, hence Queen Kristina and Gustav IV Adolf, not Christina and Gustavus Adolphus as was common in earlier English historiography. Russian and German rulers are given in their prevailing anglicised form, e.g. Tsar Nicholas, Frederick II.

The term "Baltic countries" (Swedish *Baltikum*) historically refers to the approximate area now comprising Estonia, Latvia and Lithuania; after the dissolution of the Soviet Union it refers precisely to those three countries.

CONTENTS

CONTENTS

CONTENTS

LIST OF ILLUSTRATIONS

LIST OF ILLUSTRATIONS

LIST OF ILLUSTRATIONS

LIST OF ILLUSTRATIONS

LIST OF ILLUSTRATIONS

PREFACE

Since it was first published in 2006, this book has appeared in fourteen languages. I am thankful for and proud of this international coverage, but do of course understand that such a spread cannot be due to my skills as a historian or a specific interest in Finland. It reflects a natural curiosity about how an originally poor country somewhere at the north-eastern end of Europe next to the mighty Russia was able to maintain its own culture and language, achieve and defend its independence and build up a stable and democratic society.

I wrote *A History of Finland* originally with my compatriots and Scandinavian friends in mind. But each time the book has been published in a new language I have tried to check that the text and its arguments were comprehensive for people reading the language in question. Another challenge in any such attempt at historical synthesis is the ever-expanding field of research. The numbers of academically qualified and professionally active historians in the world today have multiplied many times over in the last twenty-five years alone, and since the majority of them have specialised in the history of their own country or region, the body of material for any national history has increased exponentially.

A perhaps even greater challenge is the question of whether the writing of general histories with a national perspective can any longer be justified at all. For some decades there has been a marked trend in historiography of casting doubt on the national approach to historical studies, and of exploring instead regional, transnational or global perspectives on the past. The most recent contribution to this debate has come from postmodernist historians, who describe all forms of national surveys as collective autobiographies, in other words as products of ideology, pure and simple.

This book is in a way a response to these challenges. There is a demonstrable continuing need for national overviews, in which the results of the latest research can be presented in a succinct but elucidatory way. In many disciplines the task has been increasingly appropriated by specialist journalists. If historians are to take their social responsibilities seriously they too should play their part in this "translation" of new knowledge into a comprehensible narrative, by producing overviews and syntheses of the cumulated knowledge within their own subjects at appropriate intervals. The exercise requires the constant testing of personal professional knowledge, necessitating the selection of people, places and dates essential to the narrative and the omission of those which are more of a distraction from or even an impediment to its understanding. The structure of the presentation is integral to its accessibility for a wider readership.

If the historian succeeds in this, it is entirely possible to write a national history which also reveals the ideological and mythological dimensions of the great patriotic story. A critical or deconstructive approach to a nation's past need not involve the rejection of a traditional narrative nor the disregard of historical processes or events that have previously been viewed as significant in the growth and vicissitudes of the nation. On the contrary, a historically coherent story is often the simplest and most intelligible method of making the reader aware that national culture and solidarity are to a large extent an artificial construct.

There have been several important surveys of Finnish history published in the last three decades. Outstanding among those by Finnish historians are Pentti Virrankoski's and Jouko Vahtola's monographs in Finnish, each comprehensive in both subject and size. A somewhat older standard work, more limited in scope, is the political history of Finland from 1809 to 1999, *From Grand Duchy to Modern State*, by Osmo Jussila *et al.*, which has gone through several editions and appeared in numerous languages. Occasionally historians from other countries enter the arena. Particular mention must be made of David Kirby's exemplary contribution published in English in 2006.

My history of Finland differs from these works. It is shorter than Virrankoski's and Vahtola's books, since my aim has not been to give an exhaustive description of Finland's historical development. The intention is rather to open up perspectives and summarise longer chains of events and general trends in a manner that will enable the reader to form a picture of the whole and thus approach more specific aspects of Finnish history and society with confidence. In extent this book is closest to David Kirby's *Concise History of Finland*; in content, however, we have pursued somewhat different paths. I have woven political events into economic, technological, social and cultural contexts, whereas Kirby's book is a more specifically political history. I have also focused much more on the last few decades and contemporary events: about half of the book covers the period after 1900.

These perspectives and emphases are not a random choice. To understand how a poor and peripheral people gradually evolved into a political unity which would eventually withstand huge external pressures and build up a fully functional welfare state, there are sound reasons for a systematic examination of the economic, social and cultural structures and resources of the area. Politico-commercial interests, great-power conflicts and technological advances have undoubtedly influenced Finland's development continuously and fundamentally. But the effect of these chain reactions can only be explained with a full understanding of the prevailing social conditions.

My comparatively heavy emphasis on twentieth-century history is also a conscious choice. It was not until then that Finland became unequivocally a political entity with its own social system. Before that, decisions on the political and economic affairs of the region had been made so predominantly in Stockholm and St Petersburg that there is every reason to describe the history of Finland prior to the twentieth century as part of the history of Sweden and Russia. These connections are of course also treated in this book from many angles, but it can nevertheless be assumed that the twenty-first-century reader will be particularly interested to know to what extent Finland's Swedish and Russian legacies persisted, or were recast or restrained, after the country became an independent republic in 1917. The Finland of today is after all the result of this metamorphosis.

Proportionately more space is devoted to the period after the Second World War and especially the last three decades, since previously published surveys of Finnish history have tended to gloss over the developments of the most recent decades. The era is still rather unresearched and many historians are wary of the study of contemporary history because of the risk of premature judgements. This danger certainly exists, but my view is still that it is crucial that historians enter this arena as early as possible and offer their best interpretations, which hopefully have a more solid basis and greater independence than journalistic literature on the immediate past. Yet I have no illusions about how definite my perspective and understanding of the theme in question is. This book is not *The History* but *A History of Finland*.

If there is a central theme in this book it is the demonstration of how Finland's development from an integral component of the Swedish kingdom and an autonomous Russian Grand Duchy into a distinct nation-state has come about in constant and sometimes very dramatic interaction with other parts of the

Baltic region and Europe in general. To show what has been unique or typical in Finland's case I return regularly to how the country's natural and human resources have been exploited and how its cultural characteristics and technological awareness have contributed to its evolution. In short, this book is an attempt to set Finland in a number of different historical contexts in the Baltic region to examine how together they have shaped it into the society it has become at the start of the new millennium.

The bibliography gives a selection of the material I have found most pertinent, but it is far from exhaustive. The text reflects in one way or another the knowledge I have acquired over my years as a writing scholar and therefore obviously has the character of personal interpretation. Since the majority of the book's potential readers will have no knowledge of either Finnish or Swedish, I have endeavoured to compile a list of relevant English-language literature in both book and article form. The material is by no means plentiful. Finnish historians still publish primarily in their mother tongue, but within some decades the situation has much improved, given the constantly growing tendency among the younger generation of academics to publish in English.

I am naturally pleased that the publishing house of Hurst & Co. is publishing a new edition of this book. It includes a number of small changes, corrections and additions to the earlier text, but differs from it above all in its visual appearance due to a larger number of illustrations, which are hopefully also more interesting. The translation was supported by a grant from the Finnish Literature Exchange and was carried out in 2010 by Tom Geddes, a translator much respected in Scandinavia, for which I express my renewed thanks.

Henrik Meinander   *Midsummer 2019,*
                          Ritvala village at Vanajavesi lake

THE BEGINNINGS OF TIME

When the last Ice Age reached its most extreme point about 24,000 years ago (22,000 BC), Europe looked quite different from the way it does today. The whole of northern Europe, a great proportion of the British Isles and the Alps were overlaid by an ice cap up to three kilometres thick. The now densely populated regions of central Europe consisted of sub-Arctic tundra with permafrost, and the southern regions of the continent were covered with coniferous and mixed forest. Over the next 14,000 years the median temperature of the Earth rose, the ice sheet gradually receded, vegetation began to proliferate, immense herds of animals spread across the continent, and in their tracks came the first human beings to enter these northerly parts of the world.

The shrinking ice cap left deep impressions in the natural landscape. It is no exaggeration to say that the entire geography of Fennoscandia is one enormous monument to this retreat. The ice sheet had depressed the land, and so with the removal of the weight there began a slow uplift which continues to this day (30–100 cm a century). When the gradual rise in temperature was interrupted 13,000 years ago (11,000 BC) by a cooler period lasting a thousand years, a huge boulder moraine was formed along the southern and south-eastern edge of the ice sheet, extending in Finland from the south-

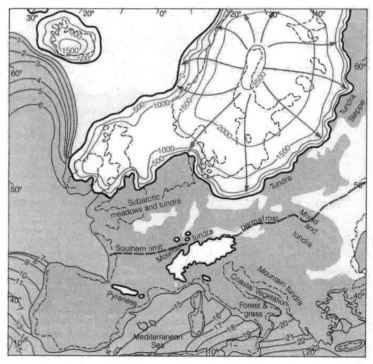

1.1: Ice Age in Europe 24, 000 years ago (22, 000 BC). The ice reached northern Germany at the time.

western tip of the country right across to its furthest eastern regions. The approximately 188,000 lakes in Finland are also a memorial to the Ice Age, since they formed in the grooves and hollows made by the ice sheet in the bedrock.

The Country's First Inhabitants

The first signs of human activity after the Ice Age in northern Europe are 10,700 years old (8700 BC), when individual hunter-gatherer communities appeared in Denmark, Skåne, the Baltic countries, southern Finland and northern Norway. The earliest traces of human habitation from this time are found in the south-eastern regions, many of which much later became Finland. Most of modern Finland still lay beneath the sea, which means that the first settlers must have arrived from the south and the south-east. As the ice caps continued to retreat, tiny hunter-gatherer communities began to inhabit the inner parts of the country. Some 9,300 years ago (7300 BC), they reached the most northern part of the country, which had already received its first population from the Norwegian Ice Sea coast 600 years earlier (7900 BC). This Sami (Lapp) population descended primarily from the nomads who had spread to northern Norway and the coast of the Arctic Ocean along the Norwegian Atlantic coast.

It cannot be known for certain what language these nomads spoke. Expert opinion is still divided on the matter. Some maintain that Finnish, which is not an Indo-European but a Uralic language, has been spoken in Finland for only the last 1,500 years. Others have concluded that even the original inhabitants used a Uralic language which was also spoken in other variants over large swathes of present-day European Russia and the Baltic countries. If the latter theory is correct, then one and the same tongue has prevailed in Finland for more than 10,000 years, since Finnish is still the major language. Genetically, however, the Finns today are the result of a continuous immigration from nearly every direction, but primarily from the south and west.

The new and larger wave of immigrants that followed crossed the Gulf of Finland around 4,500–4,000 years ago (2500–2000 BC). A corresponding influx from what is now central Sweden began a few centuries later, continuing in varying degrees well into that historical period. In any outline of the prehistory of Finland two factors have to be borne in mind: firstly, that the region was so far removed from the early agricultural societies around the Mediterranean that technical advances and new methods of production made their way this far north only very slowly and laboriously; secondly, that the climate was so harsh and nature so barren that even long after the introduction of agriculture in south-west Finland at the beginning of our own calendar era, the first 400 years AD, only a few tens of thousands of people at most could be supported.

Or to put it another way: when the historical Jesus was born, much of the Mediterranean area had thriving agrarian societies, with surpluses which provided a stable economic basis for the military dominance, administration and sophisticated culture of the Roman Empire. At that time the majority of the sparse population north of the Gulf of Finland subsisted on hunting and fishing or various combinations of primitive farming, burn-beat cultivation, stockbreeding, and traditional trapping and fishing.

Northern Europe was never incorporated into the Roman Empire, though many Roman goods, customs and innovations spread far to the north through the flourishing trade links that arose between the Empire and the Baltic region. The earliest written record of the Finns under that name—*Phinnoi*—is to be found in quotations cited by other writers from the Greek geographer Pytheas' description of his expedition to the Baltic coast in the fifth century BC. The next extant mention is in *Germania*, the work of the Roman historian Tacitus from 98 AD, where his observations on the peoples and cultures around the Baltic include the Finns—*Fenni*—living in impoverished contentment beyond the northern sea, forgotten by both gods and man.

This portrayal says a lot about how the Romans saw the barbarians of the north. But the fact is that contacts across the

Baltic were multiplying greatly at that time, as we know for example from rich finds of Roman coins in the settled areas of south-west Finland. The division of the Roman Empire and its decline in the west was a long, slow process, and in northern Europe there was little awareness of this transition period. The population and settlement of the coastal areas of the Baltic region expanded rapidly between 400 and 800 AD. Material prosperity increased and a more advanced social structure developed at a regional level. The spread of animal husbandry and agriculture brought a more stratified social order with a distinct chieftain class. In the southern half of the Scandinavian peninsula and in the Baltic countries this period saw the emergence of regional overlords vying with one another and calling themselves kings.

There were similar but only gradual and small-scale developments north of the Gulf of Finland, where until the eighth century permanent settlements were concentrated mainly in the coastal areas of the south-west and the fertile lands along the Kumo River (Kokemäenjoki) and its lake system in Satakunda (Satakunta) and Tavastland (Häme). Other growth areas of permanent settlement were Åland and the southern coastal areas of Ostrobothnia. Trade links proliferated in this period (400–800 AD), as did the movement of people to and from central Sweden, where enterprising trading centres and strong communities under local leaders evolved. Other parts of the country supported a scattered nomadic population, the Sami, who ranged over vast areas hunting and fishing, even well into the sixteenth century in southern Finland.

The extensive region that came to be called Finland only in the fifteenth century was still not a political or cultural entity. Leading families, or rather clans, ruled in the most fertile areas, and towards the end of the period (600–800 AD) they formed alliances for mutual defence and would even swear oaths of allegiance to the most powerful overlords in central Sweden. Contacts to the west and south had by that time been in existence for nearly two millennia. Many merchants and rulers must therefore have spoken Gothic, Old High German and Old Swedish, all of which left significant traces in the Finnish language. The Uralic family, to which Estonian and Hungarian likewise belong, is not Indo-European and the structure of Finnish differs significantly from the main European languages, but its many loan words show how it has developed in close cultural interaction with the Indo-European languages. The strongest influence has come from Swedish, which in the second millennium became the dominant local tongue in many of the coastal districts.

Vikings and Crusades

The first big expansionist phase of Finnish settlement and culture began in the mid-eighth century and continued until the fourteenth. Northern Europe was blessed at this time with a relatively mild climate, which together with technical advances in both agriculture and seafaring encouraged the burgeoning population to seek out new lands in the east to cultivate. So Karelia, the northern shores of Lake Ladoga and the lake district of eastern Finland began to be settled by farmers and burn-beaters from south-west Finland and Tavastland. The southern shores of Lake Ladoga were also gradually settled by Slavic peoples, with their economy centred on Novgorod. The eastward expansion of Finnish settlement resulted in the formation of a separate Karelian culture by 1000 AD. In other words, about a thousand years ago three regional communities were living north of the Gulf of Finland: Finns, Tavasts and Karelians.

These folk migrations overlapped with the Swedish Viking expeditions to the east, radiating out along the north coast of the Gulf of Finland, the River Neva and Lake Ladoga, and south through Russia to the Black Sea and Constantinople. There is no evidence that Finnish tribes systematically contributed ships and crews to these Viking forays. But what is indisputable is that the natural harbours and trading posts of the Gulf of Finland and Lake Ladoga provided staging posts for the Vikings, also known as Varangians. The Viking expeditions (800–1025 AD) are frequently described in popular historiography as plundering raids, but they also included trade, colonisation and administrative reorganisation of politically weak or previously uninhabited regions of Europe. This was the pattern both to the west and in Russia, where Varangian chieftains took over the government of Novgorod (862) and Kiev (882) and laid the foundations of what was to become the mighty Russian Empire. In Finland too the Viking period was an important economic and cultural precursor of national integration, which began to spread in the twelfth century and by the end of the thirteenth century had united much of present-day Sweden and Finland into a single kingdom.

There are no written records from the Finnish Viking period, but to compensate, a rich profusion of folklore rooted in pre-Christian society has been collected from the eighteenth century onwards. One of the earliest collectors of this Finnish-language folk poetry was Elias Lönnrot (1802–1884), who collated and arranged the songs into a literary narrative according to Classical and Romantic models, the first version being published in 1835 as the *Kalevala*. This work became a cornerstone in the construction of a specifically Finnish national consciousness: indeed it became Finland's national epic, and not simply because of its folk wisdom and the linguistic beauty of its poetry. The *Kalevala* was proof that there had indeed been a Finnish history before the political union with Sweden. For modern readers the poems also provide an insight into the society of the Viking era, with everything from influential village blacksmiths and ingenious fishing gear to bloody family feuds and folk mythology.

The fact that northern Europe was never incorporated into the Roman Empire meant an almost millennium-long exclusion from the Christian Church. It was only from the sixth century that the Church fathers began to interpret Jesus' evangelism as an exhortation to convert the barbarians beyond the Roman Empire. The first explicit evidence of Christ's message reaching Finland is indeed sixth-century, and by the eighth to ninth centuries the cross often appeared as a symbol of good fortune and unity on jewellery and high-status artefacts. Another indication that Christian customs were beginning to prevail was that the ruling classes turned away from cremation and started to adopt interment of their dead.

Similar developments were taking place in Sweden and the Baltic countries. Christian symbols and rituals were disseminated through trade links. When the Papacy decided for both spiritual and political reasons to extend active missionary work to more northerly regions of the world, the task was assigned to Ansgar of Bremen, the monk later called the Apostle of Scandinavia. He arrived in 829 in Birka, the Viking trading post in eastern central Sweden, and was eventually promoted to archbishop of the archdiocese of Bremen, which became the headquarters for the Christian conversion of Scandinavia for the next 200 years. But it was well into the eleventh century before Church practices had become firmly enough established in Scandinavian Viking societies for Scandinavia to be regarded as Christianised. In Finland and the Baltic countries the process was even slower, because organised missionary activity was not introduced into these territories until the twelfth century.

In the Baltic countries the conversion of the populace often took brutal form, forcibly imposed by crusaders known as the

Sword-Brothers, from the Holy Roman Empire. North of the Gulf of Finland the process was somewhat different. Southwestern Finland had begun its economic integration with central Sweden in the Viking era, which was a contributory factor in the spread of Christian customs and beliefs to Finland, since for diplomatic reasons the Swedish Viking chieftains were consenting to baptism for themselves, and did not prevent individual missionaries trying their luck in Finland. So the earliest Finnish parishes may well have been established in the southwest even by the late eleventh century.

There were two reasons for missionary activity in Finland becoming more organised in the twelfth century. Firstly, royal power was slowly but surely being consolidated in Sweden, which enabled the Crown to give more attention to Finland and other parts of the Baltic region. Secondly, rivalry between the Papacy and the Holy Roman Empire led the Pope to found new archbishoprics in Lund (1104) and Uppsala (1164) to supersede the archbishop of Bremen, who was much too loyal to the Holy Roman Emperor. The Pope's decision to extend systematic missionary work to Finland was one element in this power struggle, since the Holy Roman Emperor's crusaders were contemporaneously achieving territorial gains in the Baltic countries. The fear of corresponding inroads into Finland by Novgorod and the Orthodox Church was a further compelling factor in the decision.

Mediaeval documents describe three crusades to Finland, and later historians have dated them to about 1155, 1239 and 1293. Even though conversion mostly proceeded peacefully, the Church's own myth-making required it to be described as a heroic struggle between good and evil, culminating in the Christianisation of the people. The first of these known crusades in 1155 was, according to ecclesiastical tradition, led by the British monk Henry, who embarked on a missionary expedition to south-west Finland under the protection of King Erik of the Sveas. The reason this particular crusade is known to posterity is that Henry was later declared patron saint of the new Åbo (Turku) diocese, for which good deeds and miracles were a prerequisite. According to legend, the Finns were baptised by Henry after they had been vanquished by King Erik's men. Henry remained behind as bishop in the new missionary diocese, but was murdered the following year by the peasant Lalli, who of course suffered God's retribution.

The Emergence of the Swedish Realm

In the thirteenth century the struggle for political and economic control of the coastal regions of the Gulf of Finland intensified. The Danes tried to acquire a foothold on the northern shores of the Baltic countries, founding the port of Reval in 1219, now Tallinn, "Taani linn", literally meaning "the town of the Danes" in Estonian. But the town was populated mainly by Germans and by the 1280s had joined the Hanseatic League. Novgorod was expanding from the east under the leadership of Prince Alexander, who vanquished Swedish forces at the River Neva in 1240 and thus acquired the honorific epithet Nevsky. Two years later he defeated the Teutonic Order in a battle on the ice of Lake Peipus.

In central Sweden and north of the Gulf of Finland the power of the Swedish Crown and the Catholic Church over the local chieftains was consolidated to such a degree that, despite the slow progress of this centralisation through the whole mediaeval period, it was nevertheless possible to speak of a Swedish realm by the beginning of the fourteenth century, with south-west Finland as one of its core constituents. The more stable political situation was also a contributing factor in the migration of peasant farmers from over-populated areas of

Sweden to the relatively thinly populated coastal regions of the Gulf of Finland and Ostrobothnia.

Colonisation was not co-ordinated from above, but the further east the colonists ventured, the more usual it was for the chieftains or peasant leaders to organise the land clearance and ensure they kept a significant proportion of the new arable land under their own control. The immigrants hardly comprised a massive population, and even before the influx tailed off in the mid-fourteenth century the Finnish- and Swedish-speaking populace had begun to merge together through marriage and language-switching. But however small this immigration from Sweden might have been in practice, it nevertheless gave rise to a permanent Swedish-speaking settlement all along the coast which has continued uninterrupted right up to our own times.

The Swedish language became so well established in Finland because it was also increasingly the language of power. In the late 1230s the Swedish nobleman Birger Jarl led a punitive expedition to Finland's western interior, more precisely Tavastland, where the local inhabitants had allied themselves with Novgorod. The expedition of 1239 came to be known subsequently as the second crusade to Finland and was carried out in accordance with the wishes of the Pope, after the Tavasts had burned down a Catholic church. But its principal objective was to consolidate the Swedish Crown's control over Finland. Birger Jarl constructed a castle in Tavastland called Tavastehus (Hämeenlinna), which eventually became an important administrative centre for the Swedish Crown.

The Catholic Church played a crucial role in the consolidation of secular power all over Europe. It was in the interests of the Church for the Crown to be able to protect its properties and servants against attack or abuse of authority by local chieftains and regional notables. The pattern was the same in both

Sweden and Finland, which, after internal power struggles, were united into one kingdom under a single monarch in the thirteenth century. The Church was a consistent supporter of Crown interests, and when by the end of the same century the Crown's military forces were moving their outposts further and further eastwards towards Karelia, the Catholic priests were hot on their heels. In the summer of 1293 Torgils Knutsson, the Swedish constable of the realm, led a successful military expedition to the Karelian Isthmus. The local Orthodox population was converted and a castle built in Viborg (Viipuri, now Vyborg, Russia), which remained the most important eastern frontier fortress in the realm until the early eighteenth century.

This military thrust, which would go down in history as the third crusade to Finland, eventually resulted in the drawing of more distinct boundaries between the respective spheres of influence of the Swedish Crown and Novgorod. The peace treaty of Nöteborg in 1323 fixed a political border between the two kingdoms which also functioned as a demarcation between the Western and Eastern Churches. The greater part of modern Finland was thus under Swedish and Catholic control, a decisive factor in Finland's future destiny. The inclusion of Finland in the Western Church meant not only that the administration and culture of the country developed on the same lines as elsewhere in Papal Europe and were thus slowly but surely incorporated into a unified Catholic culture, but also that both administration and religious art fostered a set of values which, over the course of the centuries and above all in its later Lutheran guise, would come to shape the Finns' world view and their concept of humanity.

Nevertheless, the establishment of the Western Church did not put an abrupt end to heathen traditions and ideas. Finland was a very sparsely populated, extensive area, and the peasantry succeeded in retaining many of the ancient traditions,

exactly as in Europe generally, by giving them Christian interpretations. Perhaps most well known is the transformation of
heathen fertility rites into the Christian Whitsun celebration.
Both festivals were held at the end of spring or in early summer
and both celebrated rebirth. The heathen one made symbolic
sacrifices to regrowth, agriculture and the natural world, while
the Christian one took place on Whitsunday in praise of the
birth of the Christian Church as a consequence of the Ascen-
sion of Christ—making it easy to unify the old and the new.
This is what happened in the productive village of Ritvala in
Tavastland, for instance, where an ancient heathen fertility rite
was given Catholic garb in the early fourteenth century, but
otherwise continued into the eighteenth century in as baccha-
nalian a guise as it always had.

By the early fourteenth century the Swedish Crown had
begun the construction of three castles in Finland: Åbo (Turku),

1.2: Raseborg Castle, an administrative centre in south-west Finland
in the Middle Ages. Pastel painting from 1822.

Viborg and Tavastehus (Hämeenlinna). Olofsborg (Olavinlinna) was added at the end of the fifteenth century in the south-eastern border zone in Savolax (Savo). At the same time a number of smaller fortresses were built, as at Raseborg (Raasepori) and Kastelholm on Åland, which also helped reinforce the Crown's hold over the various regions. As in the rest of Europe, these strongholds served as military bases and as tax-collection offices for the Crown, but since the central power was still weak, a significant amount of local administration continued to be undertaken by the Church. This was particularly so in Finland, where the archdiocese of Åbo set the pace for administrative integration. The fundamental element of Church administration was the local congregation within each parish, which later provided the smallest unit for the secular authorities.

By the fourteenth century the eastern half of the Swedish realm had come to be called simply Osterlandia, the Eastland. Over the ensuing centuries the archdiocese of Åbo took on such a crucial role in political life that this whole eastern region began to be called Finland, after the south-western coastal area where the town of Åbo and its bishopric were situated. This is why that part of the country is still known as Finland Proper (Egentliga Finland, Varsinais-Suomi). The word Finland was first used officially in 1419 as a term for the entire eastern half of the realm, and it passed into the corpus of law in the 1440s.

Agriculture and Trade

Up until the sixteenth century permanent settlement was concentrated mainly in the most fertile areas of the coastal districts and in Tavastland. Here the parishes could afford what for Finnish circumstances were imposing granite churches with vaulted ceilings and brick decoration as symbols of the triumph of civilisation over wilderness and paganism. Many of these stone churches still exist today and are in active use by their congregations, as well as being topographical and cultural monuments to mediaeval Finland. Less durable have been the secular manor houses and the monasteries, which with very few exceptions have been demolished and re-used for building material.

Everyday life in mediaeval Finland was very different from the way of life of the Christian peoples of the Mediterranean. The climate rendered the agricultural yield considerably lower in northern than in southern Europe, and this had a significant effect on culture and society overall. But the involvement of the Church led in time to many common traditions within Western Christendom, resulting in the core of shared cultural values that we find in today's European Union. A major contributory factor was the standardised education in Latin and the sacraments for the priesthood offered by the cathedral schools and universities in central and southern Europe. Another important impetus for a common Western culture came from the monasteries, a network of many different orders which played a particularly influential role as a cultural channel on the peripheries of Europe, as in Finland.

The monastic system provided a sequence of staging posts both for Catholic monks from Europe and for Finnish pilgrims. The monks introduced Continental scholarship and craftsmanship, while the more worldly pilgrims brought home a range of common Christian customs and experiences. The most important destination for Finnish pilgrims was of course Rome, but there is documentary evidence of pilgrimages to many other well-known holy shrines, such as Santiago de Compostela in Spanish Galicia, Nidaros (Trondheim) in Norway, where the most famed saint in northern Europe, Saint Olav, was buried, and Saint Birgitta's grave in Vadstena in Sweden. The first Dominican and Franciscan friars arrived in

1.3: The Kalevala mythology has inspired many Finnish artists. Akseli Gallen-Kallela painting a Kalevala fresco in the aula of the National Museum of Finland in the late 1920s.

Finland in the thirteenth century. Two centuries later (1438) a Birgittine convent was founded in Nådendal (Naantali), near the seat of the bishopric in Åbo, flourishing for a brief period before the Lutheran Reformation swept across northern Europe in the sixteenth century.

Olav, the Viking leader felled in battle in 1030, was canonised as the champion of Christianity and justice in Scandinavia, and he had a prodigious number of churches named after him throughout the Baltic region. The cult of St Olav spread swiftly, and not just because of the tight hold on the Baltic by the Scandinavian monarchs and the Western Church. Equally pivotal for this phenomenon was the trade which gave rise to a string of coastal towns all around the Baltic. The impulse behind this economic transformation came from the Hansa, the federation of towns controlled from northern Germany. The principal reason for its success was the trade route between Novgorod and Bruges in present-day Belgium, which was maintained despite changing political conditions.

The influence of the Hanseatic towns on socio-political developments around the Baltic can hardly be overestimated. The origins of the federation and its three centuries or more golden age (1200–1500) were a happy consequence of a politically divided Germany, rapid population growth throughout Europe and a number of technological advances which had a decisive impact on the ease of transportation of goods and the establishment of towns. The increasing population of western Europe consumed all the grain that could be exported from the Baltic region, and payment was made in cloth, spices, wine and other products with a high status or processing value. Finland played only a marginal part in this distribution of labour, but could cover the costs of additional imports of these goods through the export of butter, furs and fish. Cloth was certainly a significant import. But most significant of all was salt, indispensable for the preservation and storage of food.

True Hansa towns were located only in northern Germany and the Baltic countries (Riga and Reval, now Tallinn), but other towns grew up which were granted the right to trade with the League. In the thirteenth and fourteenth centuries a number of towns with such rights were established in Finland. First and foremost was Åbo, which had a key role as the prime staple town for trade between south-western Finland and the rest of the Baltic region, added to which it was the bishopric and later (1640) university town for the eastern half of the kingdom. The mouth of the River Aura where Åbo grew up had been the site of a notable trading post even in the Viking period; it gradually acquired the character of a town after the Dominicans founded a Saint Olav monastery there in 1249. The construction of Åbo castle began in the 1280s, and the triple-naved cathedral was consecrated in 1300, still to this day Finland's most important religious edifice. The founding of Viborg in 1293 was followed over the next two centuries by Ulfsby (Ulvila), Raumo (Rauma), Nådendal on the west coast and Borgå (Porvoo) on the south coast of the province of Nyland (Uusimaa).

A substantial contingent of the populace in these (by western European standards) extremely minor towns consisted of Germans, or perhaps more correctly Low-German-speaking merchants, who elected their mayors and councils and formed guilds on exactly the same model as elsewhere on the Baltic littoral. In the mid-fourteenth century as many as 80 per cent of the citizens of Åbo, for instance, were Germans from the Rheinland and Westphalia. The Swedish Crown brought in a law which required at least half the mayors and councillors to be native-born, but there is every indication that this law was ignored. However, the councils looked after the interests of the merchants and guaranteed that they would adhere to their contracts. They thus cemented a bond between the citizens and their trading partners in other towns of northern Europe. The guilds fulfilled more of a social function and were in practice exclusive clubs for communal festivities and bacchanalia. There were at least six guilds in Åbo in the Middle Ages, each of which had its own particular profile and status. The most prestigious was without doubt the Guild of the Three Kings, whose members were mainly comprised of the town's priests, the upper nobility and the higher ranks of local government officials.

The guilds as an institution spread to the most fertile areas of rural Finland, but involved only the local elites of society. It has to be remembered that the kingdom of Sweden had no real system of enfeoffment. It was not the peasants themselves as vassals who were enfeoffed, but the right to tax them. In central and eastern Europe a high proportion of the peasant class was tied to the land, which was owned by autocratic feudal masters. The king gave them their fiefs in exchange for their loyalty and support in war. In the Swedish realm such a system was never fully established because there was simply not enough arable land and manpower to enfeoff. So in northern Sweden and Finland only about 5 per cent of the population worked land they did not themselves own or rent. This meant that the peasant class, especially in the eastern half of the realm, mostly paid their taxes direct to king and Church. The Finnish peasants protected their own interests assiduously, and in many cases stubbornly asserted their rights, not least if their opponent in the dispute was the Church.

Settled agriculture and stockbreeding had been pursued in the river valleys and on other productive soils in south-west Finland ever since prehistoric times. A crucial technical innovation in farming was the turning plough, which facilitated the cultivation of heavier clay soils and thus opened the way for much more clearance. A swathe of archipelago villages grew up along the south coast and on the Åland Islands, where the principal economic activities were fishing and animal husbandry. The further north and east, the more extensive the amount of burn-beat cultivation, which was a far from primitive form of agriculture. The yield was many times higher (twenty- to thirtyfold) than on permanent fields (five- to tenfold), and there were multiple varieties of the technique. The method of greatest economic significance (*huuhta*) had spread from Russia to Finland in about the eleventh century and was suited to coniferous forests on unploughed land, since the preparation of the soil required four years but then gave only one good harvest. In practice this meant that burn-beaters felled and burned new areas of forest in the same year that they were sowing and harvesting areas already prepared.

The usual subsidiary occupations for burn-beaters were fishing and to a lesser degree hunting. Stockbreeding was not widely practised. Burn-beaters ranged over huge tracts of land and thus could not have permanent barns or animal shelters. Burn-beating was very labour-intensive, and so right up to the nineteenth century households in these regions consisted of extended family groups of several nuclear families living

1.4: Slash-and-burn agriculture was widely practised in inner Finland up until the nineteenth century. Drawing from 1896.

together. This was manifest in surnames, which indicated the major clan to which one belonged.

Material scarcity also meant there was only a narrow top stratum of the upper classes or tax-exempt privileged classes in Finland. The prerequisite for this status was that a landowner could afford to arm and provide for a horseman fit to do battle for the Crown. Most of the families who attained this position were Swedish- or German-speaking large-scale farmers along the south coast, but gradually their numbers were swelled by many prosperous Finnish-speaking farming families from all over the south-west. There was in any case no particular need for an effective militia class in Finland. The peace treaty between Sweden and Russia concluded in Nöteborg in 1323 stabilised the eastern frontier of the realm for a further hundred years. Since the king lacked the means to strengthen his central power, the Crown functioned for most of the Middle Ages as a political alliance of fairly autonomous "castle counties", governed by bailiffs installed in castles which remained the property of the king.

2

THE BIRTH OF THE PRINCIPALITY

The emergence of unitary states with an undivided central power was a slow process all over Europe that was to continue at varying rates right up to the seventeenth century. The political consolidation of the Swedish realm into a principality and ulti- mately a hereditary monarchy evolved in competitive interaction with the Danish, Russian and Polish realms. In the fifteenth century Danish might predominated, but Gustav Vasa's gradual takeover of the Swedish realm in the 1520s and 1530s led to the creation of a strong principality around the Baltic, which with- stood external pressures in the second half of the sixteenth cen- tury despite the internal power struggles of his sons.

During this era Finland developed into an economically and militarily important component of the realm. Expansion was primarily in an eastward direction up to 1617, which meant that many of Sweden's fortresses were built in the eastern half of the realm and its military forces were concentrated there, especially in the second half of the sixteenth century when the prolonged war was being waged against Russia. It was also the reason for so many of the royal fraternal feuds taking place in Finland.

The Kalmar Union

A clear indication of the weakness of the monarchy was the lengthy struggle for the succession in Sweden during much of

2.1: When the Swedish Kingdom took shape in the thirteenth century, Finland was already an integrated part of it. The national symbol of Sweden, three crowns, was introduced during the next century. Woodcut from 1555.

the fourteenth and fifteenth centuries. The often precarious rulers endeavoured to establish the Crown as unequivocally hereditary. Such attempts were undermined by rival aristocratic families, forming alliances both within Sweden and with German princes to safeguard their regional and national interests. One of these influential opponents was the country's wealthiest man, Bo Jonsson Grip, who assisted Albrecht of Mecklenburg in his bid for the throne at the election of the king in 1364, and who eventually became Lord Chief Justice (*drots*), the highest official of the realm. The north German king was dependent from the outset on the financial support of Bo Jonsson Grip, so the latter was able gradually to redeem many of the king's fiefs and become the power behind the throne. His hold was strongest on fiefs in Finland, which thus became very much his own realm within the realm.

Albrecht's election as king was a reflection of the power of the Hansa towns and the north German princes over the whole of northern Europe. Their dominance was manifest in all aspects of society and, after the death of Bo Jonsson Grip in 1386, led to the decision of the Scandinavian lords to conspire against the Germans. The result was the agreement of the three Scandinavian kingdoms of Sweden, Denmark and Norway in Kalmar in 1397 to form a union, electing Erik of Pomerania as their monarch. But the real ruler of the union until 1412 was his grandmother's sister Margareta, a Danish princess who had succeeded in appropriating considerable power through marriage to a Swedo-Norwegian pretender to the throne.

In area, the Kalmar Union was one of the largest kingdoms in Europe, but its population density was very low and its financial strength minimal. Its rulers never managed to integrate the union into one centrally controlled kingdom. It held together in formal terms up to 1521 because there was consensus in principle on the resistance to Germanisation. But even on this point there were differing interests, and almost every election of a ruler was preceded by protracted negotiations. When the union introduced a trade blockade of the Hansa city of Lübeck, it collapsed because of Swedish iron exports to the Continent. In the 1430s insurrections erupted among farmers and miners throughout much of Sweden. From then on the Swedish nobility were suspicious of the union, and in 1471 the friction between Denmark and Sweden came to a head in armed conflict at the Battle of Brunkeberg, just north of Stockholm (now the northern central area of the city). The quarrel was patched up, but contributed in the long term to the dissolution of the union.

For Norway the union period represented a marked political decline, exacerbated by the severe pandemic of the Black Death. The kings of the union ensured that nearly all prominent positions in the country went to Danish, Swedish or German nobles, with the result that Norway was transformed into

25

a Danish province. For Finland the union proved more benefi-cial. The shift of power to Denmark and the ensuing conflicts gave the leading players in Finland more scope to bargain for political advantage, and Finland's economic value to the king-dom of Sweden increased substantially in the fourteenth and fifteenth centuries. That did not mean that the eastern half of the realm began to liberate itself from Sweden—it was rather that the upper echelons of society acquired greater influence at a national level and were thus able to establish Finland as one of the core provinces of the Swedish realm. From 1362 repre-sentatives of the Finnish Estates were allowed to participate in the election of the Swedish king.

Danish-Swedish rivalries led to many bloody battles between 1470 and 1520, but that was not the sole or even primary cause of the dissolution of the Kalmar Union. Innovations in weap-onry (gunpowder, firearms, artillery) and the growing volume of European trade made it progressively easier for the mon-archs of the time to subjugate regional princes and noblemen and thus consolidate their own power nationally. If they were successful, the next step was an extension of the kingdom's territory and control of strategic trade routes. The exemplar in northern Europe was the Grand Duchy of Muscovy, which subjugated the principality of Novgorod in 1477. The ensuing expansion was directed towards the kingdom of Poland-Lithu-ania, which like the Kalmar Union was a large but loose fed-eration of states. Similar developments happened in France, Spain and Britain, where the monarchs used various means to curb the influence of the upper nobility and the Church and seized control of previously independent trading towns and federations of towns. Such concentrations of power usually resulted in hereditary monarchies.

The emergence of a strong and unified Russia altered the balance of power in the Baltic region entirely. The Swedish realm's eastern border with Russia passed right through the middle of present-day Finland, but the issue was complicated by the fact that the Treaty of Nöteborg in 1323 had delineated the frontier only in the very south, on the Karelian Isthmus. As a consequence, the more northerly regions of Finland and Karelia were taxed and exploited as fishing and hunting grounds by both kingdoms. It was a sort of equilibrium which began to waver in the fifteenth century as the farmers and burn-beaters of Savolax expanded further eastwards. These areas had previously been used primarily by the Karelians, who were subject to Novgorod and Moscow. After repeated border disputes the Swedes constructed a massive castle, Olofsborg, in the Savolax lake district in the late 1470s (now known in Finnish as Olavinlinna, in the town of Savonlinna). This fortress was seen by Moscow as a provocation, since it was regarded as standing on Russian territory. A sustained sequence of armed conflicts ensued, and when the parties signed the Treaty of Teusina some hundred years later in 1595, the frontier was drawn right up to the Arctic Ocean. It followed the eastern border of Savolax settlement and unambiguously defined Lapland as Swedish territory.

It was not only the contentious eastern frontier which gave rise to a stronger central power in Sweden. At the time of the war with Russia, there was a resumption of Danish efforts to suppress the Swedish upper nobility in order to transform the Scandinavian union into a Danish enterprise. The Danes had no qualms about allying themselves with Russia if necessary. In the autumn of 1520 the Danish king of the union, Kristian II, marched into Stockholm and had eighty-two Swedish noblemen executed for having dared to defy his supremacy. Similar executions were carried out in Finland. The Stockholm Bloodbath, as it became known, set in train a reaction which Kristian had not anticipated. The Swedish peasantry were free and

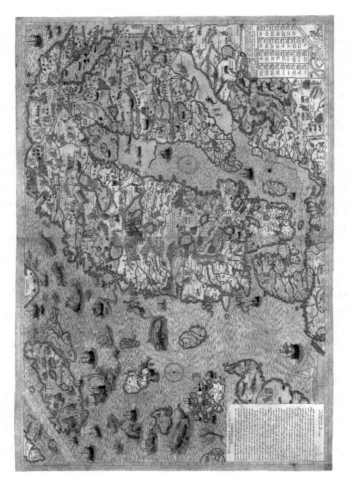

2.2: Carta Marina (1539), a map of northern Europe designed by Olaus Magnus. Finland is in this early version imagined almost as a peninsula.

independent, with a stable economic position which made them feel unthreatened by the aristocracy, and they thus had no reason to approve this wholesale slaughter. After Kristian had returned to Denmark, a 24-year-old nobleman, Gustav Eriksson Vasa, organised a peasant uprising in the province of Dalarna, which swiftly spread to other parts of the country. In August 1521 he was proclaimed regent of Sweden.

Gustav Vasa held three trump cards. Firstly, it was an easy matter to stir up the farmers of Dalarna against the Danes, who had raised taxes and thus impeded iron exports to the Hansa. Secondly, he allied himself with the Hansa leadership in Lübeck, who were at that time on a war footing with Denmark; Lübeck's military and financial support was critical, but of course also increased its influence on Swedish politics. Thirdly, Kristian II had eliminated many of Gustav Vasa's rivals among the nobility in the Stockholm Bloodbath. On 6 June 1523 Gustav Vasa swore the traditional royal oath at the Diet of Strängnäs. Danish resistance was to continue for another six months in Finland, but in October 1523 the last Danish forces surrendered in Viborg.

There was some significance in the fact that the final battles against Danish hegemony were fought in the eastern half of the realm. The Finnish aristocracy had unequivocally rallied to the support of Gustav Vasa, and when victory was assured they were frequently in a position to exploit the king's confidence in them on matters relating to the realm as a whole. The bloody dissolution of the Kalmar Union had substantially reduced the political strength of the Swedish upper nobility, which also facilitated a direct dialogue between the king and the Eastland, especially as Gustav Vasa was happy to rely on advisors and allies of lower birth. Another point was that control of Finland had proved to be essential to obstruct or avert Russo-Danish alliances.

It is easy to demonstrate that Gustav Vasa's path to the throne followed a general European pattern. Similar concentrations of power had already arisen in Russia and Denmark. His consolidation of Swedish monarchical power was crucial in the dissolution of three strong supranational networks in the Baltic region: the Kalmar Union, the Hanseatic League, and, last but not least, Catholic Scandinavia with its allegiance to the Pope in Rome. For Finland this was also the beginning of a more markedly Swedish period in the country's history.

Reformation Politics

The young Gustav Vasa's rise to power proved a good thing. He turned out to be anything but a political gadfly and was to remain on the throne right up until his death in 1560. He took his first and perhaps most effective step towards a sovereign principality at the Diet of Västerås in 1527, when he forced through a complete confiscation of the extensive properties of the Catholic Church, including a considerable portion of the private fortunes of the priests. The decision was motivated by the need for new financial resources to balance the national budget in view of the heavy debts incurred to Lübeck during the struggle against Danish hegemony. For the same reasons he had already abolished a long-established annual fund for the bishops and had begun taxing the Church.

There were of course political motives behind these measures as well. Up to then the Catholic bishops had been members of the Council of the Realm. They had also had the right to their own bodyguards and castles, which gave them independence and political influence. In the early 1520s Archbishop Gustav Trolle had openly taken the side of the Danish king of the union, an act which Gustav Vasa could not let go unpunished. Trolle was declared a traitor and sent into exile, after which certain episcopal political privileges were withdrawn at the assembly in Västerås. Simultaneously all Papal influence was removed from the election of bishops and other Church appointments. These steps had the desired effect. The bishops and clergy retained their local prestige, but were transformed into a malleable tool in the king's hands.

The reduction in the wealth of the Church certainly brought about a long-term improvement in the Crown's finances, but it did not provide a quick solution to the financial and political dependence on the Hansa city of Lübeck in which the kingdom found itself. By 1530 more than half of Sweden's debt was still outstanding. But when the Hansa demanded Sweden join them in a war against Holland and its burgeoning mercantile power, Gustav Vasa refused. This led to war between the two parties, in which Sweden and Denmark joined forces and vanquished Lübeck. In the Treaty of Hamburg in 1536 Lübeck had to renounce the remainder of its debt claims. So the Hanseatic League's dominion over Baltic trade came to an end for good.

Dutch mercantile power was to play a central role in the Baltic over the next 150 years, and would thus also have an impact on the history of Finland. But the strategy of the Dutch was quite different from that employed by the Hansa. The Hanseatic League left fully functional trading towns and contacts all around the Baltic, which made it impossible for the Dutch to take political control of commerce. The emergence of strong monarchies in much of Europe also contributed to this situation. So the Dutch concentrated instead on shipping and ensured themselves a firm grip on transport between the Baltic and the rapidly developing Atlantic regions of western Europe.

In a broader perspective, this commercial link between the Baltic and Atlantic Europe was one manifestation of the dawning of world trade. The concentration of capital and a growing population in western Europe increased the demand for grain, timber and other raw materials from the Baltic region. Payment was made in the form of cloth, wine, *objets d'art* and other manufactured products. This enormous structural change was ultimately driven by a few apparently simple technical innovations: gunpowder, the compass and printing. Gunpowder and firearms helped sovereigns to crush the power of the regional princes. The compass was an unrivalled tool for lengthy and frequent voyages across the oceans. Last but by no means least, the invention of printing opened up unprecedented opportunities for the transmission of knowledge and for universal communication.

Printing was a prerequisite for the Renaissance, that cultural shift in outlook which prepared the way for modern science and a more individually centred world view. Once the Catholic Church's monopoly on truth was called into question, its secular influence was soon undermined. The German monk Martin Luther began criticising the rule of the Pope in 1517. A mere seven years later the king of Sweden, Gustav Vasa, loosened ties to Rome with shrewd references to Luther's arguments that since the Church was the community of believers, its property must therefore belong to the people. It was but a short step from there to the confiscation of Church property decreed at the Diet of Västerås in 1527, and Church administration being placed under Crown supervision.

Gustav Vasa had done as much as he intended to reform the Church, and so he did not attempt to push through any formal split with Rome, curtailing any more radical proposals. Drastic changes in religious customs could easily lead to popular rebellion. This view was shared by his ecclesiastical advisors, who were sincere adherents of Luther's teachings but saw themselves as part of a reform movement within the Catholic

Church. One of the first Lutherans in Finland was Petrus Särkilahti, who had studied under Luther in Wittenberg and was headmaster of the Cathedral School in Åbo 1524–29. But he died prematurely and it was his fellow countryman Mikael Agricola (ca 1510–57) who would instead go down in history as Finland's reformer.

Agricola too was a student of Luther and he came back to Finland in 1539 to be appointed in his turn to the headship of Åbo Cathedral School. In 1554 he was inaugurated as bishop of Åbo diocese. As schoolteacher and priest Agricola retained Latin as the language of learning and culture and also many Catholic customs, such as the doctrines of purgatory, the Lenten fast and confession. This was natural prudence in sixteenth-century Sweden, especially in Finland, where in many respects the Catholic heritage lived on far longer than in more central parts of the kingdom. Agricola's pioneering contribution was in his writings, which in accordance with the new Lutheran teachings were based on the assumption that all fellowship with God was personal and direct.

This conviction had its roots in the piety movements of the late Middle Ages, which stressed the importance of individual faith and questioned the authority of the Church. Luther taught that only personal faith could bring the grace of God. All Christians, therefore, should be able to read the Bible for themselves. This presupposed universal literacy and access to translations, and every true reformer distinguished himself also as a translator and popular educator. Mikael Agricola in Finland certainly came into this category, laying the foundations of the written Finnish language primarily through his translation of the New Testament (*Se Wsi Testamenti*, 1548), and so did his colleagues in Sweden, whose Swedish translations of the New Testament (1526) and the complete Bible (1541) had a normative effect on the language of the whole country and helped in particular to consolidate language usage in the Swedish-speaking coastal areas of Finland.

But Agricola faced a more demanding challenge than did his principal colleague in Sweden, Olaus Petri. There was quite simply no written Finnish language on which to build. The language of the court and the aristocracy was Swedish until the nineteenth century—otherwise these circles communicated in Danish, German or French. The lingua franca of the Catholic Church was Latin, which explained why no one had considered printing anything in Finnish before the Reformation. So Agricola's first publication was *Abckiria* (1543), a Finnish-language primer, followed by a 900-page missal for services in Finnish (*Rucouskiria*, 1544).

Agricola's translation of the New Testament was his crowning achievement and has been a source of fascination for theologians, linguists and historians right up to the present day. He and his anonymous assistants used in the first instance the dialect spoken in south-west Finland, but they also took in words and expressions from other Finnish dialects. It was a rational decision, since a high proportion of the settled population lived in the south-west, and as Agricola himself emphasised in the foreword, it was only a preliminary attempt at a written Finnish language. It would not be until the 1880s that the social status and lexical diversity of Finnish would reach a level of sophistication that would enable it to overtake Swedish as the official language in Finland.

To return to the sixteenth century—how did the Reformation manifest itself at grassroots level? We must bear in mind that local clergy in the more peripheral areas of Europe had to be able to speak the language of their congregation even in the Middle Ages. The Catholic mass was held in Latin, but the rest of the service and all other communication were in the vernacular. After the Reformation what remained of the Latin

2.3: The first picture of everyday life in Finland. Woodcut from 1544 in a work by professor Sebastian Münster, *Cosmographia universalis*.

liturgy was gradually abandoned, while the priest's direct sermon to the congregation was promoted to the central element of the service. Since pre-Reformation clergy were only rarely dismissed, and since they, like their congregations, preferred to keep to the old traditions, the changes can hardly have been felt as revolutionary. To cite a concrete example: when the insistence on celibacy was abandoned, the priests were permitted to marry their concubines.

The most tangible results of the Reformation were the abolition of the monasteries, the clergy becoming local servants of the Crown, and the confiscation by the Crown of most of the church silver. There was for a long time continuing scope for various interpretations of what the Reformation actually meant. The Augsburg Confession, that pillar of the Lutheran faith, was not declared the official doctrine of the Swedish Church until 1593, and then only as a by-product of a complicated struggle for the succession. All these factors led to the Swedish Reformation gathering momentum with a generation of clergy who had not been educated in Catholic cathedral schools and universities. Yet this soft landing was by no means a foregone conclusion.

In the kingdom of Denmark, which until the nineteenth century included Norway and Iceland, the Reformation was forced through with much greater determination.

Administration and Economy

The confiscation of Church property and income gave the Swedish Crown economic stability, but to reinforce his position Gustav Vasa carried out a centralisation of government in the 1540s with the help of German specialists. It was not only their expertise that was invaluable—equally pertinent was that, in contrast to the Swedish civil servants, they did not expect remuneration in the form of fiefdoms, but were content with salaries. The same system of salaried and thus easily dismissible officials was also introduced into local administration in a far-reaching reform which increased the tax burden on the peasants. In the western part of the kingdom it was mainly commoners who were appointed as local bailiffs, while in Finland it was the lower nobility, an indication of their modest fortunes and close connections with the common people.

The tax reform and confiscation of Church silver aroused protests, and in the southern Swedish province of Småland sparked off a peasant uprising in 1542–43, known as the Dacke rebellion after its leader, Nils Dacke. The revolt was crushed with some difficulty and convinced Gustav Vasa of the need to consolidate his power further. At the Diet of 1544, hereditary monarchy was introduced on the German model. He also decided to augment his fighting forces by raising a peasant army which swore an oath of allegiance and was thus linked directly to the king. In central Europe the peasants were so suppressed that any such militia would have posed too much of a threat to the monarchy. The risk was less in Sweden, since some 90 per cent of the population consisted of freeholder peasants whose economic interests lay in maintaining the internal and external security of the kingdom.

In the mid-1550s the king's sworn troops were complemented by a similar peasant army in Finland after the Swedo-Russian border disputes had developed into outright war. The two sides agreed peace terms in Novgorod in 1557, but at a local level the peasants continued reciprocal harrying and plundering across the border. The war persuaded the king, after an extended visit to the eastern frontier in 1555–56, to strengthen the Crown's hold over the Finnish aristocracy and to improve Finnish urban administration; he also converted that part of the kingdom into a duchy and appointed his second eldest son Johan as Duke of Finland. His other three sons were given their own duchies in the western part of the realm.

Consolidation of royal power was integral to the gradual eastward expansion of the Swedish kingdom, as it was to expansion southwards. Yet this does not adequately account for such an under-populated country being able to compete so successfully with its neighbours and play such a significant part in European great-power politics in the seventeenth century. The population of the kingdom of Sweden was about 1.2 million in 1570, less than a tenth of that of Russia or France. One key to the puzzle was the relative efficiency of Swedish centralised government. Another was the modern organisation of its military forces: a militarily effective combination of well-drilled troops and a sizeable and easily mobilised peasant army.

To this must be added a critical geographical advantage, the Baltic Sea, which in the maritime era united the Swedish realm rather as the Mediterranean once linked the constituent elements of the Roman Empire with one another. Many of Sweden's chief towns lay on the Baltic shores. Stockholm did not become the official capital until the seventeenth century, but it was the biggest trading city in the country as early as

1570, when it had 6,000 inhabitants. It was no matter of chance that Stockholm became the heart of the country. Its position at the mouth of Lake Mälaren meant that a considerable proportion of Dalarna iron ore and the agricultural surpluses of the fertile region of Svealand were exported to the world through Stockholm. And since the Baltic was Sweden's elixir of life, it was entirely natural that its trading centre should face eastwards towards Åland and south-west Finland, which formed one of the principal areas of settlement in the kingdom up to the eighteenth century. The economic importance of southern Finland was also evident from the fact that Åbo remained one of the biggest cities in the realm well into the eighteenth century. At the end of the seventeenth century Åbo, with its ca 6,600 inhabitants, had twice the population of the other major towns, Viborg, Uppsala, Norrköping and Kalmar. But largest of all in the seventeenth century was Riga, in Livonia, which strictly speaking was not within the Swedish realm but in its Baltic provinces.

So control of the country's finances required control of its main trading centres. To that end, in 1550, Gustav Vasa founded a new harbour city on the northern shore of the Gulf of Finland, at Vanda fors (stream) in the parish of Helsinge. It was called Helsingfors, still its Swedish name, known in Finnish as Helsinki. Gustav Vasa was disappointed with the commercial development of Åbo and wanted to create a different centre for export trade between the Gulf of Finland and Atlantic Europe. But despite the active efforts of local government to attract merchants and citizens to Helsingfors, the new city came nowhere near to fulfilling the king's expectations. One specific intention had been to outstrip the Hansa city of Reval (Tallinn) on the southern shore of the Gulf of Finland. Only a few years later a war broke out between Russia and the Teutonic Order in the Baltic which shifted Russian export trade from Reval to Viborg, and in 1561 Reval and all of northern Estonia was annexed to Sweden's empire, completely remodelling the economic geography of the region. Newly founded Helsingfors was paralysed, but over the following two centuries its economic significance and population was to grow slowly but surely.

Yet the urban population constituted only a fraction (3 per cent at most) of the realm's inhabitants by the end of the sixteenth century. As the Crown strengthened its control over the finances of the towns, the still small numbers of urban-dwellers had to accept the fact that their influence at a local level was correspondingly diminished. The political castration of the clergy was taking place at the same time, and when during the sixteenth century the nobility too became an encumbrance to unfettered monarchical power, its ranks increased only marginally. Ennoblement became quite a rare occurrence, and the frequent wars substantially depleted the aristocracy, who earned their tax-free status through military service. Their function as the warrior class was very much a reality in Finland, and the proportion of Finnish nobility within the overall aristocracy of Sweden rose in the second half of the sixteenth century. Aristocratic titles began to be hereditary just at the time (1569) when the Finns were armed for war. In 1600 half of Sweden's aristocracy lived in Finland, but since they mainly comprised the impoverished lower nobility, their political influence was by no means commensurate with their numbers.

A study of Finland's population as a whole reveals how vital its agrarian economy was. Some calculations have shown that agriculture in Finland, with its ancillary industries, could have supported no more than 50,000 people in the early Middle Ages (twelfth century). Through continued clearances, improved agricultural methods and the opening up of burn-beat cultivation areas, Finland's population swelled to about 300,000 by

1570, just under a third of the population of the entire king-dom. There was slower population growth from then to 1750, when the world's first comprehensive census counted 427,000 inhabitants in the eastern part of the kingdom, just under a sixth of the overall population (2.3 million).

In the mid-sixteenth century almost 50 per cent of the inhabitants of Finland lived in the south-west, in Finland Proper, Satakunda and Tavastland. They supported themselves through agriculture, stockbreeding and fishing. The other half was comprised of burn-beaters and hunters, who ranged over much wider areas than the settled agrarian population and thus did not construct sizeable villages, nor even necessarily any fixed abode at all. The tax reforms in the 1540s increased the burden on the peasants, and so the promise of three years' exemption for fresh cultivation led to extensive clearances in the old agricultural regions. For the same reason, burn-beaters from the province of Savolax spread out across the wilderness regions of northern Tavastland, Ostrobothnia and even to the forested regions of central Sweden and Norway.

Gustav Vasa's decision to establish four duchies in the most inhabited regions of his realm was motivated by a desire to reduce the competition among his sons and to secure the family's hold on the succession. The Vasa dynasty kept the crown until 1654, but otherwise nothing proceeded as planned. Johan had considerable administrative autonomy in his duchy, which comprised the populous areas of south-western Finland. He also became commander of the army which fought against Russia (1555–57), with the result that under his regime the eastern part of the realm developed into something of a state within a state. Johan set up his own court at Åbo Castle and gathered about him Finland's leading nobles, who ruled over the duchy on the same principles as the Council of the Realm in Stockholm. Control over the Finnish tax bailiffs was made

2.4: The coat of arms of Finland was designed for the sarcophagus of King Gustav Vasa in Uppsala Cathedral, finished in 1583. Drawing of the coat of arms and the hard-working people of the Grand Duchy from 1712.

more effective by the establishment of a separate Treasury, and the number of bailiffs was augmented to facilitate the collection of taxes.

War and Family Feuds

After their father's death in 1560 a bitter power struggle broke out between Johan and the heir to the throne, Erik XIV. The

41

latter was angry at his younger brother's intractability, and after Johan had married the Polish princess Katarina Jagellonica in 1562, Erik had his brother imprisoned for treason. Erik had earlier approved the marriage, but when Sweden and Poland went to war that same year for control of the Baltic, he had reason to suppose that the marriage was part of Johan's own struggle for power. His suspicions were not without foundation. Johan had given his Polish father-in-law a generous loan in exchange for seven castle counties in Livonia, which Erik XIV had been expecting to conquer. Matters were exacerbated by the fact that Johan had earlier refused to make a similar loan to the Swedish Crown.

Erik XIV belonged to the first generation of European monarchs to have received a good all-round education from leading scholars, but lofty theories and social graces were not sufficient to gain control of the Swedish high nobility. Erik had inherited his father's hot temper but not his cunning. In an open schism with the nobility in 1567 he became deranged and participated in the murder of five of their most prominent members. This led the nobles to free the king's brother from prison, and the following year they elected him as the new monarch. The mentally impaired Erik was then himself incarcerated, and after nine years in prison was killed, on Johan's orders, by arsenic poisoning.

Johan III's rule (1568–92) was a period of stable relations between monarch and nobility. The king agreed to make the aristocracy hereditary in 1569, but resisted demands for any substantial increase in their fiefdoms. The system of salaried civil servants introduced by Gustav Vasa was now extended to apply to administrators and officers from the nobility, strengthening Johan's hold on power. But behind the outward calm, conflict was smouldering, and it would flare up in earnest after Johan's death in 1592. Through his marriage and close relations with Poland, he was much influenced by Catholicism and he annulled a number of Lutheran elements in the liturgy with his own "Red Book" liturgy of 1577. This greatly vexed the Protestant clergy and upper nobility, who soon found a tacit ally in the king's brother, Duke Karl.

Johan III's interest in theological matters was genuine and he arranged for gifted trainee priests to be sent discreetly to Catholic seminaries in Germany and Rome. The main reason for his ecumenical stance was its compatibility with his foreign policy, aimed at forging an alliance with Poland to drive Russia out of the Baltic. And behind this lay his ambition of making his Catholic heir, his son Sigismund, ruler of a Polish-Swedish union. The Catholic Church saw its opportunity to impose a comprehensive counter-Reformation on the whole of northern Europe, and secretly set up a Jesuit centre in Stockholm in 1576, which, however, was exposed and closed down some years later.

Johan had taken over a kingdom which had been on a war footing with Denmark and Lübeck since 1563. When he managed to negotiate an acceptable peace with the Danes in 1570, the border disputes in the east had already degenerated into open conflict with Russia. The war in the east would continue with fluctuating intensity for twenty-five years, until the Treaty of Teusina in 1595, when Russia renounced its demands for the usufruct of the great forests of Finland's interior and recognised the Swedish presence in Estonia. The frontier demarcation was now for the first time drawn right up to the Arctic Ocean. The whole of the Ladoga region and Ingria—where St Petersburg was later to be built—became part of Russia again.

The resolution of the border meant that Johan III's vision of the northern Baltic as an internal Swedish sea had almost been realised. Unfortunately he had died three years earlier. The war with Russia had required much of Sweden's military capacity to be moved to Finland. When the fighting intensified in the 1570s, all the tax revenue from the eastern half of the kingdom was actually expended on financing the war. The management of Finland's public finances was put in the hands of a separate governor with authority similar to that which Johan had possessed twenty years before as Duke of Finland.

Encouraged by his successes on the battlefield, Johan had decided in 1581 to add to his royal titles the epithet "Grand Duke of Finland", and had a coat of arms designed for the Grand Duchy which is still the official escutcheon of Finland today. The coat of arms had already been commissioned to adorn Gustav Vasa's tomb in Uppsala Cathedral. The sarcophagus was completed in 1583 and its thirteen coats of arms of the various provinces, in Renaissance style, included one of the Grand Duchy, with additional elements from two other escutcheons: the Göta lion from the national coat of arms with the straight sword of the West above the Russian scimitar from the Karelian shield. The reference to the continuing war with Russia was didactically explicit: the triumphal lion brandishing the sword aloft and trampling on the scimitar, itself a symbol of Turkish and Islamic influence.

After Johan's death in 1592 there was a struggle for the succession in which the sword was primarily pointed at fellow countrymen. Sigismund, the heir to the throne, was not regarded by the upper nobility and the clergy in Sweden as a fellow countryman, but as the representative of Poland and Catholicism. He was already king of Poland, which made it difficult for him to stay long in Sweden to defend his interests. In 1593 he had to consent to Lutheranism as the official faith of the Swedish state, and the following year he was crowned king of Sweden. The next year his uncle Duke Karl (Gustav Vasa's third son) contrived to get himself appointed regent, and an overt power struggle began between the two.

Duke Karl had some support in the Council of the Realm. But Finland was ruled by a loyal adherent of King Sigismund, the uncompromising regent, marshal and admiral of the fleet, Klas Fleming. Thus Finland was centre stage for the entire duration of the struggle for the succession in the years 1596–99. Duke Karl managed to stir up the Finnish peasantry to general uprisings against Fleming's troops, whose provisioning and quartering had made severe demands on the peasants' resources. But the peasants' revolt was ruthlessly crushed by Fleming's well-trained army, fresh from its victories on the eastern front. The final toll of what came to be known as the "Club War" was as many as 3,000 peasants killed in battle or executed, a very high figure for a European peasant insurgency in relation to the country's population (1 per cent of the total).

In the autumn of 1598 Sigismund's troops were decisively beaten in a battle in southern Sweden. Duke Karl seized power brutally and in the following year the forces loyal to the king were compelled to surrender after several large-scale battles. On capturing Åbo Castle in the autumn of 1599, Duke Karl had some forty of the leaders faithful to Sigismund condemned to death. One of the few to escape execution was Arvid Stålarm, governor of Finland after the death of Klas Fleming in 1597—he was needed for military operations in the Baltic countries. This was the duke's robust method of seeing that justice was done, and when he was appointed sovereign as King Karl IX, every remaining element of Finnish autonomy and religious ambivalence was effectively eradicated. Henceforth, the official ideology of the realm was based on an orthodox interpretation of Lutheranism, with special emphasis on the theocratic doctrine of the king as God's chosen representative.

So Finland played a prominent role in the politics of the Swedish realm during the latter half of the sixteenth century. In subsequent Finnish national historiography it would be asserted that the nobility in Finland was motivated by national interests during the "Club War". But since the 1970s some scholars have seen the "Club War" rather as a domestic class struggle and the nobility's fidelity to the king as pure self-interest. Results of recent research, however, suggest that the loyalty of the Finnish aristocracy to Sigismund was most likely to have been founded on an innate conservatism and a justified fear of Duke Karl's vengeance.

3

GREAT POWER OF THE NORTH

Sweden's Great Power period is often delineated in historical surveys as the era between two peace treaties: Stolbova in 1617 and Nystad in 1721. The Peace of Stolbova led to Russia's withdrawal from the Baltic, giving Sweden a certain amount of political security and economic stability, but it was not until the second half of the seventeenth century that it paid a dividend in the form of power and influence in European great-power politics. It is also arguable whether such influence was effective after 1700, when Sweden had been drawn into a long and destructive war on numerous fronts. It lost its hegemony over the Baltic in 1721 and Russia then became the dominant power in northern Europe.

Irrespective of how broadly or narrowly the era is dated, it is remarkable that a kingdom with such a small population and so peripheral a geographical position could attain such influence in the European arena. The two factors which outweighed these handicaps have already been mentioned: an efficiently administered central government and army, and the Baltic's function as an internal Swedish sea. Creating such a domestic waterway demanded an expansionist programme of conquest, which gradually gave Sweden control over all the strategic and economically important routes and ports around the Baltic.

Success in this military feat also required one other factor: sufficiently weak and mutually antagonistic neighbours.

Impetus for Expansion

There was no fully developed plan of action for all this in the Royal Palace in Stockholm at the beginning of the seventeenth century. Each monarch made his decisions more or less autocratically, thus constantly triggering unforeseen chain reactions. Such was the case with Karl IX's campaign in the Baltic countries in the first few years of the century. It was a war emanating from the Swedish struggle for the succession, and arose from a desire to prevent Poland gaining control over the southern shores of the Gulf of Finland and Russian export trade. The Poles allied themselves with the Russians, but it was Karl IX's good fortune that Russia simultaneously became embroiled in its own destructive struggle for the succession, which was to marginalise it in seventeenth-century great-power politics. The Swedish Crown was not slow to exploit this. In the spring of 1610 Russo-Polish resistance had been weakened to such a degree that Swedish forces were able to march into Moscow. And in the intoxication of victory, there were even plans to make the crown prince, later to become King Gustav II Adolf (Gustavus Adolphus), tsar of Russia.

Even though this castle in the air was soon demolished, the Swedish army had acquired a stranglehold on Russia which resulted in the whole of the Ladoga region, with Ingria and Nöteborg (Schlüsselburg, now Petrokrepost) and the River Neva, being annexed as provinces of Sweden in the Peace of Stolbova in 1617. The new eastern frontier was moved away from the areas of Finland that had belonged to the Swedish realm since the thirteenth century, and this brought about many significant changes in the country. Firstly, Viborg with its

Savolax hinterland lost its role as military border stronghold. Instead its function switched to that of cultural, administrative and economic centre for the entire eastern part of the Gulf of Finland and the conquered eastern provinces. One of the new border fortresses was Nyenskans at the mouth of the Neva, constructed in 1611 and given staple rights in 1642 in the hope that as a town it would become a hub for trade with the east. This was indeed to come about—but under Russian governance with the founding of St Petersburg in 1703.

The second consequence of the move of the eastern frontier far beyond the Gulf of Finland was that Finland was no longer the most important area of expansion in the Swedish realm. Through the conquests in the Baltic countries, Germany and southern Sweden, the centre of gravity of the kingdom was slowly but surely shifting south to more densely populated and fertile regions of Europe that could provide the Crown and the aristocracy with higher incomes than could Finland. At the end of the sixteenth century, the population of Finland had comprised hardly a third of that of the kingdom in its entirety. A hundred years on, the proportion had shrunk to a mere 10 per cent, even including the Baltic provinces. Since Finland, unlike the Baltic provinces, was administratively and culturally integrated into the realm—Finland was explicitly referred to as the eastern part of the kingdom—the country kept its official rank and status above that of the provinces right up until its separation from Sweden in 1809.

There was no real alternative to the Swedish policy of war and conquest. A defensive line would have required a much greater investment in fortifications and maintenance than active warfare, since the Swedish army in the seventeenth century lived predominantly on conquest and financial support from its allies, among which the most significant was France. Attack was seen as the best means of defence. But in the long term, keeping its forces on a constant war footing was an immense burden on the Crown, especially as on several occasions neighbouring states went to war against Swedish hegemony in the Baltic on two fronts at the same time.

In rather simplified terms, these wars of conquest in the period 1617–48 took the form of a protracted movement around the Baltic, from Russia to the Baltic countries and onwards to Poland and Germany. After Sweden and France emerged victorious from the Thirty Years War and had strengthened their positions in great-power politics through

3.1: During the regency period of the Swedish King Gustav II Adolf the army and central administration were considerably modernised. As a frantic Lutheran he led Sweden into the Thirty Years War and fell at the Battle of Lützen in 1632.

the Peace of Westphalia in 1648, Swedish war efforts were directed mainly towards Denmark. Swedo-Danish rivalry had begun in the period of union and would continue with varying intensity until 1814. The two neighbours fell into dispute with unusual frequency in the second half of the seventeenth century. The result of these bloody forays around the Baltic was that by 1679 the kingdom of Sweden had attained territorial dimensions that would remain intact until the Great Northern War (1700–21).

Swedish historians are still writing thick tomes in mass-market editions about the wars and monarchs of the Great Power period, and unsurprisingly the Thirty Years War is almost always the focus of attention. For this war also had a revolutionising effect on the administrative and cultural development of the country. Yet the prime motive for Gustav II Adolf joining the Protestant side in the war against the forces of Catholic Germany was military rather than religious. Catholic troops had been advancing slowly northwards ever since the outbreak of war in 1618, and by 1629 they were threatening the north German town of Stralsund, an important trading partner for Sweden, from which it sought military assistance. The Swedish king saw a chance to strengthen his grip on north Germany and landed an army of 40,000 men.

A force of that size could only be financed for any length of time through comprehensive subsidies, and thanks to significant victories at the beginning of the war, France and Holland agreed to lend their financial support. When the Swedish army reached its full strength in 1634 (150,000 men), it consisted primarily of central European mercenaries and Swedo-Finnish reserve troops. But the secret behind Gustav II Adolf's battle successes was his assiduous study of the art of warfare and of tactical innovations, principally improvements in troop mobility and the synchronisation of weaponry.

Attacks would begin with drumfire from the musketeers and artillery, then the cavalry would gallop in with drawn swords. When the enemy had given way, the horse-drawn artillery were quickly brought up for renewed drumfire. The free-formation cavalry attacks straight into enemy lines perfectly suited the Finnish soldiery, who were physically fit and well motivated but lacked sustained training in military drill. Their mobilisation was effected on a voluntary basis through the provisioning system, which allowed for a reduction of thirty *riksdaler* in annual tax for retaining a horseman armed for Crown service. The cavalry war cry "*Hakkaa päälle*" ("Cut them down") soon gave rise to the nickname *hackapeliter* in Swedish, which eventually became synonymous with Finnish fighting spirit in general.

When the king fell at the Battle of Lützen in 1632, the Swedish army lost its resolve. The war impoverished all sides and after increasingly ruthless fighting concluded in the "Swedish" army's victory and the Peace of Westphalia in 1648. This was the first pan-European peace congress and it laid the foundation for a key diplomatic principle of international politics: the importance of a balance of power between the major Continental protagonists. The peace also marked the official termination of Europe's Christian *res publica*, the unity of the Western Church, because the Papacy and its Catholic allies were compelled to recognise the existence of a Protestant Europe.

The peace also brought significant economic advantage to Sweden. Several north German ports and large swathes of Pomerania were annexed to the kingdom as provinces. In political terms the Peace of Westphalia was otherwise something of a Pyrrhic victory, since it obliged the Great Power of the north to involve itself in central European conflicts in a completely different way from before. The war had destroyed the remains of the Holy Roman Empire and weakened the

Papacy's political grip on Germany, but it also allowed scope for French and Prussian ambitions.

The Swedish peace delegation was led by the chancellor, Axel Oxenstierna, who had ruled the kingdom from 1632 to 1644 when Queen Kristina was a minor. Centralised government had been made more efficient by the administrative reforms of 1634, driven by the eternal warmongering, which required decision-making processes, taxation and the supply of troops to function at all times, especially as the monarchs in the seventeenth century were either minors or fully occupied by wars.

In the big trading nations of Holland and England, capital for war could be raised through temporary expedients. The agrarian kingdom of Sweden created a number of civil service departments, known as colleges, to the same end, most of the heads of which were members of the Council of the Realm. It was a concept concocted in haste but soon to prove its worth— indeed it still does, as "departments of state" in Sweden and "ministries" in Finland. Provincial government was rationalised in a similar way in 1635 by a more precise definition of the authority and responsibilities of provincial governors.

In the Time of the Count

In essence there was an increasing professionalism in the decision-making process, not necessarily speeding up decisions but rendering them more fully considered and more lastingly viable. This was becoming essential for the cohesion of the realm, not least since its linguistic and cultural plurality had been extended substantially through the conquest of new provinces. In the sixteenth century its languages were Swedish, Finnish, Estonian and Lappish (Sami). In the following century the affairs of German, Danish, Latvian, Polish and Russian subjects had to be administered too.

The slimmed-down administration helped to hold the expanding kingdom together, but it gave rise to new problems as well. Top civil servants and victorious generals had to be rewarded if their commitment to the monarchy was to be maintained. During Queen Kristina's reign (1644–54) three times as many ennoblements were made as in the whole of the previous century (368 compared with 116), and since the Crown did not have the resources to pay them all big salaries, fiefdoms were frequently granted in lieu. At the height of this practice in the 1650s, the nobility owned two-thirds of the total area of Sweden and Finland, and this depleted the Crown's tax revenue considerably, which led to demands from the other three Estates (clergy, burghers and peasants) for a substantial reduction in the granting of fiefs. Because of wars, reluctant rulers and another guardian regency from 1660 to 1672, any such change had to wait until the advent of absolutism in 1680.

The social development of Finland was much affected by these wars and nationwide reforms, but also had some distinct features of its own. The administration of the eastern half of the realm had wider areas of responsibility than the west's, which made supervision from Stockholm more problematical. To compensate for this, a separate governor-general's office for Finland was instituted in 1623. The incumbent was given comprehensive powers and at times functioned in as sovereign a manner as the dukes and governors of Finland in the previous century. But since the office was awarded exclusively to loyal adherents of the unity of the realm, there were no serious conflicts of interest between Stockholm and Åbo, where the governor-general's administration was based.

The first two governor-generals carried out the administrative reforms quite effectively. When the third, Count Per Brahe (the Younger), arrived in Åbo in the autumn of 1637, many of these reforms had by then become so established in

3.2: Per Brahe, twice Governor-General of the Grand Duchy of Finland in the mid-seventeenth century.

Finland that his contributions were not particularly original. The reason posterity remembered Brahe's two periods of governorship (1637–41 and 1648–54) was that he completed some important initiatives and succeeded inordinately well in asserting the significance of his own achievements. He was a member of one of the leading aristocratic families in the land, but it was his rivalry with Oxenstierna, the chancellor, that persuaded him to accept appointment as governor-general of Finland rather than remain a nonentity in the Council of the Realm.

Brahe already had considerable fiefdoms throughout the realm and would be rewarded during his second governorship with the barony of Kajana, comprising huge tracts of eastern and northern Finland. This all gave the new governor-general obvious authority and added to the status of his extensive tours of inspection in Finland, which took on more or less the character of the royal tours made by newly elected kings of Sweden in the Middle Ages. The regal impression was enhanced by his large retinue, which frequently included his wife Kristina Stenbock, daughter of one of his aristocratic colleagues in the Council of the Realm.

These travels had a practical aim too. Brahe had been charged with improving the country's legal system, armed forces, towns and taxes. On his return to Sweden in 1640 he wrote a long and effusive report on how well everything had gone in Finland under his governance. Similar reports were sent to the capital during his second period of governorship. Although much of this was empty boasting, Brahe nevertheless pushed through three important reforms, which gave some validity to the expression later common in Finland, "in the time of the Count". The Royal Mail was established in Stockholm in 1636 and within two years Brahe had set up local post offices in every town of any size in Finland and Ingria, making a real impact on communications between Stockholm and the eastern parts of the realm. And in March 1640, with Brahe's enthusiastic support, the foundation document was issued for Åbo Akademi, the university which was to play a pivotal role in Finland's academic and cultural life. But of paramount importance was Brahe's dynamic contribution to the prosperity of Finland's towns. The idea was not his own, but stemmed from contemporary mercantile theories, which prescribed that the Crown should seek control of all notable trade. The system came into being after 1610 and was primarily based on the difference between staple towns and inland towns. Only a few towns had staple rights, that is the right to engage in external trade. The others had to buy and sell their produce via the staple towns, which the system favoured through both trade and duties. All the export trade in the Gulf of Bothnia was concentrated on Stockholm, and of the towns in Finland, only Åbo, Helsinki and Viborg were granted staple rights. Another aspect of increasing control was that the Crown started appointing the towns' mayors, which of course encouraged the willingness of the local authorities to put royal orders and regulations into effect.

At the same time, in order to establish better control over domestic trade, new towns were still being founded. Brahe's predecessors had concentrated on developing the staple ports of Åbo and Viborg. Of the ten towns that Brahe established in the interior of Finland and along the coast of Ostrobothnia, nearly all became major centres of population in due course. In the summer of 1639 he made a lengthy tour of inspection through Ostrobothnia and was impressed by the settlement and potential of the region. His positive reaction was not solely the result of the season nor the fact that he had only recently acquainted himself with conditions in the interior. Shipping trade with Stockholm had already begun to make its mark on the economy of Ostrobothnia. To stimulate these developments further, Brahe founded three new ports there in his second period of governorship: Brahestad (Raahe) in 1649, Kristinestad (Kristiinankaupunki) in 1649 and Jakobstad (Pietarsaari) in 1652.

But what did the Ostrobothnians and other subjects of the Swedish Crown in Finland have that they could sell overseas? Export trade had only a minimal effect on Finland's economy up until the end of the sixteenth century, and consisted almost entirely of barter trade in furs and salmon. Only 5 per cent of the population earned a living from anything other than agriculture, hunting and fishing. Self-sufficiency was the norm and the surplus was mainly used to pay tax. Grain was exported only from the state corn stores in the Baltic countries, Pomerania, and Skåne (after 1660). The exponential growth in world trade in the seventeenth century began to make big changes in the division of labour between western Europe, the Baltic region and elsewhere in northern Europe. The rise of capitalist commerce brought an increase in urbanisation and population in Holland and southern England, at the price of devastation of the forests and shortages of timber and firewood.

These shortages benefited the more forested regions of Europe, not least the kingdom of Sweden, whose control over Baltic traffic offered plenty of scope for regulating the supply and price of various products. Distance to the commercial metropolises was a critical factor in determining which forestry products were worth exporting. Norway's proximity to Holland and Britain gave it a crucial market advantage in the export of timber products and sawn timber right up to the nineteenth century. The geographical position of the Swedish realm was more suited to a divide: west Swedish exports were similar to the Norwegian, with the emphasis on sawn timber and timber products, whereas in the Baltic area it was more economically viable to exploit the forests as a primary resource for the manufacture of three products much in demand: iron, copper and tar.

Green Gold

The international profitability of the Swedish iron and steel industry was based on its access to high-grade iron ore and vast forests. There was plenty of ore in western Europe but not enough timber that could be turned into charcoal for the foundries. So new ironworks were established in the seventeenth century all over central Sweden and in the south-west corner of Finland, to which iron ore was shipped from the

Bergslagen region of southern Dalarna and the Stockholm archipelago to be smelted. The Finnish ironworks, of which there were no more than about twenty, were often transitory because of poor profitability, and were insignificant in comparison with the more than 300 iron foundries in Sweden itself. Throughout the seventeenth century the iron and copper industries together provided 80 per cent by value of the kingdom's export trade. The relative share of copper gradually declined because of dwindling resources, but it still comprised a quarter of total export value in 1685.

Tar as a proportion of export value rose in the same period from 2 to 8 per cent. Seen from a national perspective, this may not have been much, but for the eastern half of the realm, where tar and pitch were by far the most significant export products, it was considerable: two-thirds by value of all exports. In Sweden the need for wood for the iron industry led the Crown to concentrate tar production in Finland. There were logistical reasons too. The distance from Finland to the western European markets was obviously further than from the centre of the realm in Sweden, which meant it was more profitable to process wood into the more compact tar than to ship it out into the world as timber. So three-quarters of the total tar produced came from the eastern half of the kingdom in the Great Power period, which had a substantial impact on the economy of the tar-producing provinces of Ostrobothnia, Savolax and Karelia.

The huge demand for tar was a consequence of the rapid growth of seaborne trade in Atlantic Europe and across the world's oceans. Merchant ships and slaving vessels, frigates and ships of the line, barges and rowing boats—all had hulls and decks that had to be protected and made watertight with this black viscous substance. And since in practice the kingdom of Sweden had a monopoly on tar production through its control of the Baltic, this refined product from deep in the forests of Finland was distributed all over the world.

The production method had been introduced in the early seventeenth century from Prussia, where, exactly as in Finland, there was plenty of sandy soil with a prolific growth of pine, the raw material for tar. Young pines were felled and dried, and the trunks were laid radiating outwards in circular tar pits to have their resin extracted by a slow-burning process which produced tar and pitch. Pitch was a more solid by-product which was also used to protect and impregnate, but its economic importance was marginal. Tar was collected in barrels and transported along rivers, lakes and coastal routes to Stockholm or Viborg, from where 70 to 80 per cent was exported abroad.

Production was labour-intensive but required little by way of investment. This was a welcome financial benefit, especially as the merchants provided accommodation, credit and salt in exchange for the peasants' undertaking to deliver a certain number of barrels of tar. It was in the merchants' interest to contract as many tar producers as possible. They frequently even offered to pay the peasants' tax. The system was useful to the Crown, but production figures shot up and it decided in 1647 to create a trade monopoly in a tar company in Stockholm to limit supply, regulate quality and maximise the middleman's profit.

This intervention had the desired effect. Production was kept down, prices rose, and in the second half of the century national tar export stabilised at about 110,000 barrels a year. The monopoly meant that the tar company in Stockholm was able to stipulate production quotas, which unsurprisingly gave rise to dissatisfaction among producers and the merchants in the staple towns. When the Dutch and the British disturbed the balance of the system for several years in the 1680s and a free market prevailed, the profits went abroad, whereupon the Crown was quick to renew the tar company's concession. Ostrobothnian tar from Finland was mainly exported through the capital and was given the brand name "Stockholm tar", while barrels from Savolax and Karelia were shipped from Viborg and so stamped with a "W" (Wiborg in contemporary orthography). Stockholm tar was sold primarily to the British, and thanks to its quality fetched a higher price than the Viborg product, which found its buyers as much in Amsterdam as in London.

The Great Northern War (1700–21) and the loss of Great Power status for Sweden brought to an end the dominance of its tar company on the international market. North American and Russian producers forced the prices down, and even though the combined production of the shrinking kingdom had soon risen to over 200,000 barrels a year during the eighteenth century, profit margins were steadily declining. The region that overcame this stagnation best was Ostrobothnia, where tar-burning underwent a resurgence of prosperity at the close of the eighteenth century when the national staple regulations were abolished and the North Americans lost their trade privileges on the British market. A busy shipbuilding and sawmill industry was also rapidly expanding, but tar remained the region's most valuable export right up to the second half of the nineteenth century, when steel-hulled ships and synthetic waterproofing agents eliminated the demand for tar.

By that time the sawn timber industry had already overtaken tar-burning as Finland's major export business, although the transition was a slow one. Just as burn-beating continued as a ubiquitous form of cultivation throughout the golden age of tar-burning in the seventeenth century, so tar-burning was to continue on a widespread basis right through the nineteenth century even when sawn timber was the principal form of forest exploitation. The three kinds of forestry were already co-existent in the Finnish economy in the seventeenth century. In the south-west and along the coast of Ostrobothnia agriculture and stockbreeding existed side by side with tar-burning and timber production. In the interior the combination was more likely to be burn-beating and tar-burning, while northern Finland was best suited to stockbreeding.

A Homogeneous Lutheran Culture

Economic and political realities dictated the material conditions of everyday life, but the population was also subjected to an indoctrination which brought a unified culture to the whole realm over the course of the seventeenth century. The process was conducted by the Church and the administrative apparatus of the state, both of which had been polished into efficient tools in the hands of the monarch. The role of the Church in this regard cannot be overestimated. The ideological heart of the Lutheran church service was the sermon, which in the Great Power period increasingly included political content and reminders that respect for the monarchy was inseparable from fear of God. The destructive effect of sin on both the individual and society was another recurrent theme. According to the ever more orthodox interpretation of Lutheran doctrine, unatoned sins would incur the wrath of God, which at the very worst could strike the entire country in the shape of war, pestilence or famine.

The battle against heinous sins was waged in full accord with the Crown and was initiated in 1608 when Karl IX decreed the application of strict Old Testament laws. Prior to the seventeenth century, murder, insults and various sexual crimes could be expiated by fines or monetary recompense between families. Now the Crown strengthened its hold on the courts and reinstated the death penalty, carried out in public along with a general admonition to the assembled crowd. The Stockholm Court of Appeal (Svea hovrätt) was augmented by new courts of appeal in Åbo (1623), Dorpat (Tartu) (1630) and Jönköping (1634) to bring more uniformity and efficiency to the administration of justice.

At about this time the Church was increasing ecclesiastical penances and punishments. One concrete measure was the introduction of pews, which facilitated both hierarchical placing of the congregation by rank and a register of attendance. Bans or fines were imposed for minor misdemeanours. But

3.3: The highly educated Queen Kristina was regent when the Swedish Kingdom reached its peak as a northern Great Power in the mid-seventeenth century.

exposure of marital crimes or other crimes against morality brought castigation in the form of public humiliation. The aim of course was to instil fear in the congregation and warn them that sins would be punished, but since people were only human there was actually a steep rise in the prosecution of moral offences. A further manifestation of the greater control exercised over the populace were the numerous witch trials, usually targeted at individuals who were already outcasts from their communities.

The local clergy bore much of the responsibility for ensuring that the homogeneous Lutheran culture was properly adhered to. The priest had to win the trust of his flock and speak on its behalf when the Crown wanted to impose higher taxes and levies. The priest was ex officio chairman of parish meetings, where decisions were made about parish buildings and care of the poor, among other things, all of which required a thorough knowledge of the local vernacular, the vocabulary and syntax of which varied considerably from place to place.

The material conditions of pastoral care improved in a number of ways during the seventeenth century. The construction of expensive stone churches declined with the Reformation, and this trend continued in Finland into the Great Power period, when only six churches were built of stone. The architectural innovation of the era was the timber cruciform church, made to the same floor plan as Renaissance churches on the Continent. Wood was easy for local builders to work but was of course flammable, which explains why only three of Finland's twenty-five seventeenth-century cruciform churches have survived. The decoration of the churches was largely financed by donations from local worthies.

A complete translation of the Bible in Swedish had been published in 1541, but the first Finnish translation of the Bible in its entirety did not appear until 1642. It was based on Agricola's Finnish translation of the New Testament of 1548, and it benefited from extensive study of other translations. The first edition, of 1,200 copies, was printed in Stockholm, with a portrait of Queen Kristina and all the regional coats of arms of the kingdom on the title page. It was distributed to every parish in Finland and Ingria and would prove to be normative for the written Finnish language and particularly its Lutheran vocabulary.

The equivalent religious influence on Swedish was Karl XII's Bible of 1703, which had an enormous impact on the revitalisation and standardisation of the language. At its best, the Swedish hymnal of 1695 provided a common heritage for the whole realm until the nineteenth century. Popular hymns were the hits of their day, sung communally on occasions of both joy and sorrow. The most widely known to posterity is a paean of praise to the summer landscape, with a simple but sonorous melody, still sung today in both Sweden and Finland at the end of the school year.

A vital judicial instrument in this cultural homogenisation was the canon law of 1682, which continued in force in Finland until 1869. It incorporated detailed instructions on everything from religious penalties and the duties of the clergy to church buildings and the catechism. Cultural uniformity and Sweden's expansion as a Great Power increased the demand for competent clergy and civil servants. So the Crown established a number of new preparatory schools and grammar schools throughout the country in the 1620s. Teaching underwent reform at the one university in the kingdom, in Uppsala, and as the need for more civil servants steadily grew, two more universities were set up across the Baltic—one in Dorpat (now Tartu, Estonia) in 1632 and one in Åbo in 1640. The Peace of Westphalia gave Sweden a university in the Pomeranian town of Greifswald, and after the conquest of Skåne a university was founded in Lund in 1668.

Wars interrupted academic life in Dorpat and Lund, whereas Åbo Akademi developed in much more stable conditions, so Uppsala and Åbo remained the most important universities in the realm until the early eighteenth century. Åbo had had a cathedral school—later grammar school—since the fourteenth century, and the city had been the seat of a bishopric and the administrative centre for the eastern half of the kingdom, which was reason enough to build a university there. The cause had been promoted by the town notables since the 1630s and the foundation charter was eventually issued under Per Brahe's governor-generalship.

Åbo Akademi was given broadly the same statutes as Uppsala University, with a rector who headed a senate of professors, and with faculties of theology, medicine, law and philosophy. The highest official was the chancellor, and once the seat of learning was finally inaugurated on Brahe's initiative it was only natural that he himself should be the first incumbent, a post he held until his death in 1680. He saw Åbo Akademi primarily as a solution to the shortage of civil servants in the eastern half of the kingdom, but he also ensured that students from his fiefdoms in Småland received bursaries to study in Åbo. Its dozen or so professors and 200 students had a strong Swedish component in any case at the time: most of the professors were recruited from Uppsala and as many as a third of the students came from the western half of the realm. Students from each province formed their own "nations" (student clubs) on the Continental model, under the supervision of a professor, organising festivities and other student events.

The natural sciences had not yet made their appearance in Swedish universities, but Åbo Akademi led the field in theological research at the end of the seventeenth century. So the classical languages were highly regarded even in Åbo: all dissertations were printed and publicly defended in Latin or

Greek. Academic interest in the national languages was not on the same level, despite the fact that both clergy and civil servants needed them in their daily work. Teaching in preparatory and grammar schools was conducted in Swedish. This, together with a Swedish-language central government, led to a substantial Swedification of the educated elite in Finland, which until then had been mainly recruited from the Finnish-speaking peasantry. But, unlike in Skåne, the Crown did not pursue a systematic policy of Swedification, since the Finns' loyalty to the Crown was not in doubt.

There was a similar socio-economic Swedification of the populace in the coastal towns of Finland, which became ever

3.4: The turn to Lutheran faith also resulted in the Church taking responsibility for improvement of literacy. Examination in a Finnish farmer's house.

more closely tied to Stockholm through the staple towns regulation and the amount of trade within the wider realm of the Great Power. But since nineteen out of twenty Finnish subjects lived in rural areas, these shifts had no dramatic effect on the relative strengths of the two linguistic groups. Over 85 per cent of the total population of the eastern half of the kingdom continued speaking exclusively Finnish, while a bare 10 per cent spoke only Swedish. It must also be remembered that it was not language but religion and loyalty to the ruler that created solidarity across class borders. It was the stringent control of Crown and Church which integrated the kingdom's Swedes, Finns, Danes, Germans, Livonians and Estonians into a homogeneous Lutheran culture.

Absolutism and Catastrophe

The alliance between Crown and Church was completed with the advent of absolutism at the Diet of 1680. The concentration of power marginalised the influence of the upper nobility and enabled King Karl XI to push through two major reforms: a sweeping reduction of the aristocracy's fiefdoms and a new system of conscription. The reduction invigorated state finances and freed agricultural land for distribution. Officers were given homes of their own as reimbursement for active service, and received a salary through land tax. The troops were provided by two to four households together maintaining one soldier, who was mobilised for military exercises at regular intervals.

Land distribution was primarily an economic strategy and worked well while there was peace or when wars were fought beyond the country's borders. But as fortunes turned in the Great Northern War and the Swedo-Finnish army retreated within its own frontiers, the Crown had to reintroduce the former system of compulsory conscription. Yet land distribution was retained up to the time of the Russo-Swedish War of 1808–09 in Finland (also known as the Finnish War), which ended Swedish rule in Finland. The system continued in Sweden until the full introduction of general military conscription in 1901.

Karl IX, in contrast to his predecessors, pursued a systematic policy of peace. So Sweden distanced itself from France and sought support from affluent Holland. The result was a twenty-one-year peace along all the borders of the realm—an astonishing length of time by the standards of the period. The strategy was successful principally because European great-power politics then allowed neutrality in foreign policy, but after the death of Karl IX in 1697 it soon became clear how dangerous a defensive balancing act could be. Three years later Sweden was propelled into war against all four of its neighbours (Denmark, Saxony, Poland and Russia), each reckoning on an easy victory over the Swedes, whose new monarch, Karl XII, was still in his teens. The calculations proved misguided. The Swedish army was more fighting fit than ever and Karl XII distinguished himself from the start as an innovative and fearless commander. But in the long term it was impossible to win a war on three fronts—Sweden's manpower resources were simply too limited and the geographical distances much too vast.

There was certainly no lack of self-confidence in Sweden at the close of the Great Power period. The state economy and armed forces were administered in exemplary fashion. Academics in the humanities played an active part by conceiving a real mythology of Sweden's grand prehistoric past. According to the multi-talented Uppsala professor Olaus Rudbeck, Scandinavia, with Sweden at its centre, had actually been Atlantis, Plato's ideal society, which made Sweden the origin of the whole of European civilisation. Rudbeck generously apportioned this honour equally to the western and eastern halves of the kingdom. Likewise, Daniel Juslenius, at Åbo Akademi, repeated in his dissertation *Aboa vetus et nova* (Åbo Old and New) in 1700 a story fabricated in the sixteenth century that his town had been founded immediately after the Flood by Noah's grandson Magog.

Of course, the question is how many people had the opportunity to acquaint themselves with these learned mythologies. The climate of northern Europe was exceptionally cold at the end of the seventeenth century, and those who suffered most were the peasants of Finland and Swedish Norrland, whose harvests were repeatedly destroyed in the 1680s and 1690s by frost and flood. There was famine in 1696 and 1697 and epidemics spread, causing wholesale death. By some calculations around 30 per cent of the population of Finland lost their lives, which would have amounted to about 150,000 people. Finland was by no means the only country affected. Similar food crises occurred in many regions of Europe, but because of the Swedish government's parsimonious attitude to emergency aid and the poor transport conditions in winter, crop failure and sickness escalated into catastrophe for Finland and Norrland.

Unfortunately yet another catastrophe—the Great Northern War—was lurking just round the corner. To begin with, the goddess of war was on the side of the Swedes and Finns. In February 1700, Saxon troops attacked the border fortress in Riga. Simultaneously, the Danes marched into the Duchy of Holstein, which was allied with Sweden. To the surprise of the many-headed enemy these attacks were parried without difficulty, and when a Swedo-Finnish army of a mere 10,000 men under the leadership of Karl XII himself then overcame a Russian force three times its size at the frontier castle at Narva, everything seemed to be going in favour of the Swedes.

The autocratic Karl XII refused to negotiate with his opponents, however, because in his uncompromising Lutheran view they were morally inferior Catholic and Greek Orthodox believers: in other words, heretics. The product of a strict theocratic education, the king was totally convinced he was God's instrument and he neither listened to his advisers nor revealed his plans to them. He ordered his troops onto the offensive and, having compelled both Poland and Saxony to seek peace terms, his attention turned in 1707 to Russia and Moscow. But the campaign ran into mounting difficulties with the huge distances involved and the enemy's tactical scorched-earth policy. The Swedish army was vanquished in 1709 by a numerically superior enemy at a mighty battle in Ukraine near the town of Poltava.

The king fled to Turkey, Sweden's ally, and the remainder of the Swedish army was taken prisoner by the Russians, who with Sweden's other neighbours now launched a formidable counter-attack on every front. The Russian emperor Peter the Great had already taken Ingria in 1703 and founded St Petersburg there at the mouth of the River Neva as the new capital of his expanding Empire. In the spring of 1710 the Russians embarked on their conquest of Finland, which, thanks to Karl XII's absence and total lack of interest in securing the kingdom's north-eastern flank, was successfully completed in 1714. The Council of the Realm in Stockholm should have had the resources to intervene more decisively in Finland, but its members were too powerless and desperate to be able to think about anything other than saving the heart of the kingdom and their own assets.

The occupation of Finland continued until the Peace of Nystad in 1721, and required the Russians to build up a comprehensive support system for their troops there. But it soon became apparent that the country was far too impoverished to provide for an army of occupation 25,000–35,000 strong. As much as 70 per cent of the provisioning had to be brought in by sea from Russia. The aim of the occupation had been to force Karl XII into an early peace and a new frontier demarcation, which explains the Russian army's extensive plundering and ravaging in Ostrobothnia.

Pillaging for strategic reasons was common throughout Europe and not unique to Finland. The intention was to prevent a Swedish counter-attack from northern Finland and also to furnish some recompense for the men. From the point of view of the local populace the devastation caused by the Cossack horsemen was an incomprehensible cruelty, especially as it included the kidnap of civilians. In all, 8,000 civilians were deported to Russia. Not for nothing did the occupation go down in history as "the Great Wrath". The turning point came in 1718 after Karl XII fell in battle on the Norwegian border.

On his return from Turkey in 1715 the king had refused to open peace negotiations, despite their being essential to preserving even the core regions of the kingdom. After his death peace was concluded with each enemy in turn. Prussia and Denmark ceded territory, while the principal victor in the war, Russia, was awarded Livonia, Estonia, Ingria and Karelia at the Peace of Nystad in 1721. Finland's new eastern frontier was drawn just west of Viborg, and since it had been dictated by the tsar, it came to be called the Peter the Great border. The Swedish heir to the throne was the king's younger sister Ulrika Eleonora, who soon handed over the crown to her husband Fredrik of Hesse. The Age of Absolutism was at an end. In the years 1719 to 1724 numerous constitutional laws were ratified which put all real power in the hands of the Estates.

4

STOCKHOLM—ST PETERSBURG

The kingdom of Sweden, like Poland and Holland, had to accommodate itself to the new balance of power in Europe in the eighteenth century. Russian expansion and the consolidation of Prussia took place at the expense of Sweden and Poland. The Dutch were overtaken by the British, who even began to threaten the traditional position of France as the prime power in Europe by the end of the century. Finland's geopolitical situation was all the more exposed in the changing constellation, and during the Napoleonic Wars this eastern part of the Swedish realm was finally lost to Russia.

Finland's integration into Western civilisation in the twelfth and thirteenth centuries had been the first major turning point in its history. The second was Russia's rise to dominance in the Baltic region in the eighteenth century—in the following two centuries Russia would dictate, or at least influence, much of what was to happen in Finland. The main reason for this was that the new capital of the expanding Empire, St Petersburg, was established at the mouth of the River Neva in the Gulf of Finland—a mere 300 kilometres from Helsinki as the crow flies. This proximity gave the south coast of Finland unprecedented significance for European great-power defence policies. If one particular year could be singled out as having determined Finland's fate, it would without any doubt be 1703, when Peter the Great founded his city on the Neva.

City on the Neva and Fortress of Sveaborg

Peter the Great's vision of a Russian capital by the sea was inspired by his impressions of Holland and its canals. St Petersburg was built on a number of islands in the Neva estuary, a few kilometres west of the old town of Nyen and its fortress Nyenskans. The first building, the Peter and Paul Fortress on Zayachy Island, was begun in May 1703, and since Peter had decided to transform the Ingrian marshland into a metropolis, 30,000–40,000 peasants were drafted in every year as forced labour on the enormous building project. Prisoners of war from Finland worked on it too, constructing among other things the boulevard that was to become the city's principal thoroughfare, Nevsky Prospekt.

One manifestation of the burgeoning importance of St Petersburg as a fulcrum of power in northern Europe was its population explosion. In 1710 it had about 8,000 inhabitants. Fifteen years later the number was estimated to have risen to 40,000, an impressive figure in comparison with Stockholm, which originated from the Middle Ages and yet by then had a population of only 60,000. In another twenty-five years, by 1750, the city on the Neva, with 95,000 inhabitants, had definitively outstripped Stockholm. The vast majority of immigrants were Russians, but since the immediate surroundings were home to Finnish-speaking Ingrians, and St Petersburg was also increasingly attracting workers from south-eastern Finland, the metropolis had a Finnish element (1 to 3 per cent) which would still be there well into the twentieth century. The biggest linguistic minority were Germans, but Finns came a close second, their numbers peaking at about 24,000 in 1881.

At the Peace of Nystad in 1721 a new frontier was drawn which in effect split Finland in two. Western Finland remained an integral part of the Swedish realm, while Karelia and the town of Viborg (Viipuri) were annexed to Russia and administered as the *guberniya* of Vyborg. Russia did not expand as a centralised and unified state, but as a patchwork of heterogeneous administrative cultures, which in Vyborg's case meant that the populace was allowed to retain its Lutheran faith and Swedish laws and also avoided serfdom. Proximity to St Petersburg was the key to the economic success of the *guberniya* and predominantly favoured the town of Vyborg itself, the population of which once again acquired a strong German contingent

4.1: The brave Finn. A picture in J. M. Funcke's work *Amphitheatrum* from 1723.

through contacts with the Baltic countries. It was in the eighteenth century that the linguistic diversity of the town (Finnish, Swedish, German, Russian) was at its height.

Administration and culture remained similarly intact in "Swedish" Finland, but in national politics a completely new phase began which has been called the Age of the Estates. Absolutism was replaced in the years 1719–24 by what was for the time a very radical parliamentary constitution, the only counterpart to which was in Great Britain. Legislative powers were vested in the four Estates combined. In principle they would assemble as a parliament every third year, and their political decisions were implemented by the Council of the Realm. The king had a seat and two votes in the Council, but could easily be outvoted by the rest, who were comprised of members enjoying the confidence of the Estates. The nobility remained the most influential of the Estates, but needed to seek support from the others, and this provided more influence for the peasants' Estate in particular.

The change of system gave rise to two competing parties, known as the "Hats" and the "Caps", who alternated in power and governed the kingdom through their majority in parliament. The Caps ruled until 1738 under the leadership of Count Arvid Horn, after which the Hats took over and, with some brief intermissions, ruled the country until 1772, when Gustav III reintroduced absolutism. Horn pursued a defensive eastern policy, which led those of his critics who were thirsting for revenge to describe him and his adherents as "pusillanimous nightcaps".

At the outset, the Hats' chief objective was to regain the lost territories in the east. They drew on considerable financial aid from France, in whose interests it lay to halt the expansion of Russia. Three years after the Hats took power they initiated an ill-prepared attack on Russia, which would go down in history as the Hats' War (1741–43). The offensive soon turned into a retreat and another Russian occupation of Finland, relinquished in the Peace of Åbo in 1743, in which, however, the Swedo-Russian frontier was moved westwards once again. Sweden also undertook not to enter into any alliances without Russia's approval.

This new and, if it were possible, even more humiliating loss resulted in machinations without parallel in Swedo-Finnish domestic politics. During the Hats' War, Tsarina Elizabeth of Russia, for propaganda reasons, had promised Finland independent statehood, a preposterous notion but one which made Finland an intriguing card in the ensuing diplomatic games. The Caps had no hesitation in negotiating with Russia behind the scenes, and on several occasions encouraged the Russians to retake Finland as a pawn to topple the Hat regime. The Russian occupation of 1742–43 had not been a catastrophe, but had rather shown that Russian rule could convey certain advantages, such as free trade.

The Hats attached no special importance to Finland either, but the party changed its attitude after the crushing defeat and in 1747 made systematic efforts to strengthen the country's defences and economy. The shift was marked by a nationwide investment in more frontier fortresses, financed to a large degree by French subsidies. The undertaking was seen unequivocally at the time as a necessary defensive measure, but as the Caps opposition quite rightly pointed out, it tied up such huge resources that the Crown missed a golden opportunity to modernise the army.

Construction of the coastal fortresses of Sveaborg (Suomenlinna) off Helsinki and Svartholm off the new border town of Lovisa (Loviisa) began in the spring of 1748. The work on Sveaborg would continue for the next quarter-century, primarily under the charge of the dynamic army officer Augustin

Ehrensvärd, who made the fort his own creation. He was also the man who proposed the name of Sveaborg, as the eastern border stronghold of the whole realm, corresponding to the Gothenburg defences in the west (the Sveas were one of the original Swedish tribes and the etymological root of the country's name, Sverige [Svea rike, the kingdom of the Sveas]). The original plan called for Helsinki to be surrounded by fortifications and bastions in its entirety. But after a few years all building work was concentrated on a 75-hectare site over five islands immediately to the south of the city. It was nevertheless by far Sweden's most ambitious building project in the eighteenth century, and would not be surpassed until the construction of the Göta Canal in the nineteenth century.

The purpose of Sveaborg and Svartholm was to establish such strong defensive positions in southern Finland that the army could hold out until reinforcements arrived from Sweden. Svartholm would act as the first line of resistance at the frontier, while Sveaborg was intended as the main base and provisioning fortress for both the navy and the army on land. Helsinki had been designated the appropriate place to act as Finland's lock and key as early as the 1720s. It was here that the Russian army and navy under the personal command of Peter the Great had made a decisive landing, and here too there were suitable outer skerries that could be reached easily by sea from Sweden and the Finnish coast. The mighty bastion of Gustavssvärd, incorporating Kungsporten Gate, was erected on the southern main island, and the command post of the fortress and two docks, where a substantial part of the new archipelago fleet was built, were erected on the northern island of Vargön.

The fleet was inspired by Peter the Great, whose galleys had so successfully provisioned the Russian army during its 1712–14 campaign in Finland. Under Ehrensvärd a similar amalga-

4.2: Peter the Great founded the town of St Petersburg in 1703 and thereby changed for all time the geopolitical balance in the Baltic region. Drawing from 1881.

mation of the Swedish army and navy was attempted, with the galleys put under army command as the Army Fleet. Ehrensvärd also had archipelago frigates built, an innovative vessel easier to manoeuvre and with better armaments than the low galleys. Smaller boats were constructed too, and all three types of craft contributed to the Swedish naval victory in the sea battle at Svensksund (Ruotsinsalmi, now Kotka) in 1790.

Despite both Sveaborg and the archipelago fleet being built for defensive purposes, they were a cause of increased tension between Sweden and Russia in the longer term. Finland's role as a military grey zone of little intrinsic economic or political importance was transformed into that of active border fortress against the east. The south coast of Finland, with Sveaborg at its centre, was inevitably regarded as a military problem in St

Petersburg, which was rapidly evolving into one of the leading metropolises in Europe. Its population in the years 1750 to 1800 more than doubled, going from 95,000 to 220,000.

Economic and Social Transformation

The growth of St Petersburg also had far-reaching consequences for the economic development of Finland. The political division into a western Swedish and an eastern Russian Finland did not have its equivalent in respect of trade. It was not only the economy of the Vyborg *guberniya* which slowly but surely began to look eastwards towards the city on the Neva. The greater the demand from the St Petersburg market became, the greater the city's pull on the south coast of Finland still belonging to Sweden. The Ostrobothnian coast was so inextricably linked to the national capital, Stockholm, that the region was barely connected economically to Finland at all, but like Norrland was more of a hinterland to central Sweden. Trade and commerce in the interior of Finland were directed similarly towards either Stockholm or St Petersburg, as determined by distance and access to suitable transport routes.

This development was exactly in line with the mercantile policies of the Swedish Crown and caused rising discontent in Finland, since the authorities were still endeavouring to maintain the staple regulations and combat smuggling. Criticism grew in the early 1760s and the Diet of 1765 decided to abolish the restrictions on Bothnian trade and on peasants shipping their own products. The reform was carried by the Finnish Caps of all four Estates, their leading spokesman being the Ostrobothnian chaplain Anders Chydenius, whose incisive pamphlets and contributions to debate demolished the arguments of the mercantile establishment. Best known was his *Den nationnale winsten* (The National Good), 1765, in which his cogent theories on the advantages of a total liberalisation of the economy adumbrated Adam Smith's classic *The Wealth of Nations* (1776).

The loss of the Baltic provinces boosted the ratio of iron and copper products as a proportion of the kingdom's export income. The relative export value of tar also rose somewhat (from 7 per cent to 9 per cent), and since 75 to 90 per cent of it was produced in the eastern half of the realm, Finland (particularly Ostrobothnia) remained the kingdom's principal tar producer. The abolition of the staple regulations brought a noticeable shift of income from Stockholm to the Ostrobothnian merchants, whose vessels were the predominant means of conveyance for most of the exports out of the province at the end of the eighteenth century. Trading houses established direct contacts with British and Dutch buyers and even sent their ships to southern Europe and the West Indies, influencing both consumer patterns and views of the world in the Ostrobothnian coastal towns. Finland's most significant import remained salt, but its maritime trade also introduced novel luxuries such as southern fruits, cocoa and tea.

In Russian Finland there was a marked switch away from tar-burning to the sawmill industry. One reason was the use of a new kind of fine-bladed saw which could be driven very effectively by the abundant waterfalls in south-eastern Finland. The innovation came from Holland and had started to spread around the Baltic from Ingria in the early eighteenth century. It was a technical advance that would come to have a revolutionary impact on the entire coniferous forest area of north-eastern Europe, but Swedish government restrictions on forestry delayed its progress across the Swedo-Russian border in Finland. This was very much to the advantage of Russian Finland and the merchants of Vyborg, who swiftly established themselves as sawmill owners and found lucrative markets in St Petersburg and western Europe.

The Swedish Crown abolished its ban on Dutch saw blades in 1739. Despite that, a considerable number of the sawmills which then appeared on the Swedish side of eastern Finland would export their timber onto the world market through Vyborg. Various restrictions on export trade still persisted, and in any case the Swedish merchant fleet was simply inadequate when world demand for timber, both sawn and unsawn, rose dramatically at the end of the eighteenth century.

It was not only commerce and forestry that underwent big changes. A similar upheaval occurred in agriculture in the latter half of the century, whereas there had not been any notable rise in productivity in the preceding two centuries. Higher taxation, frequent conscription, the hunger years and the Russian reign of terror in 1714–21, the Great Wrath, had lowered both the morale and the working capacity of the peasants. After that there was a recovery, which given the stable conditions and active measures by the authorities, especially after 1743, led to a substantial growth in both yield and land under cultivation.

The Crown's obstinate mercantilism gradually gave way to the physiocratic ideals of the time, which advocated investment in primary industries. More land clearances were encouraged by protracted periods of tax exemption, and the building of crofters' cottages was permitted on all farms. The reforms led to a more than twofold increase in agricultural units in Finland in the fifty years from 1750 (35,000) to 1800 (80,000), and since the upward trend persisted until the 1860s, it represented the country's biggest expansion in settlement since the Middle Ages. But most important of all the agricultural reforms was land enclosure, a decision of the 1757 Diet, which generated comprehensive improvements in agriculture and forestry in Finland and Sweden over the following half-century. In the old agrarian society every patch of land was divided into narrow strips

4.3: The cathedral and city of Åbo in the early nineteenth century. Drawing by C. L. Engel.

owned by different farmers, a system which hindered independent cultivation, so the enclosure reform sought to consolidate every farmer's strips into larger single units of land.

The repartition was implemented straight away in southern Ostrobothnia, and by the end of the period of Swedish rule in southern and western Finland. The yield of every piece of arable and pasture land had first to be estimated by qualified surveyors. At the same time as plots were redistributed into unified acreages, village or parish common land (unallocated pasture and forest) was shared out between the farmers and the state, creating sizeable areas of Crown land which could be leased or used for clearances. So the Crown, and in due course the Finnish state, became the owner of huge swathes of forest. The enclosures speeded up the drainage of the land and the introduction of new methods of cultivation, as well as encouraging clearances and more responsible forestry. Village co-operatives were replaced by individual producers. It was easy to see the process taking place in the landscape—fields were unified and buildings dispersed when peasants moved their farmhouses out onto their land.

The partitioning brought other problems, since those without property lost their right to use the commons. The dilemma was intensified by the doubling of the population in the eastern part of the realm in the latter half of the eighteenth century (from 427,000 to 833,000), which was a much bigger proportional increase than in Sweden itself (from 1,780,000 to 2,350,000). The reason for this extraordinary population explosion was the combination of a long peace and substantial agricultural reforms. Instead of being sent off to war and premature death, the peasants could marry earlier, have more children and, thanks to improved agricultural productivity, even keep them alive. The trend was to continue and gave Finland the fastest population growth in Europe for the period 1750 to 1850, with an average rise of 1.5 per cent a year. In second place came Great Britain, at 1.1 per cent.

Official censuses were introduced in the Swedish realm in 1750; they incidentally provided detailed information on the social composition of the populace. Figures compiled ten years later showed the differences between Sweden and Finland in this respect to be minimal. About 80 per cent of the population in both parts of the kingdom earned their living from agriculture. The lower urban bourgeoisie comprised a slightly greater proportion in Sweden (6.5 per cent) than in Finland (4 per cent), but on the other hand there were comparatively more administrative civil servants in the eastern half of the realm

(14.5 per cent as against 10 per cent). The remaining elements (Sweden 5 per cent, Finland 3.5 per cent) consisted of what were called persons of rank, or the gentry, which included the nobility, the clergy, the upper bourgeoisie and their servants.

The percentage of rural landless was climbing swiftly, with mounting social divisions in the countryside. But more noticeable was the friction between the three upper Estates. The aristocracy clung stubbornly to their sole rights to officers' positions and other senior posts and tax-free land. In the Great Power period there had been power and wealth in sufficient measure to distribute among the newly ennobled, not least because as a warrior class the aristocracy had been heavily depleted and were thus being replenished. When the realm began to shrink and wars became less bloody, the aristocracy sought to restrict the ennoblement of capable men from the commoners' Estates, previously the usual means of social mobility.

The problem was solved firstly by Gustav III, who in the wake of his coup d'état in 1772 began to ennoble many of his loyal followers and also opened up more civil service posts to commoners. The next step was the Act of Union and Security of 1789, in which King Gustav, with the support of the commoner Estates, removed the privilege of access to high office from the aristocracy. These measures clearly assuaged the burghers' frustration and helped ensure that the French Revolution's notions of liberty did not seem particularly relevant in Sweden and Finland in the late eighteenth century. It was not the burghers who murdered Gustav III in 1792, but disenchanted noblemen.

The Age of Utility

Increasing prosperity and Finland's new strategic importance were apparent even in material terms and were factors that made the people more receptive to outside ideas. The main point of entry for the latest customs was no longer necessarily Åbo, even though the town had a dynamic university and its population had almost doubled (from 5,700 to 10,200) in the latter half of the eighteenth century, thanks to the favourable economic climate. With the construction of Sveaborg, the fortress and city of Helsinki attracted well-educated officers and enterprising merchants, who introduced foreign gastronomy and domestic utensils, social etiquette and building methods direct from the Continent. So Helsinki's numbers shot up to

SVEABORGS GALERE_DOCKA

Hans Kongl: Maj:ts   Konung GUSTAF III.
            tillignad   af Dess

4.4: The Swedish naval fort Sveaborg outside Helsinki was constructed in the latter part of the eighteenth century with French subsidies.

3,600 by 1805, which together with Sveaborg gave a total of over 8,800 inhabitants.

Many high-ranking officers bought manor houses in the Helsinki area and started to grow new species of beneficial plants, laying out parks and gardens in the modern French and English style, and these became the model for similar ones throughout the country. The manors became meeting places for societies, and in 1763 Sveaborg acquired its first secret society, the St Carolus Carpenters' Lodge, which was a branch of the Order of Carpenters and Joiners founded in Stockholm in 1761. As far as is known, the fashionable French beverage cocoa was drunk for the first time in Finland by officers' families in Sveaborg. But for the broad mass of the populace the technique of blasting rock and the production of red paint for wooden buildings were the most practical innovations, disseminated through the land by soldiers and builders who had worked in Sveaborg.

We know when rural houses and other buildings began to have stone foundations and red walls from the parish descriptions which the authorities required the clergy, civil servants and other educated men to compile and submit to Stockholm from about the middle of the century onwards. The object of this collection of information on the topography, natural resources, buildings and culture of the various parts of the realm was the same as that of the systematic population census. The belief in rational social reform was accompanied by a gradual awareness that it should be based on reliable information, which in turn emphasised the role of the sciences and the conviction that the Age of Utility had arrived.

It was an outlook endorsed by a number of prominent scientists at Åbo Akademi. Under the direction of professors Per Kalm, P. A. Gadd and Henrik Gabriel Porthan, many detailed and methodical town and parish descriptions were produced.

Per Kalm, professor of economics and pupil of Carl Linnaeus, undertook an internationally recognised scientific expedition to North America, and on his return to Åbo established a botanical garden which became an important laboratory for the new beneficial plants. Gadd occupied the chair of chemistry and was a pioneer in agricultural research, while Porthan, as professor of rhetoric, became the forefather of Neo-humanist historical, linguistic and folklore research in Finland.

Porthan's interest in the people and natural history of the country took him on long investigative expeditions, to Ostrobothnia, Karelia and elsewhere. The results appeared in the foremost contemporary geographical works on the kingdom of Sweden. His travels opened his eyes to the extreme cultural and economic differences that existed between the littoral and the interior, and convinced him that there were two contrasting Finlands—on the one hand the developed coastal cultures, which had been in close contact with Sweden and the Continent since the Middle Ages, and on the other the immense forest and lake regions of the interior where the sparse population had managed to preserve a surprising amount of its ancient customs and language.

The interior was to become the idealised landscape for the National Romantics in the 1830s, but in Porthan's time it was rather the productive agricultural economy which was the exemplar, as was also evident in contemporary travel descriptions by foreign visitors to Finland. One of these was the Englishman Edward Daniel Clarke, who met Porthan in Åbo in January 1800 and was impressed by his fluency in Latin and his intimate knowledge of his homeland. When Clarke set out on his sleigh trip eastwards to St Petersburg some days later he saw exactly the scene Porthan must have described to him in advance, despite the snowy season. Well-tended churches and fields alternated with forests and frozen lakes, and once back in

Helsinki Clarke had an unexpected opportunity to visit Sveaborg. The animated garrison and society life there reminded him of the crowds in London's Hyde Park.

The few foreigners who came were fascinated by the virgin natural landscape of the hinterland, bearing such a visible imprint of the Ice Age, and the remarkable climate. Porthan found more than that: a unique linguistic and cultural folkloric tradition which he began to publish with a scholarly apparatus of source notes in Latin. The material formed a vital corpus for subsequent research on Finnish folklore and so helped lay the ground for the concept of Finland and its people as a distinct nation. Porthan, however, lived in a pre-nationalistic era and saw no contradiction in being a Finn in a Swedish kingdom. He expressed his love for his country through popular education and a constant striving for reform, and in 1771, with some like-minded fellow countrymen, founded Finland's first newspaper, which included historical as well as topical articles. Efforts by this same group also resulted in the establishment in 1797 of the Finnish Economic Society (Finska Hushållningssällskapet, Suomen Talousseura), later to prove so influential.

The two Russian occupations had demonstrated how exposed the eastern half of the realm was in times of war. In Porthan's circles there were hopes of a more strictly defensive eastern policy, but these views were easily dismissed as treasonable in Stockholm. So the question of Finland's future in the context of Swedo-Russian rivalries could only be discussed behind locked doors or in closed fraternities such as the Aurora Society, set up by Porthan in 1771. One example of the diminishing scope for admissible opinions was the suspension by the authorities of Porthan's new journal, *Allmän Litteraturtidning* (The New Literary Gazette), which was published for less than a year (in 1803).

Pre-publication censorship had been abolished in the Freedom of the Press Act of 1766, but reintroduced in 1774 by Gustav III. So political discussion was carried only by the Stockholm newspapers, and then often through circumlocution or metaphor. Demand for free public expression of political views was still only marginal, because the overwhelming majority of citizens were scarcely literate. Parishioners learned to read the catechism with the parish priest or in Bible classes before confirmation, but a huge step remained from that to understanding and being influenced by topical articles.

So the clergy kept their position as ideological beacons at a local level far into the nineteenth century. Lutheran doctrine and loyalty to the monarchy continued to be central themes in sermons, but there was also more of an imperative to ascribe social reforms and cultural shifts to the will of God. As academically educated people, the clergy had a fairly sound grasp of both the natural sciences and the principles of agriculture, and many of them became, like Anders Chydenius, enthusiastic spokesmen for utilitarian ideas and set a good example in their own rectories.

From the mid-sixteenth century Finland had had two bishoprics. After the loss of Vyborg the eastern bishopric was transferred to Borgå (Porvoo). But the Åbo diocese, with approximately 270 parishes, remained a considerably larger community than Borgå, whose 130 parishes were in eastern and south-eastern Finland. The autocracy had been reliant on the Church, and when the Estates took over, the clergy lost their political prestige; but thanks to economic growth they still continued to prosper, since Church tithes were linked to productivity. They had the income from their own rectories as well, which often far exceeded the salaries that clerics with scholarly inclinations would have been able to earn as professors.

An early sign of the dissolution of a homogeneous Lutheran culture was the emergence of religious revivalist movements, which in the latter half of the eighteenth century began to question the tacit uniformity of the Church and stress instead the importance of individual faith and feeling in relation to God. There was an implied criticism of the new ideals of rational utilitarianism and the general process of secularisation. The movement never split from the Lutheran Church, and indeed many of the clergy were actively involved, but the radical views inevitably caused friction between the various religious camps. By the mid-nineteenth century there were already eight separate revivalist movements in Finland. Even though each had its own individual features, there was one thing that united them all: the conviction that their specific faith was the only correct interpretation of the word of God and the only one that would lead to salvation.

Revivalist movements had arisen in the late seventeenth century elsewhere in Protestant Europe, and the phenomenon was in many ways an imported one. This religious protest became particularly widespread in Scandinavia because it coincided with the eighteenth-century agrarian reforms which brought such immense changes to everyday life in the two kingdoms of Sweden-Finland and Denmark-Norway.

The Gustavian Era

Another ideology seen as a threat to a homogeneous domestic culture in the latter half of the eighteenth century was the cosmopolitanism of the aristocracy, which was primarily French-orientated. France had been the foremost great power in Europe since the end of the sixteenth century, guaranteeing the French language its position as the shared language of the aristocracy and of European royal courts at least until the

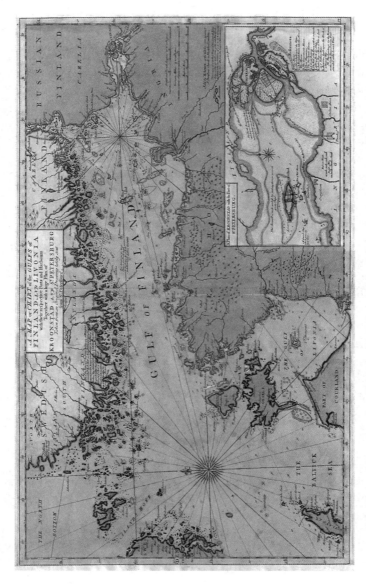

4.5: Finland between Stockholm and St Petersburg. Map of the Gulf of Finland from 1750.

beginning of the twentieth century. In the case of Sweden this influence was enhanced by the fact that for considerable periods of the seventeenth and eighteenth centuries France's political interests were compatible with Sweden's. Sveaborg exemplified this, of course, built with the help of French money, but there were extensive networks of military and diplomatic contacts, the overall effect of which was that French culture was an indisputable norm for the Swedish nobility in the eighteenth century.

After about 1760, when there was mounting criticism of this fascination with everything French, the feeling, especially among the Caps, was that it had impaired both the morality of the aristocracy and the finances of the state. But, as some critics admitted, cosmopolitanism could actually contribute to prosperity, and this became a credo for Gustav III, crowned in 1771. The new monarch had received a broad-based French education, and was well acquainted with French absolutism, the ideal he was following when he carried out his coup d'état in 1772. A form of government was imposed on the realm which transferred power back to the king and put an end to the much condemned bickering of the Estates.

The shift of power was facilitated by the fact that the economy was not burdened by expensive wars and high taxes. So the king could rule fairly independently of the Estates, and only summoned them three times in the years 1772–89. As with his contemporary rulers in Russia (Catherine II) and Prussia (Frederick II), Gustav III regarded his position as one of enlightened despotism. He brought in reforms which were systematically represented in propaganda as evidence of his progressiveness and royal solicitude. The 1774 Freedom of the Press Act may have meant in reality an increase in censorship, but in other cases, such as the Freedom of Religion Act of 1781, there was a real improvement in the people's rights, since the law permitted religious services for all Christian denominations and non-Christian religions.

Some major economic reforms had been introduced even before Gustav III's accession to the throne, but he reinforced this propitious trend with his active endorsement of the development of provincial government, urban administration and agriculture. He deliberately built up his role as a humane social reformer, and made a long journey through Finland for that purpose in the summer of 1775. This charm offensive worked beyond all expectation and confirmed the king's reputation as a genuine friend of Finland. There was some truth in this insofar as three of the four towns that were founded during his reign were in Finland: Tammerfors (Tampere), 1779; Kuopio, 1782; and Kaskö (Kaskinen), 1786. Other long-awaited reforms in the eastern half of the realm were the establishment of the Vasa Court of Appeal in 1776 and two additional counties by means of the division of both Österbotten (Pohjanmaa) county and Kymmenegård (Kymenkartano) county.

King Gustav III would go on to visit Finland more frequently than any of his predecessors, and was even reputed to have known a few courtesy phrases in Finnish. Yet behind the scenes his attitude to the eastern half of the realm was one of expediency. For him, Finland was clearly both a buffer zone that could be sacrificed if required, and a platform for possible military expeditions eastwards. In the early 1780s he contrived a covert strategy to take Norway from Denmark. The proposal was on the agenda when the king met his cousin Catherine the Great in a magnificently staged assembly of rulers in Fredrikshamn (Hamina) in 1783, but she rejected it, being interested neither in Finland nor in strengthening the natural borders of the Swedish kingdom.

Gustav III's eastern policies were explicitly defensive until the mid-1780s, but when his Norwegian dreams had been thwarted and Russia was drawn into war against the Ottoman Empire, he seized his chance and declared war on his eastern neighbour in April 1788 in the hope of regaining the lands lost in the treaties of 1721 and 1743. He also had the ulterior motive of reducing domestic political criticism of his autocratic rule through a successful military campaign. These tactics were not unprecedented: both Karl XII and the Hats Party had launched their offensives on Russia while the Turks were attacking from the south. And exactly as in those earlier wars the strategy had its weaknesses. Russia's military capacity was equivalent to the Swedish and Ottoman forces combined, and in the south the war resulted in the Russian Empire extending its boundaries to the Black Sea. The year 1794 marked the transformation of Odessa into a port city which was to be the bridgehead for all subsequent Russian attempts at further expansion towards the Bosphorus and the Mediterranean.

Gustav III's war (1788–90) could have ended in catastrophe. The initial attacks on Russian positions at Nyslott (Savonlinna) and Fredrikshamn failed primarily because the king himself had led operations. When the Swedish army had retreated in disarray to the village of Liikkala north of Fredrikshamn, a group of Finnish officers decided they had had enough. In a letter directed to the Russian empress they appealed for peace on the basis of the 1721 frontiers, and accused their own king of having gone to war illegally. The empress did not react, but the outraged king did, demanding an assurance of loyalty from all his officers. The renegade officers attested their loyalty but reiterated their conviction of the illegality of the war in a declaration signed by 112 officers in the border village of Anjala. The situation could have become completely untenable for Gustav III had Denmark not declared war at that very moment. The king was able to avert the Danish attack by skilful political manoeuvring. Fortified by that success he crushed the Anjala conspiracy and put its leaders on trial. In total seventy-eight death sentences were passed, but ultimately only one officer was beheaded, the openly defiant Finnish colonel Hästesko.

The second phase of operations was less ignominious for the Swedish forces. After minor successes for the army, the Swedish fleet won a brilliant victory in July 1790 at Svensksund in the eastern archipelago of the Gulf of Finland. The naval battle was commanded by the resolute king and ended in the loss of over fifty ships for the Russians, and only six for the Swedes. This triumph greatly facilitated Gustav III's attempts to bring the war to an honourable close, and a month later a peace agreement was signed in Värälä in which the border remained unchanged.

The king interpreted the peace as a major victory, since it diminished Russia's chances of influencing Swedish foreign policy. But the war had exposed a serious reluctance for self-sacrifice among the officer corps, and it cost the lives of over 20,000 soldiers, 90 per cent of whom were stricken down by illness or epidemic. The discontent of the aristocracy had been silenced by the suppression of the Anjala conspiracy and by the Act of Union and Security of 1789, in which the king, with the backing of the three lower Estates, further circumscribed the authority of the Council of the Realm and the privileges of the nobility. The shift of power effectively prevented the spread of revolutionary ideas from France, but came at a high price, since the king was assassinated by a clique of noblemen at a masked ball at the Stockholm Opera in March 1792.

When the next monarch, Gustav IV Adolf, came of age in 1796, he took up the powers bequeathed to him by his father. State finances were in good shape and domestic politics stable, but on the continent of Europe revolutionary events were occurring at an accelerating pace that would have far-reaching consequences for the political development of northern

Europe. Sweden's long-standing alliance with France of nearly two centuries had been abruptly severed by the French Revolution of 1789. Gustav IV Adolf had made a fresh alliance with the increasingly powerful Napoleon Bonaparte just before the united front against France was concluded, and Sweden instead entered an alliance comprising Napoleon's enemies Russia, Great Britain and Austria.

After Napoleon's forces had defeated the Russian army in a decisive battle at Friedland (near Königsberg) in the summer of 1807, the cards were shuffled once more in the game of great-power politics. In July 1807 Napoleon and Alexander I of Russia met in Tilsit and combined with Prussia to form an alliance against Britain. If the British refused to agree to an acceptable peace, Russia would compel Denmark and Sweden to join in a trade blockade against them. Denmark joined the blockade of its own accord after the unexpected and extensive bombardment of Copenhagen by the British. But the king of Sweden had painted himself into a corner: not only had he developed such a violent antipathy to Napoleon that he rejected all French and Russian overtures, firmly convinced that the diminutive Corsican was the Beast of the Book of Revelation, but in addition Sweden was receiving huge subsidies from Britain to stay out of the blockade and so continue to act as a transit country for British exports to the Continent.

The Finnish War

The Russian emperor found it repugnant to attack his former ally. But when no further pressure could be brought to bear, a slow advance was begun across the Kymmene River in south-eastern Finland in February 1808. The superiority of the Russian army pushed the Swedish troops into retreat northwards, playing for time with skirmishes while they awaited reinforcements from the west, with the result that within a month large areas of southern Finland came under Russian control. The sea forts of Svartholm and Sveaborg remained exceptions, and their task was to hold their positions until the ice had melted and the fleet could come to relieve them. This strategy was based on the assumption that the kingdom was under threat primarily from Germany and Denmark and that Sveaborg would hold out whatever the odds. But the northerly retreat of the bulk of the Finnish forces had such a devastating effect on morale that the Sveaborg officers lost heart and, with some misgivings, eventually surrendered.

The loss of Sveaborg did not alone determine the result of the war, but it substantially undermined the counter-offensive which the Swedish army launched in the summer of 1808 with flank support from guerrilla forces of peasantry. Swedish and British naval vessels managed to trap the Russian fleet in its Estonian harbour of Baltischport (now Paldiski) while the Swedish archipelago fleet was gaining a foothold in the Åbo skerries. On the mainland the Russians held their positions without difficulty, compelling the Swedo-Finnish troops to make a further and final retreat across the Gulf of Bothnia in the autumn of 1808. When Gustav IV Adolf refused to concede that the defeat was conclusive and tried to organise yet another counter-offensive, the smouldering resentment against him intensified into a coup d'état in March of 1809. The king was obliged to abdicate in favour of his uncle Karl XIII, who in practice, however, was subordinate to one of Napoleon's leading generals, the new successor to the Swedish throne, Jean Baptiste Bernadotte, in 1818 given the name Karl XIV Johan.

Bernadotte was elected in the hope of French support for a reconquest of Finland. But such expectations had to be gradually relinquished. After a last desperate attempt in the summer of 1809 to push back Russian troops who had advanced into

4.6: The Finnish War of 1808–09 was later wrongly commemorated as a heroic war. The famous Finnish journalist August Schauman is on the left in this tableau vivant from 1866.

Norrland, Sweden hastened to conclude peace with Russia in Fredrikshamn on 17 September 1809. The Russian emperor Alexander I had announced in the summer of 1808 that the conquest of Finland was immutable, and in the peace treaty it was laid down that the border of the kingdom of Sweden would now extend from the Torne (Tornio) River in the north to the Åland Sea in the south. Sweden had to surrender six Finnish counties, Åland and part of Västerbotten—an enormous sacrifice, since it meant the loss of a third of the realm in area and a quarter in population.

99

For Russia the conquest of the Finnish lands was much less significant, even though a permanent hold on Finland and the fortress of Sveaborg would improve the security of St Petersburg. The decision not to relinquish Finland had not come to fruition until the first months of war, when Napoleon's victories in Spain and Russia's defeats by the Turks increased the need for territorial expansion in the north-west. But most vital of all was to make Sweden join in the trade blockade against Britain, and that strategy indeed succeeded and marked the beginning of subsequent alliances between Russia and Sweden.

One indication of the Russian desire to retain Finland was the lack of any systematic campaign of terror or atrocities against the civilian population. Over 20,000 Swedish and Finnish soldiers lost their lives, but as in previous wars, most perished from disease or inadequate care in the camps. The attitude of the populace to the occupation showed a growing disillusion with the Swedish inability to defend Finland. The peasantry continued their guerrilla war in many parts of the country out of loyalty to the king and fear of becoming serfs. It took considerably less time for the gentry's attitude to become pro-Russian, especially when the emperor published a manifesto in June 1808 in which he pledged that the people of Finland could keep their Swedish laws, including the representation of the Estates, and would receive economic aid.

In the late autumn of 1808 a Finnish deputation attended on the emperor in St Petersburg to appeal for a Diet to be convened so that the Estates could acclaim him their new ruler and he in his turn could make his ruler's affirmation. The proposal fitted in with Alexander's plans to terminate the Finnish War in order to secure Russia's interests in the great-power game with Napoleon. He therefore issued the summons and at the same time appointed the former Swedish officer, subsequently Russian general, G. M. Sprengtporten as the first governor-general of Finland. Sprengtporten had switched allegiance in the 1780s and had actively advocated Finland's union with Russia as an autonomous Grand Duchy on the North American and Dutch federal model. So, no sooner said than done: on 29 March 1809 the emperor opened the Diet of Borgå (Porvoo) and defined the country in words that would go down in history as the birth of Finland as a nation.

5

PAX RUSSICA

The transition from Swedish to Russian authority obviously brought many significant changes to Finland. The biggest transformations were its role as Russia's military outpost in the north-west and the acquisition of its own centralised administration, the functions of which were moved to the new capital, Helsinki. But all this has to be viewed against the background of the continuing Napoleonic wars, which were causing regime change and political reforms throughout Europe and even in South America. The new order in Finland was in that respect following a more general trend. Scandinavia had only a subordinate part in great-power politics, yet nevertheless the political geography of the entire region was reshaped. Sweden finally lost Finland, but would instead, after some diplomatic jousting and a few military skirmishes, enter into a union with Norway in 1814.

At a local level the changes in Finland were much slower. Social reforms and the nationalist movement built on existing cultural traditions established in the Swedish era. The Russian authorities kept a careful watch on public life, however, and intervened immediately whenever manifestations of nationalism took on a political dimension, since they might be symptoms of a desire for separatism and a return to the Swedish

5.1: The Estates of Finland gathered in March 1809 in the mediaeval town of Borgå to meet the Russian Emperor Alexander
I. The main ceremony took place in Borgå Cathedral.

fold. For the same reason the Estates were not reconvened after
the 1809 Diet of Borgå until 1863.

Union with Russia

The Diet of Borgå fulfilled the expectations of both the new
rulers and the four Estates. Alexander I appeared for the first
time with the highest title of the conquered country: Grand
Duke. In a formal ceremony, he declared his sovereign pledge
to the Estates, who reciprocated by giving their oath of loyalty
to the new regent. This procedure followed the traditional
mediaeval ritual used to mark a change of ruler, which was a

common practice in Europe until the 1830s. The parties attested their intention to abide by the prevailing laws and governance. In the case of the Finns, this largely entailed adhering to the Lutheran faith, the Swedish legal system and the special privileges of the Estates. The Russian occupying forces had already extracted two oaths of loyalty from the general populace in the first year of the war. Thus, the emperor's pledge as ruler—which was given in French and translated into Swedish—expressed gratitude for these oaths, and ended with his own promise to retain the country's constitution.

His reference to the existing constitution would subsequently be interpreted by Finnish legal experts as a treaty and official recognition of Finland as a state, not least because the emperor's speech at the conclusion of the Diet included a magnanimous expression referring to the country's inhabitants as being "placed from this time on amongst the rank of nations". The speech was given wide distribution in printed form, which reinforced its long-term effect and provided scope for later reinterpretations. In reality he had merely uttered a few brief courtesy phrases, which cannot be taken as a treaty in the modern sense. The Diet had only been required to submit "straightforward advice" on how the Grand Duchy's defence, taxation, monetary system and government should be administered.

Irrespective of the emperor's actual intentions, Finland's annexation to Russia ensured that the country's external borders and administrative status as a separate Grand Duchy were now recognised by both the old and the new central power. Over the period of more than 600 years that Finland had belonged to the Swedish realm it had been gradually incorporated as an integral part of the whole kingdom, evolving and changing in organic interaction with the western half of the realm. In certain times of war or transition the Eastland had been administered as a separate entity, but when further internal consolidation took place in the eighteenth century the entire kingdom was governed by a single undivided centralised administration.

The lack of any equivalent Russian administrative tradition gave the emperor and his principal adviser, Count Mikhail Speransky, no reason to dismantle Swedish civic structures in the Finland they had annexed. In other areas of westward expansion of the Russian Empire in the eighteenth and nineteenth centuries the vanquished regions were also permitted to keep their previous administration and culture. In the case of Finland, the Empire's decision-makers in fact displayed a positive inclination to remodel Russian administration on the Swedish pattern, and they hoped Russia itself might develop along the lines of Finland. It was not to be. Finland, on the other hand, had a unique opportunity to become a state within a state, and some hundred years later in the whirlwinds of the First World War had matured sufficiently to sever the bonds that tied it to Russia and declare itself an independent republic. The fact that its annexation marked the beginning of a protracted period of peace which came to be known as the *Pax Russica*—the Russian peace—was of course a major contributory factor in this respect.

It was not Alexander I's intention, however, to allot the Grand Duchy of Finland a special autonomous position within his expanding Empire, as is evident from the long list of his titles in the preamble to the peace treaty of Fredrikshamn of 1809. As well as being emperor and autocrat of all Russia, and tsar of Astrakhan and elsewhere, he was "Grand Duke of Smolensk, Lithuania, Volhynia, Podolia and Finland". The significant element was not which regions he reigned over, but his multiplicity of titles. The aim was to create a Finnish government closely bound to Russia, but various chance factors prevented it going beyond an administrative solution, which turned out to be anything but.

When Sprengtporten was appointed governor-general of Finland in December 1808 he drew up a proposal for a Finnish governing council unequivocally subordinate to his own office. But as a former traitor to his country and a difficult personality, Sprengtporten aroused universal antipathy and was replaced in the summer of 1809 by General Mikhail Barclay de Tolly, who had led the conquest of Finland and would go on to distinguish himself as field marshal in the war against France. He had previously been adamantly against a separate Finnish governing council, but realised as governor-general that such a body could be of benefit in administering the country. Special regulations for the governing council were accorded high priority, and were confirmed by the emperor in August 1809.

The regulations had been drafted for approval at the Diet of Borgå by a Finnish committee chaired by the bishop of Åbo, Jakob Tengström, and bore distinct traces of the hand of the influential minister Mikhail Speransky. They included two administrative arrangements which transferred power from the governor-general to the governing council, which in 1816 was renamed Imperial Senate of Finland. Speransky had already been instructed in 1808 to refer Finnish matters for the emperor to the governor-general of Finland first of all, and made sure this rule was stipulated in the regulations. When Speransky's workload became too onerous, a separate post of state-secretary for Finnish affairs was established in 1811 to produce reports with the aid of a Committee for Finnish Affairs in St Petersburg. This solution was strongly recommended by Alexander I's Finnish adviser, Gustaf Mauritz Armfelt, previously a favourite of Gustav III, and when Speransky fell into disfavour with the emperor shortly afterwards, Armfelt became the first incumbent in 1812 and was able to push through many special measures advantageous to Finland.

5.2: The Russian Emperors and Finnish Grand Dukes Nicolaus I,
Alexander II and Alexander III. Russian memorial medal from
1882.

The governor-general's freedom of action was also restricted
in other ways. The regulations gave him the ex officio position
of chair of the Senate, which consisted of two departments,
law and finance. But Speransky made sure that the governor-
general did not have voting rights on civil matters, of which
much of the administration of the country consisted. The
governor-general's field of responsibility was therefore in practice control of the Grand Duchy's military forces. But he had
the right to express his personal opinion on the Senate's proposals to the emperor, which frequently resulted in the emper-
or's acceptance of his suggestions.

This division of responsibility was reinforced in 1812 in special regulations for the office of governor-general. The dualism
was accentuated by the fact that the governor-general's office
was staffed by Russian-speaking civil servants predominantly

from Russian Finland, while the members of the Senate were recruited from among civil servants from Swedish Finland who did not know Russian. The objective was to school a new Russian-speaking elite in Finland, but attempts to implement this were too clumsy to succeed. The outcome was that only the first two incumbents, de Tolly and Fabian Steinheil, presided over the meetings of the Senate, and even then they chaired the proceedings in French.

It was by no means unusual for conquered regions of the Empire to be governed by direct representations to the emperor. But Finland was the only part of the Empire except Poland whose affairs were represented by its own state-secretary. The creation of the office in 1811 was a crucial factor in the separation of the Grand Duchy's administration very early on, and in its gradual development from province to state. The years 1811–12 also saw the passing of other notable administrative reforms tending in the same direction.

Further civil service departments were set up, and in March 1812 the emperor decided to move the capital from Åbo to Helsinki, which, being adjacent to the fortress of Sveaborg, had distinct strategic advantages. At least as significant was the imperial decree of 1812 incorporating the *guberniya* of Vyborg into the Grand Duchy of Finland. The amalgamation brought the laws and administration of Swedish Finland into effect in Russian Finland, often called Old Finland after 1809. This decision stemmed partly from a wish to simplify the administration for domestic political reasons, but there were also good foreign policy arguments in its favour. The Russo-French alliance was already creaking at the joints, and there was every reason to send a signal that Russia regarded the annexation of Finland as irrevocable.

In the spring of 1812 Tsar Alexander and the Swedish crown prince Karl XIV Johan entered into a secret alliance against Napoleon. The treaty was made public in August of the same year when the two met in Åbo to agree a common strategy against Napoleon, who had begun his attack on Russia a few weeks earlier. Karl Johan had let the Russians know even before his election as successor to the Swedish throne that his strategic aims did not include the return of Finland, but rather the conquest of Norway. The Russian emperor endorsed this in exchange for Swedish support against Napoleon and a definitive renunciation of any policy of vengeance directed eastwards. The agreement was reached under pressure of circumstances and might well have been annulled if Napoleon's campaign had prospered. But it failed, and the year 1812 went down in history as the catalyst for Sweden's eastern defence policies. After a few skirmishes emanating from the Swedo-Norwegian union of 1814, Sweden entered a long period of peace which has lasted for nearly 200 years. In other words, the loss of Finland was the key to Sweden's good fortune.

The Imperial Stamp

The break-up also had its advantages for Finland. In the early days, the attitude of the people to the rupture with Sweden was decidedly negative, and armed resistance continued from the peasantry even after the battle was irrevocably lost. But attitudes began to change as the Russian authorities started giving out positive indications of a civil status quo. The shift occurred soonest among the gentry in key positions, such as Bishop Jakob Tengström and some of the upper aristocracy, and their flexibility was rewarded with high posts in the new administration. Tengström was appointed archbishop, and the clergy followed loyally in his footsteps, their task as the messengers of authority remaining of the utmost importance far into the twentieth century.

The most visible and durable sign of the emperor's charm offensive was the new heart of Helsinki, transformed in two decades with Russian help into something of a miniature St Petersburg in all its architectural glory. Helsinki had been ravaged by a devastating fire in the autumn of 1808 and thus stood in need of comprehensive reconstruction. As soon as the emperor had moved the Grand Duchy's administration there, a building committee was selected, which under the leadership of Johan Albrekt Ehrenström devised an urban plan and in 1816 appointed the German architect Carl Ludvig Engel to carry out the project in its entirety.

The combination of Ehrenström and Engel proved ideal. Ehrenström, a civil servant of wide-ranging education, had once served at the court of Gustav III and was fully aware of the political symbolism that architecture could bring to the Grand Duchy. Engel was a blend of innovative visionary and well-organised professional. He had trained in Berlin at the same seat of learning as the renowned K. F. Schinkel, whose monumental edifices in the Prussian capital are unsurprisingly reminiscent of those which Engel designed for Helsinki. The taste of the times was for the Empire style advocated by Napoleon with appropriate references to imperial Rome, and Engel had already designed buildings in that idiom in Russia before his arrival in Helsinki.

The city nucleus was built up around Senate Square. Large public buildings decorated in neoclassical style started going up in the square and the nearby streets, and hills and valleys were levelled to make way for the city's grid plan. Storgatan (High Street) was renamed Alexandersgatan in the 1830s, and the road from the north was given the name Unionsgatan as an enduring memorial to the Grand Duchy's union with the Russian Empire. The emperor had decided on this himself when he entered the city on that road in 1819 from an extensive tour of Finland and caught sight of the Senate building being constructed among "bushes and hovels". The plan to relocate the university to Helsinki was put into effect following the fire in Åbo in 1827. The university building rose on the other side of Senate Square and was inaugurated in 1832 amidst much festivity. The university library came into service eight years later. But the tallest of all the buildings was to be the Lutheran St Nicholas Church, work on which was slow and protracted for a variety of reasons, and only concluded in the early 1850s.

By that point the rest of Engels' Empire-style city was complete. Civil servants and university teachers with their families were transferred from Åbo as Helsinki shouldered its responsibilities as capital, and by 1840 the two towns had equal populations of some 13,000 inhabitants. In their footsteps came the students, whose tendency to political opposition and attachment to the former motherland had been contributory factors in the decision to transfer the university to Helsinki. To maintain a hold on the administrative elite, salaries were substantially raised and special uniforms introduced for both students and all those in the public sector. Standardisation failed in one important respect, however. In 1812 the authorities imposed a regulation that all aspiring civil servants would have to pass a public examination in the Russian language. But when the time came the students erupted into such violent protests against the requirement that it was decided to shelve the scheme. Correspondence with the government in St Petersburg would be acceptable in French or German or through translations, which gave employment to a growing band of translators.

This language barrier would later become a serious obstacle to Russian attempts at integration, but in general Finland had an unusually loyal civil service compared with elsewhere in Europe. It was not simply a matter of improved salaries, higher status and elegant uniforms. Finland had not had national traditions of its own, like Poland, but only acquired them through its union with Russia. The top civil servants understood and accepted their dependence on the imperial power, and at an early stage established a system by which they avoided conflict with the Russian authorities and anticipated the emperor's likely responses, in order to retain some freedom of action in domestic affairs.

Finnish loyalty was also attributable to the fact that the country's gentry were a class consisting to a great extent of civil servants and officers, who were not big landowners like the upper classes in the rest of eastern Europe. There were no groups outside the civil service to compete for power, so the Finnish social elite identified closely with the state and national ideology. Comparison with developments in the Baltic countries serves to clarify Finland's distinctive position: the power of the Baltic aristocracy was based on substantial landholdings, and they had no interest in strengthening state control or allying themselves with the peasantry, so the emergence of any strong national coalition would have been much more difficult.

There were also more tangible reasons to obey the imperial power. The Russian authorities intensified their surveillance of the populace throughout the Empire after the end of the Napoleonic wars, especially the students, who were deemed to be particularly susceptible to revolutionary ideas. The importation of political literature was prohibited, censorship of foreign newspapers increased, and in 1817 Finland's first police force was established in Åbo. Ultimately, order was kept by Russian military units in Finland, who had been given their own staff officers and the governor-general as commandant. Despite the peaceful situation prevailing in the whole Baltic region through to the 1850s, a division of 15,000 men was permanently stationed in Finland, because of the proximity of its south coast to the imperial capital of St Petersburg.

Barracks were built in various locations in southern Finland to accommodate the division. The largest were in Helsinki, where Engel's Åbo Barracks, Naval Barracks and Barracks of the Finnish Guard remained conspicuous landmarks on the outskirts of the city until the 1870s. Sveaborg continued to function as a naval base as before, and the fortress and the rest of the barracks were inaccessible to the unauthorised, the segregation reinforced by linguistic and cultural differences. Contact with the civilian population was mainly limited to parades, troop movements and changing of the guard. The Russian officer corps took part to some extent in society life, but even here there were boundaries that were not transgressed.

The conscription system from the Swedish era was abolished after the union with Russia, and the peasants' mandatory provision of soldiers was replaced by taxation. That prevented the emergence of any separatist force in Finland and dispelled any concern at the possibility of having to fight against the former motherland. When Napoleon attacked Russia in 1812, three regiments (3,600 men) were recruited from Finland and stationed in St Petersburg, and so never went into battle. But the gesture was appreciated and led to their transformation into three Finnish sharpshooter battalions which were attached to the Russian forces in Finland.

The military traditions of the Finnish aristocracy nevertheless continued even during the Russian era, through the setting up of the Finnish Cadet Corps in Fredrikshamn in 1819. It provided the majority of the approximately 3,000 sons of the Finnish nobility who became officers in the imperial army and served all over the expanding Empire until 1917. More than 4,000 Finns in total made their careers as Russian officers, and of them as many as 300 rose to the rank of general or admiral, afterwards in many cases to return to high civilian posts in Finland. In some subjects, such as modern languages, topography and mathematics, cadet-school education was almost on a par with the university's, and since Russian was a compulsory subject for the cadets, it created an extremely important professional link between Finland and Russia.

The Long Farewell

The journalist August Schauman described in his memoirs how in his youth everyone in the Finland of the 1830s assumed that integration with Russia would continue to advance inexorably. No one dared hope for the opposite—as was entirely natural given the dominant position Russia had in Europe until the 1850s. The old motherland of Sweden remained in the memory as a nostalgic yearning for bygone days, not as a vision for the future. So Finland took on the form of a Russian province with its own national characteristics, but the country's separate administration ultimately resulted in real autonomy. The close interaction of its economy and culture with that of Sweden well into the nineteenth century was a contributory factor to progress in this direction. Militarily and politically, 1809 was a critical turning point in Finland's history. But in other respects Finnish society continued to develop in parallel with Sweden, and this has led historians to describe Finno-Swedish relations after 1809 as a long farewell.

Tsar Alexander announced at the Diet of Borgå in 1809 that the Grand Duchy was freed from the obligation of passing on tax revenues to the Empire's national Treasury. The surplus from the Finnish economy was totally insignificant by Russian standards, but the decision was accepted with profound gratitude, because it meant that all public funds could thenceforth be used for Finland's own needs. The country would later receive some loans from the Russian state, and at the beginning of the twentieth century was burdened with new taxes, but these outgoings were not at all on the same scale as the transfers to the Swedish Treasury had been. The customs, monetary and export policies of the Grand Duchy were laid down by the Russian authorities. In theory there was a distinct imbalance in Finno-Russian trade, since only Finnish goods were subject to duties, but in practice this posed little problem. The customs duty did not apply to agricultural products and other Finnish raw materials. And goods of Finnish origin were accorded substantial duty-free import quotas in Russia.

5.3: A Finnish peasant in Häme with his family and farm in the background. Drawing by Eero Järnefelt (1896).

Finland's domestic economy, however, was handled fairly independently by the Senate finance department. The chairman of the department was the country's unofficial prime minister, since he acted as the vice-chairman of the Senate and until the late 1890s even chaired it, because the proceedings were held in Swedish. Another institution of importance was the Bank of Finland, which the tsar established in 1812 for the introduction of the rouble and the dismantling of Finno-Swedish credits. Up until the 1850s the economic policies of the Senate tended to be characterised by the mercantile attitudes inherited from the Swedish era. In the first few decades state finances were concentrated on the development of agriculture, but in the 1830s under the leadership of Lars Gabriel von Haartman more comprehensive reform measures were put into effect. The aim was to reduce Finland's economic dependence on Sweden, augment state revenues to allow more systematic investment in civic projects, and above all to invest in industry.

Trade between Finland and Sweden had continued steadily after the separation in 1809. Russia accepted an eight-year duty-free transition period between the two countries and permitted them domestic duty privileges even after that; thus Stockholm long remained a profitable market for the farmers of south-west Finland, and the import of Swedish iron ore and various consumer goods proceeded as before. The low level of duty made it hard for Finnish industry to compete, however, and of course involved a significant loss of duty revenue for the Finnish state. So with the full support of Russia, the levels of duty between Finland and Sweden were standardised in the years 1834–44, which gave the Finnish Treasury a welcome boost.

At the same time the dual-currency system was abandoned, having been kept in force because trade across the Baltic was so prolific. Even by the end of the 1830s the *riksdaler* was still a more widespread currency in Finland than the rouble, not least because with the escalating importation of Russian grain the roubles flowed back to Russia. This reform was considerably facilitated by the reintroduction of silver coinage by both countries in the 1830s. The redemption of *riksdaler* for silver roubles was terminated in southern Finland in the autumn of 1843, while in the northern parts of the country the transaction continued until 1850.

The currency reform brought a palpable improvement in the Senate's ability to pursue a national economic and monetary policy. The extra income from duties gave the Bank of Finland the resources to make substantial enhancements of credit provision. State investment in roads and canals was also increased. In the period 1835–60 twelve canals were dug, of which the Saima Canal linking the Saima lakes with the port of Vyborg was by far the most significant. Finnish decision-makers were rather conservative and cautious and no railways were built until the late 1850s, but otherwise, from an international perspective, state investment in infrastructure was unusually comprehensive.

Government initiatives were one answer to the glaring dearth of private capital to stimulate the country's industry and economic growth. Active efforts were made in the 1820s to create an iron industry based on bog iron in eastern Finland independent of Swedish iron ore imports. Even though the state soon withdrew from the project, the constantly expanding weapons industry in the St Petersburg region guaranteed a good profit for these ironworks, which passed predominantly into Russian ownership. Russia's iron production was itself located far to the east in the Urals, and besides that, Russian import duties were an effective protection against western European competition.

Textile manufacture was another of the industries which managed to establish itself in Finland because of the proximity to St Petersburg, and it became really profitable after Russian capitalists acquired the textile business of Finlayson & Co in Tammerfors (Tampere) and transformed it into the biggest industrial complex in Scandinavia. The success was contagious and led to the birth of a number of other textile factories in Finland. None of them reached the size and profitability of Finlayson, which resulted partly from cheap water power, partly from the tsar's granting of duty-free status to Tammerfors in its trade with Russia. It kept this privilege until 1905, but in one respect the entire Finnish textile industry was favoured: duties on raw materials (cotton and linen), shipped over from North America, were lower in Finland than in Russia, giving the Finnish factories a clear competitive advantage.

Typically enough, three of the country's five largest industrial companies were owned in the mid-1840s by Russian capital. Their contribution to the Finnish economy was marginal, however, since nearly 90 per cent of the population earned their living from agriculture and forestry before the 1860s. At the beginning of the Russian period, about 95 per cent of Finland's export income came from agricultural produce and tar and timber products. The rapid population growth (from 863,000 in 1810 to 1,770,000 in 1870) reduced agricultural surpluses, and thus also their share of exports, in favour of forest industries and especially timber, by the 1830s Finland's major export product. Ocean-going wooden ships were being replaced by steel-hulled vessels, and by 1860 tar had finally lost all significance on the export market. In the 1870s agriculture had regained its place as the major source of export production, because the exponential urban growth in Russia and central Europe was multiplying demand for milk and other animal products. The textile and iron industries' share of export income rose to nearly 30 per cent for the same reasons.

So rural life was subject to both continuity and change. Continuity was represented by the Lutheran Church, local customs and Swedish administrative procedures, which in essence went through the same development as in Sweden itself, as for example in the prominent role accorded at this time to parish meetings as platforms for local self-government. Change was driven by a number of structural shifts, caused above all by population growth and the expanding markets of St Petersburg. The availability of cheap Russian grain induced the farmers of eastern Finland to abandon their burn-beat cultivation and tar-burning in favour of the export of butter and firewood to St Petersburg. Everywhere else in agrarian Finland the amount of land under cultivation was increasing at the same rate as the population.

National Awakening

To what extent did the people of Finland themselves shape their homeland into a nation in the first half of the nineteenth century? The union with Russia brought many visible changes in public life, but the question is whether they were regarded at the time as an expression of a Finnish national spirit. Most people identified first and foremost with their church community and their sovereign. The senior ranks of the civil service assumed that integration with Russia would continue and were convinced that the Empire opened "broader vistas" for the economy and the Finnish people. It therefore required a very conscious and long-term effort from the country's intellectuals to bring about a national revival and involve the wider general public, especially since nationalism was really an ideological product of the Napoleonic wars and in Finland's case would even require the active creation of a national past.

The motto "Swedes we are no longer, Russians we cannot be so let us be Finns" would later be attributed to the Åbo historian A. I. Arwidsson, who had to leave for Sweden in the 1820s after taking too radical a standpoint in the nationality debate. In fact the thought had already been articulated in 1811 by the first state-secretary of the Grand Duchy, G. M. Armfelt, who had witnessed Tsar Alexander's exhortation to the people of the conquered territories that they should now be Finns. The tsar meant that they should not live in the past, and Armfelt thought it was their duty to put the tsar's wishes into effect.

The tsar's attitude was political and had nothing to do with the linguistic situation in the country. Yet the union with Russia meant that the Finnish language began to be seen in a completely different way. The separation from Sweden and the transformation into a distinct administrative entity put Finnish for the very first time in the position of a majority language, and one of which the authorities had to have a better command than previously in order to do their job properly. A new enthusiasm arose for research into the grammar and vocabulary of Finnish, and in 1826 a clergyman named Gustaf Renvall published a substantial Finnish-Latin-German dictionary which provided the standard for the slowly burgeoning written Finnish language throughout the nineteenth century.

Renvall, like the sixteenth-century Bible translator Mikael Agricola, gave precedence to the western Finnish dialect, which was the most widespread and contained an abundance of Swedish loanwords. Opposed to him was the folklorist Carl Axel Gottlund, who advocated the eastern Finnish Savo dialect, spoken in the vast inland regions and thus described by him as purer and more authentic. He was an early representative of nationalism in its Romantic guise, and, in the German tradition, he began to make a comprehensive collection of Finnish folk poetry, in order to seek out the soul of the people. It was Elias Lönnrot who published the Finnish national epic, the *Kalevala*, in 1835, but we have to remind ourselves that Gottlund was the man who in 1817 first expressed the idea that Finland's ancient folk poetry might be moulded into a literary whole.

It was symptomatic of the situation that it was in Swedish that Gottlund gave utterance to this vision. At the beginning of the nineteenth century more than 85 per cent of the population spoke various Finnish dialects, but despite the mounting interest in Finnish, Swedish was still the language of both home and workplace for the academic and administrative elite up to the 1880s. This was the educational legacy from the Swedish era, which paradoxically enough was reinforced in the nineteenth century by state investment in university and higher-level school education, since the language of tuition by and large remained Swedish until the 1870s, for lack of a realistic alternative. In any case, only a minor proportion of the Swedish-speaking population consisted of the social elite: the farming and fishing communities of the south and west coasts continued to speak their eastern Swedish dialects exactly as before, and in urban areas Swedish remained the first language of ordinary townspeople for as long as it was the language of school and of trade contacts, still predominantly with Sweden.

The national awakening in Finland was thus given momentum by cultural circles who did not necessarily use Finnish actively themselves but admired the language and were convinced of its intrinsic national spirit. There was a similar situation elsewhere in Europe, such as in the Baltic countries and Russia, where the upper classes communicated in German or French and paid no attention to the language of the common people until the era of National Romanticism. At least in Finland the educated classes were more likely to speak the vernacular, since they would often have grown up in entirely Finnish-speaking districts or be of Finnish-language descent. Such language switching had been occurring continuously since the thirteenth century, and in many bilingual regions took place in both directions.

German scholars' interest in folklore had inspired Finnish academics like Porthan towards the end of the previous century, but it was not until the 1820s that it was fully realised in Finland that the national language could be a political bone of contention. Arwidsson's newspaper articles in 1821 were the turning point. He, in common with the students, protested against the imposition of Russian as the language of the civil service, and argued that socio-political developments in Europe presented more of a case for giving that status to Finnish. This was an overt reference to the civic and republican ideals associated with political nationalism in central Europe. His articles were taken as a criticism of the Russian authorities and precipitated his dismissal from the university and exile to Sweden. From then on St Petersburg kept a careful eye on the whole nationality debate in Finland, one result of the tighter control being the transfer of the university itself to Helsinki.

So in order to be able to express themselves at all, the main proponents of Finnish nationalism had to avoid any form of negative criticism of Russia, and preferably throw in a few phrases of loyalty to the tsar. The organic unity of the people could be stressed, but their primary collective virtue had to be an unflinching faith in God and sovereign. The boundaries of the permissible were firmly imprinted from an early stage on the minds of the group of young intellectuals who were to be in the vanguard of the national revival movement in the years to come. It was only a few months after Arwidsson's dismissal, in fact the autumn of 1822, when the trio of Elias Lönnrot, J. L. Runeberg and J. V. Snellman began their university studies in Åbo.

Johan Ludvig Runeberg (1804–77) made his debut as a poet of National Romanticism in 1830. His poems soon fulfilled the expectations of the educated public for a poetry which captured the essentials of the Finnish national spirit. As a young

5.4: The Finnish philosopher and statesman J. V. Snellman (1806–81) pictured on a 100 Finnish mark bill from the 1970s.

student in Åbo, he had been by no means uncritical of an all-too-ingratiating loyalty to Russia, but as lecturer and poet in the Helsinki of the 1830s and husband of the niece of Archbishop Tengström, Fredrika Tengström, he had learned the rules of the game. In his epic poem *Elgskyttarne* (*The Elk Hunters*) he depicted the spartan but contented everyday life of the peasant farmers in the lake landscape of the interior in a classic simple style that was to be his inimitable hallmark. The climax of his literary career was the major poetic cycle *Fänrik Ståls sägner* (*The Tales of Ensign Stål*), published in 1848 and 1860, in which he pulled off the trick of describing the patriotism and sacrifice of the Finns in the war of 1808–09 without offending the Russian authorities.

Elias Lönnrot (1802–84) became the key figure in Finnish folk poetry with the publication of his *Kalevala* (1835, 1849). His achievement was not limited to meticulously transcribing the age-old folk songs collected on his extensive wanderings through the interior of Finland and bringing them into print. Like many other national epics which appeared in Europe that century, the composite whole entitled *Kalevala* was to a great extent the creation of its collector. Lönnrot was one of the founders of the Finnish Literature Society in 1831, a body which over the years became a central forum for the national revival, and within that circle there were fervent hopes that Finland's early history would find a worthy narrative. Lönnrot's *Kalevala* was the answer. Admittedly its Finnish was frequently so complex that even the educated public in the nineteenth century mostly made its acquaintance through Swedish or German translations.

By the 1840s the concept of Finland as an independent nation was beginning to establish itself among these same educated classes. Runeberg and his literary friends had started the newspaper *Helsingfors Morgonblad* (Helsinki Morning News) in 1832, and it remained the country's only intellectually stimulating and nationalistic organ of the press until 1844. Two Finnish-language provincial newspapers, *Oulun Wiikko-Sanomia* (Oulu Weekly News) and *Sanansaattaja Wiipurista* (Viipuri Messenger), had been published in the 1830s, but both collapsed for lack of subscribers in 1841. In that same year a group of academics centred on Lönnrot launched the linguistic journal *Suomi* (Finland); and in 1844 J. V. Snellman founded the Swedish-language journal *Saima*, as a radical language platform which assumed quite a different significance for Finnish society, becoming a focus for popular nationalism (the "Fennomane" movement) well into the twentieth century.

Johan Vilhelm Snellman (1806–81), having lived for some years in Sweden and Germany, had been influenced by the way the liberal press combined nationality questions with demands for an egalitarian civic society. Snellman referred to the social theories of the German philosopher Hegel to argue for a kind of nationalism firmly anchored in the common people. The seedbed of the state was a nation comprising a single linguistic community, one people who spoke the same language. The well-being of the state required a conscious investment in the national culture which would open up channels of influence for the people. Snellman believed the problem with Finland was that it lacked a vernacular literature around which a national culture and public life could be built up. He was the headmaster of a school in the little lakeside town of Kuopio in northern Savolax when he began publishing *Saima*, but his radical motto, "One nation, one language", was so revolutionary that the journal immediately sparked off animated discussion in the Helsinki press and inspired the like-minded to nail their colours to the mast.

The majority of the participants in this ongoing argument agreed with Snellman that it was both desirable and necessary for Finland's public life in the future to be Finnish-speaking, but many questioned his impatience to introduce Finnish into secondary education and were amazed that he could so sweepingly describe the country's Swedish-language literature and education as not national. How could anyone assert that Runeberg's poetry was not part of the nation's literary canon? Predictably, this entire public debate took place in Swedish. Despite his radical demands, Snellman himself never learned to compose his published writings in Finnish, and in practice Finnish was not used at all in such public dialogue until the 1870s.

Yet his contemporaries were well aware of the revolutionary nature of Snellman's argument. In the spring of 1845 the newspapers reported a student festival in Helsinki where several of the guests of honour, including Bishop Ottelin of Borgå, had given substantial speeches in Finnish. This met with widespread approbation and was reported with eminent satisfaction by Snellman in *Saima*, though he could not resist pointing out the amusing aspect of all the fuss. An uninitiated foreigner would hardly have understood why it was so remarkable for a Finnish bishop to speak Finnish in public.

The Crimean War

But the authorities were quick to perceive the significance of Snellman's comments. In the autumn of 1846 *Saima* was closed down on the grounds of its seditious effect on the students. Press censorship was still in operation, and the greater the political ferment in central Europe in the late 1840s, the more the Senate and the governor-general clamped down on the students, who were very conscious of ideological currents and political arguments in other countries. Sweden played a major role in this regard, since Finland's political dissidents usually fled across to the former motherland and continued publishing contributions to debate which were then distributed illegally in Finland.

The best-known public debate among dissidents took place over the years 1838–43 and related to Finland's constitutional position within the Russian Empire. Some (Israel Hwasser, for instance) described the Diet of Borgå of 1809 as a proper treaty between Russia and Finland; others (such as A. I. Arwidsson) raised cynical objections. Even though their arguments could not be aired publicly in Finland at the time, they were not forgotten and formed a starting point for the constitutional debate that was taken up in Finland twenty years later. But equally important for Finland's national consciousness was the fact that in the late 1830s the 1808–09 war began to feature increasingly in Swedish memoirs and history books, which were widely read in Finland and helped shape the receptive intellectual climate for Runeberg's epic war poem, *Fänrik Ståls sägner*, the first section of which was published for Christmas 1848 and immediately achieved huge popularity.

These "Tales" have been described as the fundamental text of Finnish patriotism, and not just because the work so strikingly highlighted the stoical heroism of the Finnish people. It was also seen as a successful response to Snellman's demand for a literature that was more nationalistic and folk-based, yet without being too radical for the country's cautious civil servants. Runeberg's skilful balancing act was at its most evident in the opening poem, "Vårt land" (Our Land), which had already been introduced at a student festival in the spring of 1848 as the country's new national anthem.

It was set to music by the German composer Fredrik Pacius, who was working in Finland, and given a fashionably Romantic tone. Runeberg had written the verses in 1846, when Snellman's pleas for civic patriotism were still able to be made in the public arena. That explains why the poet constantly refers to the communal spirit of the people and in the final stanza paints his vision of the future of their native land: "Thy bloom, a tender bud till now, / Shall burst its bounds ere long". Some critics have pointed out that the poem lacks revolutionary slogans and have thus concluded that Runeberg's motives were reactionary. But why would he even have considered writing a song which for political reasons could not be sung?

When the authorities actively encouraged the students to sing "Vårt land" after the spring of 1848, it was not primarily because of the nuances in Runeberg's text. The aim was to prevent them singing the Marseillaise and other politically subversive lyrics. The social unrest in central Europe had escalated into a wave of real revolutions in the spring of 1848, shaking the whole political order that had been created by the Congress of Vienna in 1815, the ultimate defender of which was autocratic Russia. The echoes from the barricades were soon resounding through northern Europe too—in April 1848 a big civic festival was organised in Sweden, where Russia was explicitly referred to as the last bastion of conservatism.

The barb was well directed inasmuch as the European revolutions were crushed the following year at the instigation of the Russian tsar Nicholas I, who had ruled the Russian Empire with a rod of iron since 1825. The tsar's attitude towards Finland had been neither particularly sympathetic nor antagonistic, due no doubt to the fact that the loyal senior civil servants had put in place preventive measures to discourage political demonstrations against the regime. These had worked for the Polish rebellion in 1830, and again in the "mad year" of 1848–49. In 1846–47 revised rules on censorship were introduced, and in 1848–49 stricter limitations were imposed on societies. In March 1850 censorship was made even more stringent by the regulation that only books on religion and economics could be published in Finnish.

This latter restriction was intended to prevent the spread of revolutionary ideas and religious heresies into rural areas, where the speed of population growth and widening social gaps had provided fertile ground for religious revival movements with political undertones. The authorities were also keeping an increasingly close watch on the students, who in the spring of 1849 had demonstrated their displeasure at a political appointment in the university and plans for the Finnish Guard to take part in the Russian suppression of the uprising in Hungary. The tsar's threat to convert all universities in the Empire into vocational colleges was averted, but in 1852 Helsinki University, like many other seats of learning in the Empire, was given new statutes which had a similar effect in some respects, with courses of study specialising in either the humanities or the sciences. The reform raised academic standards of teaching, but the students' political activism was not notably diminished, and that had been the principal objective.

So, exactly as before, Finland was affected by the political and ideological upheavals of the great powers in central

Europe, albeit with a certain time lag, and by the general con-
clusions drawn by the tsar in St Petersburg and his opponents
on the Continent. The pattern was the same in the Crimean
War of 1853–56, which was in essence about the struggle
between Russia and the Ottoman Empire for hegemony over
the Bosphorus and thus over the whole of the eastern Mediterranean. The conflict escalated into a European great-power
conflict after Russian troops had conquered Ottoman territory
in the southern Balkans and the Turkish fleet had been sunk
in a naval battle in the Black Sea. The Turks had support from
Great Britain and France, both of which declared war on Russia in March 1854 with the intention of reducing its dominance of the European political situation. Behind this too lay
Britain's fear that in the longer term the Russian naval
advance into the eastern Mediterranean would threaten the
Pax Britannica, British superiority on the world's oceans and in
world trade.

The Western powers' decision to attack Russia by way of the
Baltic as well was dictated by the same logic that had once
guided Swedish wars of aggression towards the east. A war on
two fronts would compel Russia to divide its forces and so opti-
mise its enemies' chances. The Russian military command had
foreseen this and begun strengthening the sea defences of St
Petersburg, including the reinforcement of the forts along the
south and west coasts of Finland and augmentation of Russian
troops in the country to a total of about 70,000. And sure
enough, in the summer of 1854 Western naval forces attacked
a number of Finnish ports and also completely demolished the
fortress of Bomarsund in the Åland Islands.

Russian anxieties about Finnish separatism turned out to be
quite groundless in this campaign. The Russian tsar, with
some justification, interpreted Sweden's passive endorsement
of the Western powers as an interest in retaking Finland from

5.5: The Russian naval fort in the Åland archipelago, destroyed by the British-French fleet in 1854.

Russia, but any such plans ultimately foundered on inadequate guarantees of more permanent military backing from the Western powers. In Finland loyalty to Russia was boosted not just by anger at the Western powers' coastal attacks, but also because their navies paralysed Finnish shipping almost entirely, bringing significant financial loss to the export trade of the coastal towns. The newspapers consistently supported Russia in their coverage of the war, but that did not prevent liberal circles from privately adopting ever more critical attitudes towards Russia.

By then the outcome of the war was becoming self-evident. In the late summer of 1855 the Western powers launched powerful offensives in both the Gulf of Finland and the Black Sea. Between 9 and 11 August Sveaborg suffered a 46-hour bombardment from the Western fleet, whose guns had twice the range of the Russians' and so could fire on the fortress with shells and incendiary rockets to their hearts' content. The great

131

invention of the day was the telegraph, which allowed the Western press to report the engagement as it was happening, and this was the first time that Finland as an individual nation achieved widespread international publicity. The offensive could be used for propaganda purposes, since the Western fleet had deliberately avoided shelling Helsinki itself, where the inhabitants had been able to watch the macabre fireworks from the shore of Brunnsparken (Kaivopuisto). Once their task was complete the attackers weighed anchor without a single significant landing. The primary purpose had been achieved—Russia's loss of prestige.

A few weeks later Western forces captured the main theatre of operations, the Russian fortress of Sebastopol on the Crimean peninsula. With that, the war was over, and peace was declared in March of 1856, with Russia having to relinquish its naval bases on the Black Sea and in the Åland Islands. The conclusion of peace put a definitive end to Russian dominance in European politics. This turning point was further accentuated by the fact that "Europe's gendarme", Tsar Nicholas I, had died in the middle of the war and been succeeded by his son, Alexander II, whose reign (1855–81) brought major social reforms to the whole Empire.

6

GROWING AUTONOMY

Russia's defeat in the Crimean War was also a turning point for Finland. The tsar allowed the country's parliament to meet again regularly from 1863, and over the next four decades politics became public, with political parties and debates, the latter concentrating on the language question, the modernisation of society and Finland's constitutional status within the Empire. The social reforms helped bring economic growth and an accelerating pace of industrialisation, with a corresponding increase in geographical and social mobility. At the same time, Finland was being transformed into an ever more articulate civic society, which bolstered the country's sense of its own national autonomy within the Russian Empire. A protracted constitutional battle was waged from 1899 to 1917 between the Russian central government and Finland about the country's rights and duties within the Empire. It came to an abrupt end in the autumn of 1917 following the October Revolution in Russia, when the Finnish Senate decided to declare Finland's independence.

Parliament Revitalised

Even though many of Alexander II's reforms were imposed on him by the Crimean defeat, cumulatively they had a wide-ranging effect. The most important was without doubt the modernisation of the army, which also strengthened Russian central government. More attention, however, was accorded to the abolition of serfdom in 1861 and the introduction of *zemstvos*, a form of communal self-government, which despite their inherent faults became a genuine focus for democratic expression. The new tsar had been partly brought up by that earlier patron of the Grand Duchy of Finland, Speransky, who convinced his pupil that the Empire could not be governed without a proper administration. Nevertheless, Alexander II had no plans to limit his own power. He opposed any suggestion of representation of the people in Russia and put through reforms with the aid of his compliant civil servants, who transformed Russia in the second half of the nineteenth century from a despotic to a bureaucratic autocracy.

Finland was in many respects to be an exception. The senior ranks of the civil service and the population as a whole had shown their loyalty during the Crimean War, and so the tsar proved willing to agree to a special reform programme for the Grand Duchy. It had five aims: development of trade and shipping; investment in industry; extension of school education to rural areas; improvement of communications; and raising civil service salaries. Such a comprehensive programme required legislation and budget approval, which under the still prevailing Swedish laws from the eighteenth century could not really be passed without recalling parliament.

Alexander II would have preferred to use purely administrative measures, but when a similar reform programme for Poland disintegrated into outright rebellion in the spring of 1863, he felt obliged to conform to Finnish expectations in order to prevent such unrest spreading to Finland. The freer atmosphere in society had paved the way for a more liberal press, which emphasised Finland's constitutional autonomy within the Empire and argued that the Grand Duchy should

Helsinki — Helsingfors.
Saksalainen kirkko — Tyska kyrkan.

6.1: The German church in southern Helsinki was built in 1864 and got a higher tower in 1897. Postcard from the early twentieth century.

maintain a neutral stance on the Poland issue. The argument was interpreted quite correctly in the western European media as a sign of incipient Scandinavianism and Western-orientated public opinion in Finland. So to counterbalance the brutal intervention in Poland, the tsar decided to make Finland a shop window for Russian liberalism, and in 1863 convened its parliament for the first time in fifty-four years.

The situation was very reminiscent of the years 1809–12, when tensions in great-power politics had persuaded Russia to adopt different tactics for the newly conquered Finland. On the formal opening of parliament in September 1863, the tsar pledged that the Estates would thenceforth be summoned regularly to decide their own taxes and to propose motions on any subject except constitutional law. He also promised a revision of the constitution of the Swedish period. But the review came to nothing, since in reality the tsar opposed any substantial shift in power. The sole exception was the Parliament Act of 1869, which replaced the Swedish constitutional law of 1617. Parliament would meet once in every five years as a minimum; in practice, it met every third year from 1882.

The attempt to abolish the mediaeval division of Estates failed. The system of separate assemblies for the nobility, the clergy, the burghers and the peasants remained in operation until the 1906 parliamentary reform, when practically overnight Finland acquired the most progressive representation of the people in Europe. According to the 1869 Parliament Act the different Estates were intended to represent the whole people, but there were still enormous contrasts in comparison with Sweden, for instance, which had a two-chamber parliament from 1866 with a much broader democratic base. Until the beginning of the twentieth century only the wealthiest strata of the rural population in Finland (4.5 per cent) had voting rights for parliamentary elections. Over the next few decades suffrage was expanded, especially among the burghers, and together with other social reforms it led to the gradual dismantling of the Finnish Estates. The most important of these reforms were the 1865 and 1873 Local Government Acts, which substantially extended voting rights in both town and country.

The tsar's object with these reforms was to tie Finland closer to Russia. He could still autocratically decide which reforms he wanted to put through by decree and which should be debated as bills in parliament. The notion of the ruler being bound by the constitutional laws of the Swedish era was so potent, however, that it was taken for granted in Finland that the tsar would always seek parliament's approval on major topics such as the constitution, taxation or monetary policy. If at least three of the four Estates gave their support to a bill it was referred to the tsar, who would then ratify it if he felt so inclined.

As there was no similar procedure elsewhere in the Empire, every law that was ratified exclusively for the Grand Duchy actually implied a recognition of its special status. This widened the latent gulf which had always existed between Finland and the Empire. One example was the Empire's universal reform of military service in the late 1870s, which was adopted in Finland in 1878 through a Finnish law specifically drawn up by the Finnish parliament. Uniforms, calibres and the language of command were to be identical throughout the Empire, but the Finnish officers and men were to be enlisted exclusively from among Finnish citizens, and not to be sent beyond the country's borders—a regulation that soon came in for criticism by Russian nationalists. And this force's only organic link to Russia was the governor-general, who functioned as commander of both the Finnish conscript army and the country's military districts.

But perhaps the main factors contributing to Finnish separatism were the currency reforms of 1865 and 1877, which led to Finland gaining its own currency—the mark and the penni, based on the silver standard and protected by new tariff regulations. The reform was pushed through like so many other special measures, as a result of skilful preparations by the state-secretary, Alexander Armfelt. In 1864 he was able to persuade both the tsar and the governor-general, backed up by the Russian finance minister, Michael von Reutern, who felt it would boost the Russian economy, hard hit by inflation. Whether it had the desired effect is doubtful, but over the course of time the currency switch certainly benefited Finnish exports to the West, particularly as in 1877 the mark was tied to the gold standard and to the value of the French gold franc.

National and Global Politics

Altogether the Finnish Estates parliament passed as many as 400 laws in the years 1863–1906. Most of them prepared the ground for democratic society and the expansion of capitalism. Two rival political groupings came into being from this long work of reform: the Nationalists ("Fennomanes") and the Liberals, whose leaders took turns as powerful figures in the Senate. The Nationalists were favoured principally by the peasant and clergy Estates, while the Liberals relied on the nobility and the burghers. The Estates made their decisions independently of one another, which gave scope for different emphases within the two groups. On many critical issues the positions of the individual Estates were still determined by narrow factional interests.

The obvious leader of the Nationalists was J. V. Snellman, who was appointed professor of philosophy after the Crimean War and acted as vice-chairman of the Senate from 1863 to 1868. He attested his loyalty to the tsar as unambiguously as was expected, and in return received endorsement from the Russian authorities for his Fennicisation programme. The Russians did not really believe that Finnish could develop into a language of state, but they could see that the dominant standing of Swedish in Finland's public life rendered the country susceptible to politically inflammatory ideas from Sweden. Their intermittent active support for the Fennic movement was due to their long-term aim of replacing Swedish with Russian as the country's official language. When Alexander inspected Russian troops in Finland in the summer of 1863, he received a visit from a delegation led by Snellman, to which he granted his assent for an edict raising Finnish to equal status as a language of administration after a twenty-year transition period.

This reform made the language question a political bone of contention once again, and gave impetus to a national

6.2: The Grand Duchy of Finland had by the end of the nineteenth
century in many ways developed into a state within a state. The
Russian authorities were of a different opinion. Map from 1896.

consciousness movement under Snellman's banner: "One nation, one language". The object was the total Fennicisation of public life in Finland. This vision was not shared by the Liberals, who thought it unnecessary and hazardous, since Swedish was a guarantor of the Western cultural tradition and of contacts with Scandinavia. It must be noted that both groups were motivated by patriotic and nationalistic sentiments. The dispute was about how best to further Finland's cause; in other words, how to prevent the country being swallowed up by the Russian state and culture.

In many European countries in the nineteenth century nationalists were committed liberals, since they saw political emancipation as the precursor of popular emancipation. In Finland the situation was more complicated, for uncontrolled political emancipation could easily drive the country closer to Sweden, a situation which neither the Fennomanes nor the Russian authorities desired. So Finnish nationalism in its Fennomane incarnation included a powerful element of loyalty to the state and the authorities. In its liberal version it was characterised by an ardent belief in the letter of the law, since the law was seen as the surest safeguard against any extreme Russification.

The dispute gave rise to competing perceptions of Finland's history and constitutional relationship to Russia. Both groups regarded Finland as having developed into a state by the early 1860s, but that was based for the Fennomanes above all on the fact that the Finns' national consciousness had been able to flower during the Russian period. Professor Yrjö Koskinen, who became leader of the Fennomane Nationalists in the 1870s and subsequently also a senator, argued that the Swedish era had entailed a sustained repression of and discrimination against the Finnish people. Nationalist historians began to write about the whole of Finland's history in this spirit, and the Finnish-nationalist press, with *Uusi Suometar* (New Fenniciser) in the vanguard, laid the ground in the 1870s for the official use of Finnish nationwide.

The Liberals, on the other hand, referred to Israel Hwasser's interpretation from the 1830s that the Diet of Borgå in 1809 had been a treaty of statehood and union, and stressed the significance of the eighteenth-century Swedish laws and Finland's Swedish heritage in particular. The leading spokesmen for this viewpoint were August Schauman, newspaper editor, and Leo Mechelin, professor of politics and senator. Schauman had been at the head of the liberal wing during the Crimean War and went on to spread the message through *Helsingfors Dagblad* (Helsinki Daily News) and *Hufvudstadsbladet* (Metropolitan News) that Finland was joined to Russia only in a personal union through the tsar. Mechelin's 1886 French-language survey of the government and administration of the Grand Duchy took the same line, and it soon appeared in a Russian edition with critical commentary. That became the scholarly prologue to the Finno-Russian schism that flared up into open conflict in 1899 and informed Finnish political life right up to 1917.

The Nationalist movement's offensive set off chain reactions in domestic politics. In the 1870s a group of outspoken Swedophile academics, known as "Suecomanes", began demanding more vigorous support for the continuance of Swedish in society. Extremist proponents maintained that Swedish-speakers were a distinct nationality, but most of them saw Swedishness rather as a cultural attribute. When the Liberals failed in the early 1880s to consolidate themselves into a linguistically neutral party, the majority of them united with the Suecomanes to form the Swedish Party, with its strongest constituency in the Estates of the nobility and burghers. Among the Fennomanes there emerged around this time a younger generation with the student leader Lauri Kivekäs at their centre, looking for more drastic means to bring about a programme of Fennicisation. Two new parties arose in the 1890s, the Young Finns and the Socialists, both of which came to be key players on the political scene.

Ultimately the political agenda was still dictated by the Russian tsar's attitude to the Grand Duchy. Alexander II was building up his bureaucratic autocracy with the aid of increasingly professional advisers who were responsible for the efficient functioning of the Empire in its entirety and therefore preferred homogeneous solutions. This integration policy was gradually intensified after Alexander II was assassinated by Russian extremists in 1881. His son, Alexander III, determined to tighten internal political controls, and at the same time Russia had to contend with ever weightier challenges in great-power politics. The unification of Germany in 1871 had taken place with Russian backing, but after the dissolution of the Russo-German alliance in the 1880s there was increased risk of a war between the two countries. This made St Petersburg's situation all the more exposed and highlighted Finland's strategic position as a military buffer zone.

Furthermore, Russia, like the other European great powers, was being transformed between 1870 and 1910 into an empire with interests ranging far beyond Europe. The Western powers' colonial domination was expanding mainly in Africa and south-east Asia; Russia completed its Siberian conquests and in the 1890s started vying with the Western powers for control of China. This escalation in the pursuit of new colonies was to a large extent due to technical advances such as railways, the telegraph and electricity, which, in combination with the rapidly regained battle-strength of the European armies and navies, gave the indigenous populations no chance whatsoever. There were non-European pressures too: the United States and Japan had emerged as serious rivals, and political unrest in the colonies was hovering just round the corner, requiring an increase in military presence and resources.

It was inevitable that these shifts in great-power politics would reduce the sympathy of Russian decision-makers for any special measures in Finland, especially as the Slavophile press in Russia was accusing Finland more and more vociferously of deliberate separatism, which was difficult to deny for anyone who had their finger on the pulse of the political elite and the democracy movements. Alexander III certainly did, and despite his coronation oath permitting Finland to keep its former constitutional laws, he would in no way tolerate its inhabitants regarding their country as any kind of separate state. When the Finnish Senate proposed a number of special Finnish amendments to an Empire-wide customs regulation, the tsar enquired sarcastically if it were not the case that Russia belonged to Finland rather than vice versa. A year later the Finnish postal service was closed down, and steps were taken to integrate the Finnish conscript army with the rest of the Russian armed forces.

The Dawn of Industrialisation

One important instrument in this Empire-wide integration policy was the railways. They were particularly significant in Russia because of its vast landmass. Work on the Finnish rail network was begun in the late 1850s, and the St Petersburg to Helsinki line came into operation in 1870, very soon providing a stimulus to trade and to Finland's economic development. The high investment costs delayed rail connections to the other ports until the 1880s, but by the early 1890s it was possible to take a train from Uleåborg (Oulu) in northern Finland to Odessa on the Black Sea. To facilitate long-distance troop transport, the gauge was the same throughout the Empire, and rail junctions became garrison towns, even in Finland.

The construction of the railways was in progress at a time when northern Europe was afflicted by several years of famine

143

that caused over 100,000 deaths in Finland alone. The situation spiralled into a catastrophe in Finland because, despite three years of poor harvests (1862, 1865, 1867), the Senate was too late in abandoning its austere monetary policy and procrastinated too much before deciding to finance the import of grain. Cheap grain from Russia had lulled decision-makers and the general public into a false sense of security. The façade cracked when the hunger years went on longer than expected and borrowers had difficulty repaying their loans. The situation was exacerbated by the fact that the price of corn shot up all over Europe and the winter again arrived early in 1867. Hordes of the hungry travelled far and wide, begging as they went, but as food was scarce everywhere there was little help for them. The movement of people spread a variety of epidemics, and it was these, together with malnutrition, which accounted for most of the deaths.

The famine years of 1867–68 uncompromisingly exposed the structural problems of the rural economy. After a slow recovery in the early 1870s there was a pronounced shift in Finnish agriculture from arable towards stockbreeding. The change had begun earlier in eastern Finland and was facilitated primarily by the constant improvements in rail connections, which ensured a supply of grain from the corn stores of southern Russia and Ukraine and made it profitable to sell meat and dairy products to St Petersburg and more distant cities in the mother country. Agriculture became very much more market-orientated and cost-effective. Fields were increasingly given over to the production of fodder, and by the turn of the century in 1900 a dense network of mechanised dairies had been established, predominantly owned by farmers' co-operatives.

Forestry also assumed a far greater importance in the years 1870–1914. The output and profitability of the sawmill industry rose in parallel with the rapid expansion of the building

6.3: In the late nineteenth century, the Finnish dairy industry gained a profitable market in the St Petersburg region.

industry in central Europe in the same period. Steam-driven saws represented a major innovation: investment costs were quite low and they could be set up anywhere on the coast or in any other logistically suitable spots. The steam engine was not an innovation in itself, but as the authorities feared devastation of the forests it was banned as a source of energy in the timber industry until 1857. The change of policy resulted not just from the general liberalisation of the Finnish economy but equally from the realisation that their competitors would otherwise gain a lead. Similar bans were discontinued in Sweden in 1848 and in Norway in 1860.

More than half the earnings from the proliferating timber exports went to the forest owners, who for the most part were farmers. The influx of capital eased the transition to

145

stockbreeding and the mechanisation of farming methods. The cash flow stimulated rural demand for consumer goods too, and gave the farmers the resources to have their children educated for professions requiring qualifications. Many forestry magnates came to prominence in this same period, buying up forest from the farmers for less than the market value and processing the timber in their own sawmills for export—but the trend was never as universal as it was in Sweden and Norway.

The consumption of timber likewise rose exponentially from the 1860s to the 1880s when more modern techniques were introduced, enabling the transformation of wood into paper on a grand scale. Logs were floated through the country's immense lake system, and so factories had to be built adjacent to waterways and railways. Water power was employed to grind the wood into the raw material for paper pulp. The pulp was boiled up with chemicals to improve its fibrous structure, and the viscous result pumped out onto the rollers of the huge machines that pressed and dried it into paper, glazing it if required. These inventions had a revolutionary effect on Finland's economy, since the country's prime raw material was and would remain its forests. After some experimentation, as many as seven paper mills were established in the early 1870s in various parts of the country, and they immediately found lucrative markets in Russia, thanks to the good rail links.

The paper industry had been exempted from Russian import duties in 1859, and even after that commercial advantage was terminated in 1885 the industry more than held its position on the Russian market. One obvious reason was that the import of paper from other countries was burdened with considerably higher duties. But Finnish paper was also better quality than Russian, so ensuring steady sales on the Russian market and inducing the Finnish manufacturers to form cartels to push up prices. By 1910 some 25 per cent of all paper for Russian consumption was produced in Finland.

So withdrawal of exemption from Russian tariffs in 1885 was not disastrous, but nevertheless made the Finnish paper manufacturers actively seek fresh markets in the west. Their efforts bore fruit and by the beginning of the twentieth century over 30 per cent of Finnish paper products were being exported to central and western Europe. The proportion rose over the next few decades to nearer 40 per cent, but when the First World War broke out and exports to the West ceased, the Russian market dominated again. The bulk of exports to the West (80 per cent) were wood pulp and low-grade paper, while nearly all exports (90 per cent) to Russia consisted of high-quality bond.

The paper industry required considerably more initial investment than the timber industry, and by the end of the nineteenth century that capital was increasingly provided by domestic banks. The main lenders were Finlands Föreningsbank (Suomen Yhdyspankki, Union Bank of Finland), founded 1862, and Nordiska Aktiebanken (Nordic Commercial Bank), founded 1873, but in 1889 a group of nationalist ("Fennomane") businessmen set up Kansallis-Osake-Pankki (National Commercial Bank), which competed with the older banks for the really profitable clients. Regional savings banks formed another significant category of credit providers, but they mostly served private households and small industrial borrowers.

Even though the paper industry was the fastest growing, it was timber, both hewn and sawn, which accounted for upwards of half the value of the country's export trade at the outbreak of the First World War. The paper industry represented barely one fifth of export income, but an almost equal amount came from animal products, with butter as the chief element (14 per cent), for which steamer traffic had opened up a wide market in Great Britain. Exports to the British Isles in 1913 reached nearly the same level as total sales to Russia. As far as imports were concerned, Germany had achieved a pre-eminent position with a market share of over 40 per cent. It was principally corn, metal products and machinery, but as living standards rose, German-manufactured consumer goods were also greatly in demand.

The beginnings of industrialisation and improved transport connections created excellent conditions for domestic trade, which was shifting from markets to grocery stores and other specialised shops. This trend was considerably enhanced by the proliferation of shops and chains of co-operatives owned by the producers, and the emergence of an efficiently organised wholesale trade controlled by wealthy urban businessmen. Once basic sustenance was assured, even the masses could afford the regular enjoyment of exotic delicacies such as coffee, sugar, white bread and tobacco. The consumption of coffee trebled and sugar consumption multiplied ninefold between 1860 and 1913, which implied that morning coffee was already being regarded as a necessity even in rural areas by the 1890s. This period marked the inception of that abiding Finnish ritual of modest enjoyment: a coffee and a bun.

Civic Society

The composite effect of accelerating industrialisation between 1860 and 1913 was a near-tripling of the country's GDP. This increase was by no means equitably spread over the populace as a whole, but it helped reduce infant mortality and extend the average lifespan. The population was continuing its rapid growth. The most dramatic increment had actually occurred in the first few decades of the nineteenth century when the birth rate peaked and the population more than doubled (from 863,000 in 1810 to 1,770,000 by 1870). Between 1870 and 1910 it rose at a rate of 300,000 per decade, and by the outbreak of the First World War Finland had a total of about 3 million inhabitants.

The rise was primarily in the Finnish-speaking population. The proportion of Swedish-speakers declined in the same period from 14 per cent to 12 per cent, partly because of increased language-switching to Finnish, but also because of a lower birth rate. The Grand Duchy's Russian-speaking civilian population remained at a moderate level all through the nineteenth century and amounted to about 6,000 in 1900, to which can be added the Russian troops stationed in Finland, fluctuating between 10,000 and 20,000.

As transport communications continued to improve and industry's need for manpower escalated, ever-mounting numbers of people moved into the towns of Finland or to the St Petersburg area. The population of the city on the Neva climbed above a million in the 1890s. Helsinki more than trebled its inhabitants between 1880 and 1910 (from 39,000 to 127,000) and the expansion was even greater in Vyborg (from 11,000 to 43,000), which due to its good connections to the east had the same rate of growth as St Petersburg, itself always having had a Finnish minority. Indeed, by 1880 the intake of Finnish workers was at its height and the Finnish residents of St Petersburg reached some 24,000, outstripping even Finland's own second largest town, Åbo. At this time about 37,000 Finnish citizens lived in Russia, but by the outbreak of the First World War the number had practically halved.

The mobile workforce was moving in greater numbers to the industrial centres of Finland in the period 1880–1910 and official statistics show the urban proportion of the population going up from 9 per cent to 15 per cent. Another almost equally significant population movement was emigration to North America, which in the same period accounted for some 280,000 people. The majority emigrated from Ostrobothnia.

With its seafaring tradition and often inimical attitude to Russian rule, the province had a labour surplus that was inclined to seek opportunities across the Atlantic. Over 100,000 of those emigrants would eventually return, and Finland thus gained a significant injection of expertise which was to benefit both its economy and its cultural life.

By 1910 the urban population of Finland was actually well in excess of 15 per cent, since many of the new industrial and built-up areas were not officially designated as towns. About 65 per cent of the population earned their living from agriculture and forestry, while only 20 per cent could be classified as urban working class. The remainder consisted mostly of the urban middle (7 per cent) and upper classes (2 per cent), so nearly a third of the country's inhabitants could be classified as town-dwellers.

Accelerating migration to the towns required large-scale investment in urban infrastructure. Even though this process got under way later than in central Europe, by the beginning of the twentieth century the major towns in Finland had attained roughly the same level of services as similar urban areas on the Continent. The principal innovations—electricity, the telephone and the internal combustion engine—steadily reduced the relevance of geographical distance for the development of society. The benefits were especially pronounced in the sparsely inhabited peripheries of northern Europe, where social planners and decision-makers had continually improving facilities for keeping abreast of technical progress and new applications. One sharp-eyed observer of this speedy transformation was the writer Angel Ganivet, Spanish consul in Helsinki in 1897–98, who published his impressions of Finland in the Spanish press. He described the country as having a naïve but efficacious enthusiasm for all technological advances, ultimately because it was not burdened by an ancient and intractable culture.

An essential prerequisite for the populace to be able to exploit and modernise its infrastructure was the raising of the general level of education. Until the 1860s, public education was administered by the Church, but in 1869 the state authorities set up the School Board, as a means of creating a nationally regulated school system. The ground had been prepared by the Elementary Schools Act of 1866, which gradually provided a path to knowledge for more and more children, even from rural areas. The reform was led by the educationalist Uno Cygnaeus. Yet for a long time his active campaign for a basic education for both boys and girls met with resistance, since education had to be financed by local taxation. By 1900 about half of all rural children attended elementary school, and compulsory education was introduced in 1921.

Another element in the national standardisation of the educational system was the reorganisation of the state grammar schools on the French and German pattern. Classical education was replaced by modern languages, the sciences and practical subjects, and special priority was accorded to national history and the mother tongue. The Fennomanes quickly realised the contribution the grammar schools could make to the creation of a Finnish-speaking public life, and from the 1870s started establishing Finnish-language private grammar schools. These efforts began to bear fruit in the 1880s when grammar school pupils became schoolteachers and influential figures in society. Between 1870 and 1917 the number of students at Helsinki University swelled from about 700 to almost 3,000.

In fact this represented a professionalisation of the expanding middle class, while fewer students were being recruited from the upper social classes; but the other reason for the rapid surge in student numbers was that higher education was gradually being made available to women. The authorities had introduced separate girls' schools from the 1860s, but since these did not lead to school certificate examinations, the route for girls to university and other higher-education establishments was chiefly through private co-educational schools. Finland's first female student was Marie Tchetschulin, daughter of a successful Russian businessman in Helsinki, who was allowed to sit the school certificate examination in 1870 after making special application. Hard on her heels followed Emma Irene Åström, subsequently herself to become a well-known educationalist, who went up to Helsinki University in the autumn of 1873. For the right to study at university, female candidates had to continue to make special application, indeed to the tsar himself, until 1901, but by then the restriction had ceased to be meaningful since a quarter of registered students were women (400 out of 1,650).

It was from these ranks of the highly educated that the pioneers of the emerging civic society arose. Until the 1860s the growth of voluntary organisations had been prevented by regulations that were founded on a fear of political unrest. When the prohibition was lifted a rich flora of diverse societies and national organisations burst forth, which despite their varied aims gave the concept of Finland as a nation a solid social context. There were already well-organised mass movements in Scandinavia and Great Britain, giving the popular movements in Finland a ready-made model to emulate.

There can be no doubt that nationalism ("Fennomania") gave rise to the popular movement which attracted the largest membership and had the widest range of activities. A sizeable proportion of its programme was introduced or administered at the outset by the People's Educational Society (Kansanvalistusseura), the establishment of which in 1874 prompted a series of educational campaigns, evening lectures and folk festivals across the country. In the 1880s the initiative was increasingly adopted by local activists, who began setting up individual societies based on foreign paradigms for everything from temperance, youth work and women's emancipation to sport, local history and the ever more pressing labour question. In northern and central Finland these associations would be dominated by local Fennomanes until long into the twentieth century. In the predominantly Swedish-speaking coastal districts and the industrial urban areas, the first step was more likely to be taken by individuals connected to the Liberal, Suecomane (Swedish-orientated) or Socialist camps, but it was equally common for these associations to be led by generally respected people who were enthusiasts for a specific cause and also efficient organisers.

The most revolutionary aspect of these associations, however, was that they forged links between individuals and groups who had not previously been able to mix on equal terms. Since the process coincided with the spread of school education, the activities of such groups often took the form of a broad educational programme, ultimately oriented towards building up social cohesion. Their figureheads were successful businessmen, dynamic schoolteachers or self-taught workers, who succeeded in promoting a vision of the interconnectivity of the local and the national. So nationalism was reshaped into civic awareness almost as a system of belief.

The same applied to workers' associations. Well into the 1890s their activities were focused on temperance, with Christian and patriotic overtones. The labour movement itself stemmed essentially from the temperance movement. A more radical approach developed in many respects when the labour movement began to ally itself with the international class struggle, but otherwise many of the original patriotic ideals lived on within the Social Democratic Party, formed in 1903, and that was a decisive factor when Finnish civic society was mobilised in the years 1899 to 1905 to defend the country's autonomy in relation to Russia.

Cultural Expression

One reason this vision of Finland as a nation with its own historical orbit made such a pervasive impact on all sections of society was that it appeared in so many different guises, reinvented and adapted to the demands of the time. It was popularised above all by the writer Zacharias Topelius, whose poems, tales, novels and schoolbooks were published in huge numbers and thus very effectively disseminated the concept of Finland as a nation with a past and a future of its own. There is no doubt that the most influential was *Boken om vårt land* (*The Book About Our Country*), 1875, which he wrote for use in elementary schools and which continued to serve that purpose right up to the 1940s. In the main, Topelius elaborated ideas already expressed by Runeberg and Snellman, but as a versatile writer he had that rare ability to clothe them in lively new literary form. A considerable portion of his output was translated into Finnish, a necessary requirement for the national status it was to achieve.

Whereas Topelius was the populariser, Aleksis Kivi was the real literary pioneer in the Finnish language with his novel *Seitsemän veljestä* (*Seven Brothers*), published in 1870. Its humorous but classic depiction of the confrontation between Finnish peasant culture and modern civilisation became an exemplar for the country's twentieth-century narrative prose. But his contemporary readers found it difficult to stomach his burlesque parody and racy language. So it was not until the 1890s that the book attained greater popularity, when a specifically Finnish culture had become more established and there was scope for national self-irony. Another valuable contribution to Finnish-language public life was a vibrant theatre, which really took off in the 1880s with the Ibsen-inspired plays of Minna Canth. The theatre in general was important for the incipient

6.4: Aleksis Kivi wrote the novel *Seven Brothers* (1870), which was the first modern novel written in the Finnish language.

civic awareness, and in 1902, after various temporary locations, the National Theatre moved into the magnificent art nouveau building on Station Square which it still occupies today. In a similar way, Canth's novels and stories of emancipated women and the social insecurities of the middle classes opened the gates to a burgeoning social criticism in literature.

Influences from Scandinavia persisted in the final decade of the century, when a new generation of Finnish-orientated authors, not least Juhani Aho, began writing fresh and straight-forward journalistic prose, literary criticism and novels in the mould of August Strindberg and Georg Brandes. An equally significant but now often forgotten source of inspiration were the illustrious names of Russian literature, Turgenev, Tolstoy

155

and Chekhov, whose writing made an impact on Arvid Järnefelt and Joel Lehtonen in particular.

Broadening contacts with Scandinavia, Western Europe and
Russia made a potent impression on art and culture in turn-of-
the-century Finland. The Scandinavian artists' colonies in
Berlin and Paris were creative focal points for such interchange,
where first drafts or ideas for many of the great national works
originated. The principal movements in the arts on the Continent in the early 1890s were Symbolism and National Romanticism. It was no coincidence that Jean Sibelius wrote many of
the initial versions of his world-famous *Kalevala* compositions in
the cafés and restaurants of metropolitan continental Europe.

Aho and Sibelius, together with a handful of productive
pictorial artists, formed the nucleus of the group of "Young
Finns" who managed to revitalise the national epic, the *Kalevala*, for a wider public, simultaneously making it part of the
"Modern Breakthrough" in Finland's cultural life. The new
direction was not just a reaction to the dominant patriarchal-
Christian social structures, but was also in some ways a rejection of an uncritical belief in progress in the wake of the
technological advances of the 1880s. Many of these early
Modernists were National Romantics and nature worshippers,
who made pilgrimages to deepest Karelia.

Ironically, much of the commercial artistic success of these
so-called Karelians arose from innovations in printing and
transport technology. Books could be published in bigger and
cheaper print runs, and it was possible to make high-quality
reproductions of famous works of art, allowing the innovative
exploitation of historical and national painting for both educational and political purposes. A prime example of this was the
magnificent volume on nineteenth-century Finland published
in 1893 (*Finland i 19de seklet*) in which the country's transformation
from the poor man of Europe into one of its most progressive

nations was described and illustrated by a number of pre-eminent writers and artists. The editor was Professor Leo Mechelin, and there was no doubt that the object was to emphasise Finland's position as an autonomous state within the Russian Empire.

The most prestigious artist of this circle was Albert Edelfelt, who had already achieved international renown and whose illustrations to Runeberg's *Tales of Ensign Stål*, in an edition of 1898–1900, would ensure the continued existence of that work as a national icon. It was not only his unrivalled ability to evoke the Russo-Swedish war in Finland of 1808–09 with historical and dramatic fidelity; just as the book was being published, the smouldering constitutional dispute between Finland and Russia flared up into overt political conflict, giving fresh topicality to Runeberg's patriotic texts and Edelfelt's illustrations. A notable parallel to this were Akseli Gallen-Kallela's numerous illustrations to the *Kalevala*, where the figures were much more warlike and defiant than in earlier editions of the national epic. When Finland had its own pavilion at the World Exhibition in Paris in 1900, it was Gallen-Kallela's spectacular *Kalevala* frescoes that were very much the centre of attention.

After the upheavals of 1899–1905, which also exposed domestic conflicts of political interest, national motifs had to make way for new subjects and new ventures in cultural life. Within the increasingly self-aware labour movement a working-class culture was crystallising, with a dynamic press and multifarious educational activities, among which amateur dramatics and sport were the primary attractions for the young. The same pursuits drew members to rural youth associations, which usually had a decidedly conservative and patriotic political profile. The next rung on the educational ladder would most usually be one of the country's many folk high schools, founded on the Danish model as a civic provision of further education.

6.5: The famous composer Jean Sibelius (1865–1957) wrote some of his most archetypally National Romantic symphonies in central Europe.

The undisputed luminary of Finnish-language literature at the turn of the century was Eino Leino. His powerful verse was influenced partly by the revived *Kalevala* vogue, partly by European Symbolism and Nietzscheanism. There were likewise hints of the strong but isolated superman in the contemporary poetry of L. Onerva and Otto Manninen, where the relationship of the individual to society and nation was much more detached than in late nineteenth-century literature. The process was evident too in Finland's Swedish-language literature, which in step with the Fennicisation of public life and the political turmoil began to show signs of a studied melancholy, giving rise to the appellation "flaneur literature". The most celebrated Swedish-language poet of the next decade and beyond was the modernist Edith Södergran, who in her free verse avoided conventional national and historical subjects completely. But contemporary bourgeois taste was more appreciative of Bertel Gripenberg's traditional poetry, where such elements proliferated.

The most tangible attempt at national expression was Finnish Art Nouveau (Jugend) architecture, which thanks to the speed of economic growth between 1895 and 1915 was able to manifest itself in buildings throughout the country. Entire districts in some of the bigger towns were designed in Art Nouveau style with irregular layouts, ornamental decoration and materials inspired by Finnish or Scandinavian mythology and naive art. Public buildings of particular note from around that time include Tampere Cathedral (1907) and the National Museum (1916) and railway station (1919) in Helsinki. They were all three intended as composite creations involving the foremost architects and artists of the day.

Despite this architecture being regarded as a manifestation of national culture, it was to a large extent in the international Art Nouveau style, its main concept a return to natural materials and organic construction. Finnish architects started using rough-hewn native granite for façades after having become aware of the technique in Scotland. Typically, it was only there that their eyes were properly opened to the granite construction of their own mediaeval churches. Art Nouveau style also went hand in hand with increasingly modern building techniques. Granite and wood-carving could be employed to disguise cast iron and concrete. This was the mode adopted for Helsinki railway station, the architect of which, Eliel Saarinen, gave the building an austere form that combined both Neo-Classicism and Functionalism.

Opposition and Rupture

The years 1899 to 1917 are frequently described in Finnish historiography as a protracted period of Russification and oppression. The concept is correct insofar as the Russian authorities from 1898 onwards redoubled their attempts to bind the Grand Duchy more closely to the Empire, but the era as a whole enjoyed a social and cultural vitality that was more evocative of a golden age. Paradoxically, it was precisely this positive development of society that gave rise to the conditions for the organised resistance which was mobilised on the Finnish side. The more successfully both business and civic society thrived, the greater the amount of economic and ideological resources that could be freed to defend the country's gradually more outspoken independence within the Russian Empire. It is ever thus with historical processes: they occur simultaneously and frequently overlap; they develop in different directions and are as often as not mutually contradictory, leading in the end to unexpected consequences and conflicts.

The premature death of Tsar Alexander III in 1894 had brought to a halt the efforts at integration that had begun in the 1880s, but as soon as his son Nicholas II had found his feet the project continued, with three overarching objectives. Firstly, the Russian authorities wanted to make a clear distinction between laws of Empire-wide application and those that applied only within the Grand Duchy. Secondly, they intended to abolish Finland's own army, which was not duty-bound to defend the other borders of the Empire, and in the worst-case scenario might even turn its weapons on the capital, St Petersburg. Thirdly, the governor-general's powers were to be substantially enhanced and Russian was to be used as the official language in all public contexts.

In the summer of 1898 the single-minded General Nikolai Bobrikoff was appointed governor-general to push through these reforms. When it became obvious six months later that the Finnish parliament was being recalcitrant, the tsar signed a manifesto in February of 1899 stipulating that the Grand Duchy was subject to the laws of the Empire. In compliance with this, new statutes that applied only to Finland but had relevance to national policy would be handled by the Russian authorities. The manifesto was received with dismay by Finnish public opinion, belief in the country's constitutional autonomy having been reinforced during the latter half of the nineteenth century as civil society expanded and contacts with the West were consolidated.

The manifesto was aimed at the political influence the Finnish parliament had acquired since 1863. The swiftly mobilised

6.6: Helsinki Market Square and the Russian orthodox cathedral in the background. Photo by Signe Brander, from the early twentieth century.

mass protests against it were organised by leading figures of many political factions which for various reasons described themselves as upholding the constitution. The constitutional argument was that the tsar was breaking his own royal affirmation, which, in accordance with tradition, had included a vague promise of respecting the country's existing laws. In the course of a few weeks a petition to the tsar had collected more than half a million signatures, expressing concern at the consequences of the manifesto. The country's journalists, academics and artists also alerted friends and colleagues overseas, who submitted their own appeals and expressions of solidarity with Finland to the tsar.

The protests did not come as a surprise to the decision-makers in St Petersburg, but their sheer volume nevertheless commended a certain caution. Bobrikoff, however, as governor-general, pursued the policy vigorously, and in the summer of 1901 an imperial edict was issued on military service, in line with the objectives already announced. Finland's own army was replaced by pan-Russian conscription, with five years' active service for all conscripts, in Russian-led units, which were expected to take part in the defence of the Empire in its entirety. The edict prompted a further wave of protest with public demonstrations, culminating in the refusal of nearly half of those called up to report for duty in the spring of 1902.

This was something utterly novel in a Grand Duchy which had previously been so loyal to the Emperor. When Bobrikoff raised the tempo over the following two years, abolishing the Finnish Cadet Corps, strengthening the position of Russian in the administration, and finally acquiring new powers to suppress the Finnish opposition, resistance was further radicalised. Passive resistance was complemented by a conspiratorial activism which forged contacts both with Russian revolutionaries and with Japanese spies, who had started financing the formers' illegal activities after the outbreak of the Russo-Japanese War in 1904. A series of political assassinations took place, of which the murder of Bobrikoff in June 1904 aroused the greatest furore.

But the major turning point was brought about by the huge demonstrations and strikes that swept over the whole of war-weary Russia from the spring of 1905 and pushed the tsar into making concessions. The Finnish military service law was rescinded that same year and later replaced by an annual tax to the Imperial Treasury. After the Russian defeat in the war, demands for civil rights and suffrage reform were intensified in October 1905 by an Empire-wide general strike. In November the tsar gave way on other issues too. Russia was to have an elective National Assembly (Duma) and increased freedom of expression. In Finland other 1899 reforms were withdrawn and preparations begun for a comprehensive review of the parliamentary system. In the summer of 1906 Finland's four-Estate parliament was replaced by a single-chamber legislature, and the following year its first 200 members were elected by universal and equal suffrage. The number of those qualified to vote shot up tenfold overnight (from 126,000 to 1,300,000), and the women of Finland were the first in Europe to have the right to vote.

The election result was an interesting summation of the political turbulence of the preceding year. The largest party by far was the Social Democrats (SDP), with eighty members. The alliance of the labour movement with the constitutional front against further Russian integration had been a gradual development, and was decisive for its success in 1905. The alliance guaranteed the effective mobilisation of the masses and prevented social unrest degenerating into internal political conflicts like those which had occurred in Russia and the Baltic countries, subjecting them to extensive plunder and murder in the year of revolution. The labour movement's nationalistic stance also made it easier for right-wing elements to accept parliamentary reform, and appealed to the voters, who had mostly been brought up in the spirit of the nationalist Fennomane movement.

The second largest party was the conservative wing of the Fennomane movement, the Old Finns (fifty-nine seats), which despite its tactical readiness to meet Russian demands had managed to retain broad support among the people thanks by no means least to its unwavering views on the language question and further land reforms. The result was much worse for the Young Finns (twenty-six), the Swedish People's Party (twenty-four) and the Agrarian Union (nine), whose prominent commitment to the constitutional front paid no noticeable dividend, since the political agenda was rapidly filled with questions which shattered any hope of national unity.

The chief merit of the parliamentary reform was that it created a common and representative arena for political debate. Legislation, on the other hand, was much impeded by the tsar's refusal to ratify a number of reforms which were important for both social and political reasons, triggering fresh elections. The tsar in fact retained his right to dissolve parliament, reject draft Finnish legislation, and enforce his own will through edicts. That was what happened in 1908 when he transferred the presentation of the Grand Duchy's draft laws from the Finnish state-secretary to the Russian Council of Ministers, simply by means of a decree. That marked the beginning of a renewed integration policy which was to continue up to the February Revolution of 1917. In 1910 the tsar approved a bill that subjected all Finnish draft laws to committee approval in the Russian Duma, and in 1912, two years later, an equality law was enacted that gave Russian subjects full citizenship in Finland. The Senate was thenceforth made up solely of the governor-general's trusted appointees, which in practice meant that it consisted of Russian military officers and civil servants.

Such interference consolidated the political schism that had opened up between the Empire and the Grand Duchy over the previous decades. From the point of view of the Russian authorities integration was fully justified; the mistake lay in the requisite steps having been taken too late. From the point of view of Finnish civil society, however, now well-established, it was completely unacceptable for autonomy in legislation to be removed just when the country had acquired its democratic representation of the people, and the further the Russification went, the more aversion to all things Russian developed. Widespread Russophobia surfaced in the climate of relatively unlimited freedom of speech Finland then enjoyed. The acrimonious tone was admittedly applied even to Finnish opponents. Language fervour, class hatred and racism could now suddenly be articulated openly, and since in any case the compromises of domestic politics were always torpedoed by the Russians, public debate was marred by ominously aggressive language.

The outbreak of the First World War in August 1914 brought with it numerous restrictions in public life which effectively subdued the rhetorical fever. Military preparations in Finland were gradually building up to a force of some 100,000 men—because of fears of a German attack on St Petersburg via Finland. Coastal defences were strengthened and a chain of militar bases and earthworks installed. The male population of Finland was not mobilised, but in the first few months of the war there were many spontaneous expressions of sympathy for beleaguered Russia and over 500 men joined the Russian army as volunteers. Meanwhile, academics in Helsinki sympathetic to Germany launched a secret recruitment of some 2,000 men for the German army. They would go down in history as the Jaeger Brigade (the Royal Prussian Rifle Battalion).

In the first three years of the war, Finland came off quite lightly. The war blocked Western markets, but in compensation the demand for paper and steel products in Russia increased. That secured the supply of Russian grain, and Finland's trade prospered until the autumn of 1916. But in March 1917 military defeats eroded discipline in the Russian army and there was a glaring lack of both food and determination on the home front. The result was revolution. Tsar Nicholas II had to abdicate and the autocratic monarchy was replaced by a provisional government which assuaged public opinion with a number of

6.7: Bread ration stamps from January 1918.

reforms and in Finland issued a manifesto revoking all the integration measures which had been introduced since 1899.

This was the beginning of a complex process in which by the late autumn of 1917 Finland came to sever its bonds with Russia and declare itself an independent republic. The notion of total liberation from Russia had been taking root among radical activists even under Bobrikoff's regime, but was generally regarded as likely to be abortive as long as the country was controlled by the Russian military. When the army lost its grip on the situation, the ideal of independence gathered momentum, and in June 1917 the Finnish Social Democrats announced their objective to be total national sovereignty. The Russian Bolsheviks were inciting the various minority peoples in the Empire to civil disobedience and promising them national liberation if the Bolsheviks came to power. Expectations rose even on the Right, and on 18 July 1917 parliament passed a sovereignty law which removed from the provisional government in Russia the authority to decide on any matters except foreign policy and military affairs. This was unthinkable for the Russian government, which was endeavouring to hold the Empire together, and so it immediately dissolved Finland's parliament. Such a response simply encouraged Finnish demands for independence, and led to the definitive rupture of ties with Russia just a month after the Bolsheviks had seized power in St Petersburg in the October of 1917.

The liberation from Russia would later be described in national historiography as a pre-ordained fulfilment of the national awakening, but for contemporaries these dramatic events appeared in quite a different light. Despite Finland having developed during the nineteenth century into a state within a state, the country's economy and external security had become so tightly bound to the motherland that any liberation, however welcome in itself, had to be regarded as full of complications in nearly every respect. How would the country survive without Russia's huge markets, and above all, how would it survive the ongoing world conflagration with its independence intact?

7

WAR AND INDEPENDENCE

Many of these questions came to the fore in the spring of 1918—when the Russian Revolution spread to Finland. A short but bloody war between the revolutionary and bourgeois troops was waged, which resulted in victory for the latter forces, who had the crucial support of German troops. After the defeat of Germany in the First World War, Finland became a republic with a system of government that was to remain unchanged until the beginning of the new millennium. The occasionally volatile relationship with its Soviet neighbour affected the country's domestic and foreign policy in various ways in the 1920s and 1930s. By the mid-Thirties a social harmony was achieved which was to be of the utmost importance for the country's morale in the Second World War. Finland was sucked very quickly into that war, the real test of maturity for the independent nation. The disengagement from Russia was not the catastrophe that might have been feared, since Finnish goods soon found other markets in Europe and further overseas. Cultural life was shaped partly by the traumatic experiences of the Civil War, and partly by the Modernist movement advancing on all fronts.

Revolution and War

Late in the evening of Sunday 27 January 1918 the Red Guards seized power in southern Finland, set up a People's

Commissariat as the new government and issued orders to imprison the Senate, though they all had time to flee. The coup took place without great loss of life, but in the course of the next few days the crisis exploded into armed conflict between the White and the Red Guards, soon involving German and Russian troops. The confrontation was given many different names from the outset. Nowadays, it is commonly referred to by Finns as the Civil War, even though it was in fact a peripheral offshoot of the ongoing World War. The Revolution in Russia was part of a chain reaction to the defeats inflicted by Germany, and when the chaos within the Empire intensified in the summer of 1917 a power vacuum arose which spread in all directions and escalated into military conflict even in Finland.

Both the non-socialist and Socialist camps had begun forming their own military guards in the summer of 1917 as protection against internal and external threats. When in the autumn of 1917 the home-grown strikes and demonstrations degenerated into pillage and murder, the two sides began an arms race, each blaming the other for plunging the country into civil war. The Finnish Declaration of Independence on 6 December 1917 was triggered by the non-socialist Senate's fears that the Russian Revolution was on the point of extending to Finland. On New Year's Eve of 1917–18 Lenin signed the Bolshevik government's recognition of Finland's national sovereignty, though this was not to endorse the Finnish bourgeoisie society, but rather to urge on the revolutionary process in the country. In mid-January 1918 the Finnish parliament voted by a narrow non-socialist majority to approve the Senate's proposals for strengthening the forces of law and order, and when the White Guards were appointed to this role just days later, it was interpreted within the Socialist camp not only as an attempt to halt the Revolution, but also as a sign that the Conservatives were even less willing to consider social reforms.

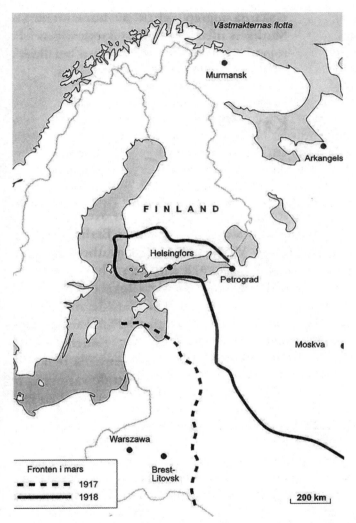

7.1: The 1918 war in Finland was a peripheral part of the First World
   War. Its development was crucially a chain reaction provoked by
   the changes at the German-Russian frontline.

The majority of the Finnish Social Democrats were reform-ist, but when the situation took this turn they gave in to the Russian Bolsheviks' and domestic party radicals' frenetic demands for a Finnish revolution. They could see no other way forward. The non-socialist parties had increased their contacts with Germany during the autumn of 1917 and there was no doubt that the Senate's objective was to seek German backing to safeguard the independence attained. Finland was just a pawn in the peace negotiations between the Bolshevik govern-ment and Germany that had been in progress throughout the previous year. Lenin was being urged to fulfil his promises of peace, while the Germans wanted an end to a ruinous war on two fronts. Both sides could see that control of Finland was strategically vital in view of its proximity to Petrograd (St Peters-burg). It was therefore in the interests of both that their allies should seize power in Finland without delay.

So, the war in Finland broke out while Russo-German peace negotiations were still being held. The Red Guards acquired plenty of weapons from the remaining Russian troops in Fin-land, among whom the majority sympathised with the Bolshe-viks. On the commencement of hostilities 30,000 Red Guards were mobilised, primarily from local workers' associations, and with material and ideological support from the Russian troops in their rail-junction garrisons they swiftly gained control of southern Finland. Their numbers grew steadily and by the final phase of the war amounted to some 70,000 men.

At the beginning of February there were about 75,000 Rus-sian soldiers left in Finland, but they were somewhat reluctant to take up arms: some 10,000 at the outside actively engaged in hostilities and even then primarily as trainers, officers, or for fire control in the field. The paucity of experienced officers and functioning military organisation was a severe handicap for the Red Guards from the start. The situation was further exacerbated in that respect after the Russo-German peace treaty of Brest-Litovsk on 3 March 1918, when the Bolsheviks included an undertaking for the immediate withdrawal of their approximately 35,000 soldiers still in the country.

At the outbreak of war the White troops comprised a total of 38,000 men, and the number rose through conscription to nearly 60,000 by April. Even though they succeeded in disarming the Russian troops in Ostrobothnia and eventually set up their own importation of weapons from Sweden and Germany, they suffered shortages of arms throughout the entire war. In compensation they had a professional leadership, which afforded them a distinct advantage in military strategy. The general staff were dominated by Finnish officers from the disbanded Imperial army. Their commander-in-chief was General Gustaf Mannerheim, who had grown up in Finland. He was a remarkable combination of professional soldier, clear-sighted politician who understood security policy, and worldly aristocrat with experience of the Imperial court. At the end of February 1918 the lower ranks of officers were significantly augmented when the Jaeger troops trained in Germany returned and were placed in command of many of the units. The Jaegers' courage now bore fruit and they became folk heroes, especially as, in contrast to the so-called "Russian officers", they had a decidedly negative attitude to everything Russian and also had been recruited from a broad spectrum of society.

Over the first few weeks of the war a front line was drawn from northern Tavastland to Karelia that remained more or less static until mid-March. The towns and industries of southern Finland were under Red control, while the Whites had their firmest foothold in Ostrobothnia and set up their political headquarters there in the coastal town of Vaasa (Vasa). The war was fought predominantly by amateurs who lacked both weapons and military discipline, and so distinct front lines appeared only near strategically important towns, rail junctions or main roads, making the conflict in Finland quite different from the total war in central Europe.

Since the war was an offshoot of the Russian Revolution, the Reds liked to emphasise its class warfare aspect, which appealed to their largely proletarian soldiery. The Whites depicted the war as a liberation struggle against the Russians, but not just from ideological conviction: their soldiers had been recruited from all levels of society and so had to be welded together under the banner of a liberation war. Most were the sons of peasant farmers or the middle classes, and after conscription was introduced the proportion of crofters and workers began to rise. As deaths mounted and resentment grew, both sides were induced into atrocities, resulting in at least 11,800 people being executed behind the front lines, either directly after they had surrendered or through decisions of hastily convened field courts. At the outset of the war, Red terror was pre-eminent, but when the fortunes of war were reversed, the Whites took their revenge to the full—some 10,000 of the victims were Red Guards.

Events changed course after the signing of the Treaty of Brest-Litovsk, when the German military leadership chose to bring the warfare in Finland to an early conclusion with a strike on Red forces in southern Finland. On 3 April a German division landed on the Hanko (Hangö) Peninsula on the southwest coast, and only eleven days after this their troops were parading through the centre of Helsinki. It was an irony of fate that the lightning attack followed the railway lines laid in the Russian era for the very purpose of warding off coastal landings. Red resistance was quashed elsewhere in Finland too: on the same day that the Germans landed in the south-west, White troops began their capture of Tampere (Tammerfors), where the Red Guards had stationed a considerable proportion of their troops.

With that, the outcome of the Finnish war was a foregone conclusion, even though fierce battles raged in south-east Finland until early May. Some 10,000 soldiers fell in the war (5,300 Reds, 3,400 Whites, 600 Russians, 300 Germans). If all the victims of execution, atrocities and sickness are included, the death toll came to about 38,500. A third of these (13,500) died of disease or malnutrition in camps where the Reds were held prisoner. The global epidemic of Spanish flu struck Finland in earnest just as the war ended, and the victors collected together as many as 80,000 Reds in huge camps in barracks and fortresses in the south of the country. By the time each outbreak was discovered it was usually too late to intervene. Since most of the war survivors had been given conditional sentences and more than 60,000 of them were not even eligible to vote in the parliamentary elections in the spring of 1919, the bitterness against the White "butchers" did not really begin to abate until the 1930s.

In a broader perspective, the German intervention was decisive in shortening the conflict in Finland in favour of the Whites. Elsewhere in the crumbling Russian Empire the White counter-revolutionaries continued their resistance for several more years, but since the Western powers' pledges of substantial military aid came to nought, in the end the Bolshevik victory was absolute. Finland's White Senate had no difficulty in acknowledging the crucial impact of the German intervention, since they had been urging this very thing ever since the late autumn of 1917. The alliance with Germany was seen as a guarantee for the permanence of the liberation from Russia. Finland's defence and economy was thus willingly subordinated to German interests.

Immediately after the war a new Senate was formed under the leadership of J. K. Paasikivi, of the Old Finn Party. Together with the temporary head of state P. E. Svinhufvud, the Senate abandoned the republican principles drawn up in December 1917 and by a small parliamentary majority pushed through a monarchical constitution. Practically all the Social Democrat members had lost their parliamentary seats because of their alignment with the Reds. At the beginning of October 1918 the German prince Friedrich Karl of Hesse was elected the country's first king, but Germany's capitulation a month afterwards turned this into a political cul-de-sac.

The saviour at hand was once again Mannerheim, who as a former Russian officer had always been averse to any German inclinations in Finland. He was now appointed head of state to repair shattered relations with the victorious Western powers. He succeeded brilliantly. After the parliamentary elections the following spring a republican form of government was adopted which was ratified by Mannerheim on 17 July 1919. The experiences of the Civil War were still fresh in the memory, and this was one of the main reasons the non-socialist parties gave the president the strongest authority and a long mandate (six years), as a counterbalance to a possibly too radical or disunited parliament. This was to have far-reaching consequences for domestic politics, in that the constitutional laws remained in force until 1 March 2000.

The first elected president, with a safe majority, was K. J. Ståhlberg, a widely respected liberal parliamentarian well-versed in law, who had himself led the drafting of the new form of government. Mannerheim stood as the alternative candidate, but for obvious reasons he was not in great favour with the Social Democrats, who had won back their position as the largest party in the parliamentary elections in March 1919. In addition, his active efforts to involve Finland's army in the Russian Civil War had also aroused distrust of him within the non-socialist camp, which was not prepared to have the country dragged into further armed conflict.

Finland's road to independence had been marked by high drama and many chance factors which could easily have steered its development along less propitious lines. A prime element was of course the heartfelt popular endorsement of emancipation from the Russian Empire, but the decisive political impetus was the Bolsheviks' seizure of power in Petrograd. It afforded Finland the opportunity to sever its bonds and reduced Russia to such impotence in its Soviet incarnation that its subsequent attempts to retake Finland were doomed to failure.

Towards Parliamentary Democracy

The sovereignty of the new Republic had been recognised by all its neighbours, but in the autumn of 1919 there were still many problematic issues on the foreign policy agenda. The political map of central and eastern Europe had been completely redrawn after the First World War, and the consequences of that had an impact on relations between European states in the years to come. Like the other smaller countries that had stepped forward out of the ashes after the war, Finland needed to have its borders firmly and unambiguously fixed. Relations with Bolshevik Russia had been strained both by the 1918 war in Finland and by the participation of Finnish activists in the subsequent fighting in Russian Karelia. In the summer of 1920 the two countries opened negotiations in the Estonian university city of Dorpat (Tartu), and after some delays a peace treaty was drawn up which gave Finland a land corridor to the Arctic Ocean, beyond what had been the Grand Duchy's historical territory since 1812.

Finland also won a protracted dispute with Sweden on rights to Åland when the question was referred to the League of Nations in 1921. Åland's monolingual Swedish-speaking population had unequivocally expressed its desire to be annexed to

Sweden in 1917. But when an undertaking was extracted from Finland that the islands would remain a demilitarised zone and be granted comprehensive home rule within Finland, Sweden was content to acquiesce. From the Swedish viewpoint a guarantee of military neutrality for the islands addressed its principal concern.

Behind the Åland dispute lay the Swedish government's extremely muted stance on Finland's struggle for independence. Sweden's defensive policy towards the east had paid excellent dividends during the nineteenth century, so its government was consistently unwilling to involve itself in Russo-Finnish squabbles about the autonomy of the Grand Duchy, and even refused to give official support to the Finnish Whites against the Revolutionaries in 1918. That was one reason why in the early 1920s Finland tried to establish co-operation on security policy with the other newly independent border states, Poland, Lithuania, Latvia and Estonia. The attempt soon foundered on internal conflicts of interest, though some limited covert collaboration with Estonia developed in military preparedness and intelligence.

Bitter memories of the war in 1918 cast their shadows over domestic politics too, which explains why the whole of the 1920s was dominated by short-term governments and profound ideological hostilities. Despite the imprisoned Red Guards being granted a belated amnesty, it was inevitable that the mistrust between the Socialist and Conservative camps would persist, complicating co-existence in their shared Republic. The vast majority appreciated the recently won independence, but far fewer were willing to budge from their own vision of how it should be used.

The fact that none of the first four presidents held office for more than one term contributed to the political turbulence. K. J. Ståhlberg's (1919–25) successor Lauri Kristian Relander

(1925–31) was from the Agrarian Union. Next came the Conservative candidate, P. E. Svinhufvud (1931–37), who had acted as head of state in 1917–18 and therefore had the authority to restrain the arrogant leaders of the radical right-wing Lapua Movement. The presidential term (1937–40) of the Agrarian Union's Kyösti Kallio was interrupted by illness, and so he had even less time than his predecessors to become undisputed leader of the Republic. Notwithstanding the principle that authority was vested by the constitution in the president to direct the country's foreign policy, this responsibility was in practice shouldered by the prime minister or foreign minister between the wars. Emphasis was instead placed on the ceremonial role of the presidential office, for lack of monarch and royal house.

How did domestic politics develop? An open breach arose within the Socialist camp in 1922 when the Communists, under the aegis of the Soviet Union, broke away from the Social Democratic Party, the leadership of which had since 1919 advocated a reformist path to Socialism. On the Conservative side a schism arose over control of the White Civil Guards, which had established itself as a voluntary defence force with considerable stocks of weapons but without any clear-cut ties to state authority. The result was that the state took stricter control of the White Civil Guards and circumscribed the former activists' ability to exploit it as a means of extra-parliamentary pressure. But even so, it was regarded, especially on the Left, as a latent threat to democracy throughout the interwar period.

Another potentially explosive political issue continued to be the position of Swedish as an official language in Finland. The Fennomane cultural campaign had been successful and the 1906 parliamentary reform brought the pre-eminence of the Swedish-speaking elite in political life to an abrupt end. In the period 1880–1940 the process of Fennicisation continued and Swedish-speakers decreased from 14 per cent to just 10 per cent of the population. But to the annoyance of many of the ardent supporters of Finnishness, the Swedish-language element was still strong in many particular areas of society. In the early 1920s more than half of the business elite had Swedish as their mother tongue, and there was also a manifest over-representation in the sciences, arts and cultural life in general.

The parliamentary reform had made the language dispute more strident and given further stimulus to the political and organisatory consolidation of the country's Swedish-speakers, leading their most radical protagonists in the period 1917 to 1921 to advocate a language-based self-rule. To aid definition, the epithets "Finland-Swedish" and "Finlander" came into common parlance, as a linguistic distinction from "Finn", which in the domestic context had always been the appellation of Finnish-speakers. Since Finnish and Swedish had been classified in the constitution of 1919 as the country's two official languages, and parliament in 1921 had passed a very liberal language law, even the most introverted Swedishness gave way to a positive desire to be identified with the new Republic.

The reaction was quite the opposite among radical Fenno-manes, the so-called "true Finns" (*"äktfinnar"*), who in 1924 started pursuing their demands for Fennicisation principally through a student association, the Karelian Academic Society (Akateeminen Karjala-Seura). The society was originally inspired by activist dreams of territorial expansion for Finland, into an area termed Greater Finland, but through to the late 1930s confined itself more or less exclusively to the total Fennicisation of Helsinki University. After parliament approved a revised university statute in the spring of 1937 asserting the prime position of Finnish but at the same time guaranteeing the continuation of teaching in Swedish, the language question faded away. The social levelling between the elites of the two linguistic groups was already well advanced. In addition, the government was calling for an active peace in the language dispute to facilitate its Scandinavian orientation in security policy.

The common denominator in all this antagonism was a reluctance to comply with the rules of parliamentary democracy, which required the acceptance of compromise and respect for lawfully taken decisions. Governments tended therefore to be short-lived minority coalitions—there were thirteen in the Twenties alone—and it did not help that none of the right-wing parties were prepared to co-operate with the Social Democrats, who had sole responsibility for government in 1926–27. The passing of new legislation functioned satisfactorily while the country was enjoying economic growth, but when the world economy entered a long period of recession after the stock exchange crash on Wall Street it had severe repercussions for Finnish business and politics.

The crisis was accentuated by the bitter ideological feud of the late Twenties in most eastern and central European states between Communists loyal to Moscow and nationalist anti-Communists. In the Baltic countries and Poland the fear of Communism led to the rejection of representative democracy in favour of various kinds of authoritarian right-wing regimes, while the process went even further in Italy and Germany, which turned into Fascist regimes. Finland was similarly affected by this fear of Communism, which was hardly surprising against the background of the traumatic experiences of the revolutionary war in 1918 and the close contacts of the extreme Left with Moscow.

The authorities had already stepped up their fight against the underground activities of the Communists. In 1929 tensions were heightened by several Communist-led strikes and demonstrations. They precipitated a country-wide anti-Communist reaction which took organised form in the autumn of the same year in the Lapua (Lappo) Movement, named after a small municipality in southern Ostrobothnia. Its symbolic leader was the Ostrobothnian farmer Vihtori Kosola, and it found its adherents mainly among farmers, the White Civil Guards and representatives of the export industry.

Initially it garnered sympathy in broader non-socialist circles too, where there was genuine concern that Communist agitation might develop into yet another revolution. The legal restrictions were regarded as altogether too lame, and in the spring of 1930 the Lapua men began to press their demands for a complete ban on all Communist activities through mass meetings and brutal expulsion of known Communists and Social Democrats to the eastern border. At first the police adopted a rather passive attitude to this terror, since it tended to be instigated by the local White Civil Guards and rich farmers. In July 1930 a Lapua march was organised, bringing 12,000 men to the capital. This forced a change of government which that same autumn passed a law prohibiting all public Communist activities.

With that, the ever more undisciplined Lapua Movement had exhausted its wider popular support. After the ignominious failure of an attempted coup in the spring of 1932 which brought legal retribution, the Movement was transformed into a radical right-wing party. But it never managed to pick up more than 7 per cent at most, of the votes in the three remaining parliamentary elections in the Thirties, and so the country's parliamentary system slowly regained its credibility. The experiences of the Lapua years noticeably increased all parties' willingness to compromise and paved the way for cross-party majority governments. Developments took the same course as those in Sweden and Denmark, where the Social Democrats and the Agrarian parties had managed to form broad-based coalitions in 1933. In the spring of 1937 Finland got its first Centre-Left coalition (known as the "Red-Earth government"), which set out to create a democratically regulated welfare state.

The main reason Finland's political system survived the crisis of democracy, in contrast to, for example, Poland or the Baltic states, was undoubtedly its well-functioning civic activities. Even though all Communist gatherings were prohibited, working-class culture continued under the Social Democratic umbrella, which ensured that most citizens could identify themselves with the nation and a state governed by laws. The civic movements were still strongly influenced by the Scandinavian countries and were thus a factor in Finland's own more Scandinavian mode of socio-political evolution.

This also gave legitimacy to the change of direction in the country's security policy in the mid-Thirties. With Hitler's assumption of power in Germany, the League of Nations gradually lost any credibility as a world peacekeeping organisation, and as the Soviet Union was then showing signs of military recovery, there was an obvious risk for all border countries of being caught between two dictatorships sooner or later. Finland therefore sought an alliance with the Scandinavian countries, whose neutrality policies had worked so superbly in the First World War.

Negotiations had been opened with Sweden for a joint remilitarisation of Åland, with a view to a Finno-Swedish defence pact that would deter the Soviet Union, but when in the spring of 1939 the latter indicated its disapproval of the fortification of the Åland Islands, the plans did not materialise. The result was that Finland, exactly like the other border countries, was left entirely without military support in the autumn of 1939 when Hitler and Stalin in collusion began their simplification of the political map of eastern and northern Europe.

Growth and Technology

The Lapua Movement originated in part from adverse economic conditions, but generally speaking Finland's growth in GDP in the Twenties and Thirties was much swifter and more regular than that of most European countries. At the outbreak of the First World War Finland's GDP per capita was still somewhat below the European average. Between the world wars its economy grew by nearly 5 per cent a year, so that its GDP per capita in 1938 had reached the same level as that of long-prosperous countries such as France or the Netherlands. In practice this meant a doubling of production value. The achievement was all the more remarkable given the fact that Finland, in common with other new border states in eastern Europe, had carried out land reforms in the early 1920s which slowed down both industrialisation and urbanisation.

One important reason for Finland's upturn was that its agriculture and forestry quickly adapted to a capitalist market. The Crofter Act of 1918 made it advantageous to redeem leasehold land, and four years on a Land Acquisition Act (*Lex Kallio*) was passed giving the same opportunities to the rural landless. In the mid-Twenties the prohibition on company purchase of private woodland was tightened up (*Lex Pulkkinen*). Farmers became significant forest owners and began to receive a respectable share of the rising export income from forestry. The explicit aim of the reforms was to reduce rural social inequalities, and within ten years over 100,000 more agricultural units came into existence. There were further widespread clearances, which together with innovative methods of cultivation and improved communications led to a marked increase in the yields even of small farmers.

The impetus behind the transformation of food production was nevertheless the forestry industry. The profits from these

7.2: Jolly dance on the steamboat Suomi. The standard of living improved in Finland in the twentieth century more swiftly than in the other parts of eastern Europe.

exports were channelled to the farmers via the timber trade and provided them with the resources to invest in fodder, artificial fertilisers and agricultural machinery. In the other border countries of eastern Europe the regeneration of agriculture was prevented by the lack of a competitive export industry that could give the farmers a secure supplementary income. The forests continued to be Finland's green gold, as is evident from the fact that forestry accounted for over 80 per cent of the country's export income through the whole interwar period.

185

Russian markets had been lost in the Bolshevik takeover, but conversely demand for timber and paper was multiplying in central and western Europe, and so Finland's export trade became as exclusively Western-orientated as its foreign policy. The paper industry's relative share of exports grew fastest. Active investment in bigger and more modern factories quadrupled paper production in twenty years, making the business responsible for more than 40 per cent of the country's total export income by 1938. The creation of national cartels to co-ordinate exports and capture new markets overseas contributed to this positive development. By the outbreak of the Second World War Finland was one of the world's leading paper exporters.

When the country first gained independence, two-thirds of the population earned their living from agriculture and forestry. The proportion shrank during the following two decades to just over 50 per cent, but was still large enough for the self-employed farmer to embody independent Finland. Land reforms turned the agricultural proletariat into market-conscious smallholders with a heightened sense of community. In the same period industrialisation augmented the proportion of the working class in the population to nearly 20 per cent. Another expanding category was service sector employment, which rose from 10 per cent to 16 per cent of the populace.

The fact that soaring prosperity was spreading more equitably than before was not simply a result of the land reforms. Industrial workers' real incomes were climbing fairly steadily, and in 1920 parliament brought in a progressive income tax which may have had a ceiling of 20 per cent, but indisputably gnawed away at higher incomes. The real incomes of the economic elite followed the ascending fortunes of industry, but things were worse for public employees, whose salaries did not rise as they had in Russian times. Salaries were laid down by parliament, which was not especially minded to squander tax-payers' money on these "gentlemen" who could look after themselves. This hit the upper ranks of the civil service particularly hard, where real salaries had tumbled in the First World War and in 1939 were still a third less than in 1914.

If smallholders achieved changes in rural areas, the burgeoning middle classes had similar success in the towns. The Republic was quick to build up its defence, administration and service sectors, with a trebling of state and local council employees between 1910 and 1940 (from 21,400 to 56,200). The educational system, similarly expanding, was fulfilling its function well. The number of grammar schools rose steadily and in 1940 Helsinki University, where the majority of those obtaining academic qualifications studied, had twice the number of students as in 1917 (up from 3,400 to 6,200), which made the proportion of the population in higher education one of the biggest in Europe. Students still came primarily from middle- and upper-class homes, but even so the expansion clearly stimulated social mobility.

These social shifts have to be seen against the background of Finland's surge in population from 3.1 to 3.7 million between the wars. Despite a fall in the relative numbers of those in agriculture and forestry, absolute numbers carried on climbing until the Second World War. Numerical growth had continued at this rate since 1870 (300,000 per decade), which meant actual growth was decelerating. With more urbanisation and improved welfare, the birth rate was gradually declining. Mortality was also falling as a result of medical advances and better nutrition. These factors together meant that the age structure of the population was changing from a pyramid to a square—children were fewer and adults were living longer.

One of the much-discussed but failed social reforms of the 1920s was the so-called Prohibition Act, a total ban on the sale and consumption of alcoholic drinks. The demands for such a law had mounted in parallel with better standards of living which facilitated access to alcohol but at the same time reduced public tolerance of unbridled drunkenness. The law came into force in the summer of 1919 but soon proved ineffectual and was repealed in 1932, after a referendum in which some 71 per cent voted against the continuance of prohibition. In practice the police had had little success in preventing restaurants from serving alcohol. The Act also resulted in large-scale smuggling of spirits from Estonia, which seriously undermined people's respect for the law.

Urbanisation and the increase in mobility went hand in hand with the expansion of transport systems and various technological advances. Domestic long-distance transport continued to be principally by rail, which had doubled its freight between the wars. For local traffic the main innovation was the motor car, use of which grew rapidly and in turn required the extension and improvement of the road network. From 1922 to 1938 the number of cars shot up from barely 2,000 to over 47,000, which created problems in the towns, where motor vehicles were concentrated. But since the private car remained a luxury until the 1960s, it was bus transport which had the most influence on geographical mobility. Comparatively few people in rural areas had access to the railway or public lake transport. Steamships still accounted for a large proportion of traffic abroad, even though the Aero Company introduced regular flights by seaplane from Helsinki to Stockholm and Tallinn. In the latter half of the Thirties several regional airports were built and a domestic air service established.

All those motor vehicles required fuel, and the import of refined oil rose steadily, no longer coming from the Caucasian oilfields after the Russian Revolution, but from the Western oil giants Standard Oil (Esso), Gulf and Shell. Distribution was so efficient that the Government did not contemplate building a refinery in Finland until the late Thirties. Plans were interrupted by the war, but put into effect in 1948. That was when the state oil company Neste was formed, soon becoming one of the country's largest industrial firms. The industry sector ensured its spiralling energy needs were met as early as the 1920s by constructing its own power stations on all the major rivers of southern Finland. It sold electricity to some private households, but most domestic supplies were provided by a nationwide state electricity network that came into use in 1929 when the hydroelectric power station in Imatra was inaugurated. By the end of the Thirties practically the whole of southern and western Finland was receiving electricity from this grid.

Social and geographical mobility underlined the significance of good telecommunications. Private initiatives accounted for the rapid proliferation of telephone companies from their beginnings in the 1880s—by the mid-1920s there were about 600 companies or co-operatives involved. The business required only a state licence, but in the mid-Thirties the state took over all long-distance calls, mainly for security reasons. This division continued into the early 1990s, when the telecommunications sector was swiftly deregulated and opened up to competition.

The most important mass media invention of the interwar years was the radio. As in the majority of European countries, broadcasts were soon put under state control when their significance for opinion-building and news was realised. It was not only a matter of safeguarding the dissemination of unbiased information, but also of strengthening national unity and if necessary steering it in the right direction. That was very much the case with the Finnish Broadcasting Company (Yleisradio), which was formed in 1926 from a number of cultural organisations to further popular education and the communication of useful knowledge. Another feature shared by all these state-controlled radio companies was that their remit included linguistic correctness and refinement of popular taste. This was not always appreciated by ordinary people, who would rather have listened to popular music and comedy programmes than lengthy symphonies and lectures.

In the spring of 1928 a state radio transmitter was erected with a 150-metre mast on Salpausselkä Ridge near Lahti. It immediately enhanced reception over the whole of southern Finland and boosted the sales of radios. The real increase in sales, however, occurred in the later 1930s, when domestic production got under way and direct broadcasts from abroad were possible. Many listeners found the broadcast from the Olympic Games in Berlin in 1936 one of their most memorable, the high point being the report of Finland's triple victory in the 10,000 metres.

National, Modern, Popular

Finland's sovereignty, achieved by dramatic means, was for obvious reasons a constant theme in the cultural life of the young Republic, and since the war in 1918 had given victory to the non-socialist side, the cultural sphere was in thrall to a vision of a White and predominantly agrarian Finland, whose military preparedness and fervent belief in the future would guarantee national survival. This vision was in many ways rather exclusive, since it allowed minimal scope for the Socialist sympathies of the working class, and it was often extremely "true Finnish", which scared off the Swedish-speakers. Yet there were also many elements of the national image that were of an older and more generally accessible character, such as the idealisation of the people and the lake landscape, with frequent literary references to Runeberg, Lönnrot and Topelius.

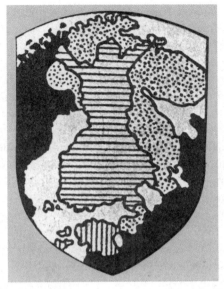

7.3: Finnish ultra-nationalists dreamed in the interwar period of a political integration of Finno-Ugric-speaking peoples.

The symphonies of Jean Sibelius and the paintings of Akseli Gallen-Kallela had a broader idealistic range, but it was nevertheless inevitable that as exalted artists they would be seen as figureheads for White Finland, in the case of Gallen-Kallela not least because he designed many of the young Republic's official medals and emblems. Sibelius' attitude to the nationalistic fervour was more ambivalent from the start. His composition of *The March of the Finnish Jaeger Battalion* (1917), an overwhelming favourite with the White Civil Guards, assured him a place of honour everywhere. Before his creativity completely ebbed away towards the end of the Twenties he went on to compose four of his most significant works, all with a universal perspective.

191

Many of Wäinö Aaltonen's sculptures achieved the same universality, featuring national figures in classical form. The best-known example must be that of Paavo Nurmi, the Olympic runner, which was unveiled in 1925 and soon became one of the most durable symbols of Finland. Nurmi undeniably had an athletic physique and an economical running style, but Aaltonen's work transformed him into a classical demi-god radiating everything the new Republic wanted to be associated with—youth, beauty and stoical willpower. The respect in which sculpture was held in Europe between the wars stemmed from a craving for tangible monuments to the collective will. In Germany and Italy these monuments would be given a high profile in Fascist propaganda. In northern Europe Aaltonen and his Scandinavian colleagues Carl Milles and Gustav Vigeland portrayed a vaguer image of national self-sacrifice which was open to more varied interpretation.

But nationalism could all too easily become high-flown and bombastic. A cosmopolitan Modernism began to exert its influence on the younger generation of writers and artists in the early 1920s. To a large extent the precursors were painters, whose Cubist and Surrealist creations represented a resounding break with national tradition. In the literary field the trend found its initial momentum from the Finland-Swedish Modernists Gunnar Björling, Hagar Olsson and Elmer Diktonius. Their Dadaistic experiments and fragmentary impressions of urban life elicited a swift response in literary circles in Sweden.

Hard on their heels followed the Finnish-speaking writers' group Tulenkantajat (Torchbearers), whose journal of the same name was filled with both adulation of technology and an urban Romanticism, along with Modernist texts of Socialist or "true Finnish" conviction. The group was united by its observant social commitment, but since it was ideologically diver-

7.4: Sunny days for young Finns in the lake district sometime in the 1930s.

gent, a split was ultimately inevitable. The writer who aroused the most interest was Olavi Paavolainen, with his topical articles contrasting the chic fashions and radical ideas of the Continent with Finland's own bucolic Romanticism.

Paavolainen's depictions of Hitler's Germany (1936) and Stalin's Soviet Union (1939) expressed an honest ambivalence. On the one hand these were totalitarian regimes with a brutal machinery of suppression; on the other, they were technologically innovative social experiments which led him to draw parallels with the United States. This attitude was not at all unusual among intellectuals in the Europe of the 1930s. Alvar Aalto (1898–1976), who was to become an international name after the Second World War with his nature-inspired Modernism, was similarly enthused by both Soviet and Swedish architecture. In Soviet achievements he was impressed by form and vision, in the Swedish by the feeling for style and the "home of the people" cradle-to-grave welfare concept, which demonstrated that human-scale and technically functional architecture could thrive in a planned national economy.

Despite the language conflict, Finland maintained close cultural ties with Scandinavia, and above all Sweden, in the interwar years. Communication was easy because up to a tenth of the population of Finland (360,000 in 1940) still had Swedish as their mother tongue. The upper strata of society were virtually bilingual, partly because Swedish was a compulsory subject in grammar schools, partly because it was a living cultural heritage in many families and sectors of society. A number of pan-Scandinavian associations for civic and professional endeavours had been set up at the end of the nineteenth century when the foundations of modern society were being laid. The co-operation was mainly of a practical character and involved the Finns even though the country was not yet independent. When national sovereignty had been achieved, interaction was further promoted in many spheres, especially between the countries' workers and sports movements, which for various reasons saw a Scandinavian context as the most natural one. Social Democratic contacts spread the Swedish "home of the people" ideology within Finland, while co-operation in sport gave rise to regular national competitions and assiduous press coverage.

Popular culture was completely open to Swedish influence. Swedish magazines, hit records and feature films were hugely successful and became models for similar products in Finland. Illustrated weekly magazines really took off in both countries in the Twenties, when printing technology brought high-contrast photography in mass-market print runs. The best-selling title in Finland was *Suomen Kuvalehti* (The Illustrated Finland Magazine), which started in 1917 and soon found its market with a balance of political news and informative entertainment. Of the women's magazines, the most popular were the rather domestic *Kotiliesi* (Hearth and Home) (1922–) and the more urbane *Eeva* (1934–), appealing successfully to their distinct readerships. The same applied to the White Civil Guards magazine *Hakkapeliitta* (see p. 52 above), whose multi-coloured martial covers signalled a confident patriotism and a readiness to take up arms in defence of the country.

Even though Swedish popular culture was highly regarded, musical hits and film were both dominated from the early

7.5: Ansa Ikonen and Tauno Palo, the iconic Finnish love couple in drama films of the 1930s and 1940s.

Twenties onwards by German and American titles. German was the first foreign language throughout Scandinavia until the Second World War, which gave German products an unrivalled advantage in the entertainment industry and guaranteed German popular music a loyal audience in Finland. Finnish recordings were usually made in Berlin's state-of-the-art music studios, and a significant proportion of the melodies were of central European origin, so they could almost be said to be a semi-German product. The majority of the "moving pictures" were imports, and since they were silent films until the late 1920s, the Hollywood film industry soon achieved a leading position in the Finnish market which would endure, even through the war years.

The first feature-length sound film from Finland, Erkki Karu's *Tukkipojan morsian* (The Logger's Bride) had its premiere in 1931. Within a decade Finland had its own film industry and its own film stars, with the ubiquitous loving couple Ansa Ikonen and Tauno Palo leading the field. During the war years popular culture was an important tool for boosting morale both in the armed forces and on the home front. People needed comfort and entertainment more than ever, which not only increased sales of radios, record players and film projectors, but also brought about the definitive breakthrough of a national, and above all classless, popular culture. And not only that—the Second World War meant that listening to the radio was akin to a study of global geography. When the war was over people throughout the world knew the location of Suomussalmi, El Alamein and Hiroshima.

Lessons of the Winter War

In many regards the Second World War followed on as a chain reaction from the First, a fact which has led some historians to describe the years 1914–45 as a single war with an unusually long truce. As on so many previous occasions, Finland was drawn into war against its will. Independence had been attained a mere twenty years before because Russia and Germany had happened to be weak concurrently. In the late summer of 1939 the situation was the exact opposite. Both great powers had recovered and were hungrily waiting to reconquer, and ideally even extend, their pre-1914 domains. When Hitler's Germany began to expand in the mid-Thirties by forced annexations, Great Britain and France tried to negotiate an anti-German alliance with the Soviet Union, which Hitler, in his early manifesto *Mein Kampf* (1923), wanted to turn into a source of raw materials for Germany. The negotiations petered out when the Western powers refused to agree to the Soviet Union taking control of the Baltic states "as a preventive measure".

Moscow instead entered a non-aggression pact with Berlin on 23 August 1939, to which the foreign ministers Molotov and von Ribbentrop added a secret supplementary protocol marking out a mutually acceptable demarcation line through eastern Europe. Finland, the Baltic states and eastern Poland would come within the Soviet sphere of interest, while Germany was to annex the greater part of Poland. The Molotov-Ribbentrop Pact was a trigger for the Second World War, since the Western powers this time, against all expectations, declared war on Berlin when German troops marched into Poland a week later. But it was a positional war on the western front until April 1940. The centre of operations during that first winter was in the east, or more precisely on the Finno-Russian border.

Why then did the Soviet Union attack neutral Finland? The main reason was that Stalin feared Hitler would invade Leningrad and the northern Soviet Union across Finnish territory. It made no difference that in the Moscow talks in the autumn of 1939 the Finnish government had declared itself ready to counter any German attacks. Stalin believed the Germans could make a landing in Finland irrespective of whatever assurances the country's government might give. There was also a deep mistrust between the two parties which could not be overcome in such a brief period. The Soviet Union had actively supported subversive Communist agitation in Finland, while many Finnish politicians, academics and officers were German-orientated and kept up close contacts with professional colleagues in Germany.

Negotiations were broken off in early November when the Finns refused to agree to Soviet demands for frontier adjustments, considered essential as additional security for Leningrad. Similar demands had been put forward unofficially since 1938, but they had been ignored by the Finnish government. Foreign Minister Eljas Erkko had been able to convince his colleagues right up to the outbreak of war that Moscow was applying scare tactics. Finland in this respect acted quite differently from the Baltic countries, which by the end of September 1939 had already acceded to the Soviet Union's demand for military bases.

One cause of the Finnish obstinacy was its tendency to cling to its faith in Sweden and the Western powers coming to its aid in times of danger. The fact that Sweden had confidentially made it clear that no military help could be expected apparently made no impact. Wishful thinking was deep-rooted and was fed by popular Russophobic opinion, which would have regarded even the tiniest territorial concessions as high treason. There also seemed to be every indication that armed conflict was inevitable. Moscow's long-term objective was to regain control of Finland. When diplomacy failed to achieve this, Stalin gave orders to the Red Army to invade. Four days before the attack a "Finnish" border provocation against the village of Mainila on the Soviet side of the Karelian Isthmus was staged.

It was a pretext to renounce the two countries' non-aggression treaty of 1932 and declare war.

On the morning of 30 November 1939 the Soviet air force began bombing raids on built-up areas in southern Finland. The Red Army simultaneously streamed in over the border on the Karelian Isthmus and along the isolated forest roads in the east. The attack came as a shock to the populace, who despite the increase in tension and the mobilisation of the army had been lulled into the belief that the conflict could be resolved by diplomacy. But after the first panic-stricken reaction, a sense of national unity emerged with a staunch resolve that there was only one thing to do—fight to the bitter end. So Stalin's decision to install a Finnish puppet government, and Soviet propaganda claiming that the attack was in defence of the Finnish working classes, were wasted efforts.

The Finns' determination to defend themselves was revitalised by the appointment of the 72-year-old Field Marshal Gustaf Mannerheim as commander-in-chief of the army. He had made a comeback as a soldier in 1931 when he was designated chair of an advisory defence council, and from that position he had been an active participant in the decision that Finland should pursue a Scandinavian neutrality policy from the mid-Thirties. The aim had been to avoid the very war that the country was now being drawn into. One aspect of the same campaign had been Mannerheim's class reconciliation programme, which made him an accepted figurehead even among Social Democrats. Despite his critical attitude to Finland's inflexibility in the autumn of 1939 and his advocacy of tactical concessions, it was not hard to make him change his mind when it mattered.

Two days after the outbreak of war, Risto Ryti, head of the Bank of Finland and a respected Liberal, was appointed prime minister of a coalition government that frantically tried to resume talks with the Soviet Union, while at the same time appealing to the League of Nations to intervene. Sweden gave considerable practical support and sent over a detachment of volunteers, but no substantial reinforcements beyond that. The greatest help in Finland's hour of need was the season and the unusually cold winter, which rendered the ill-synchronised Red Army march towards the Gulf of Bothnia even more fraught with difficulty. In the second week of the war Finnish troops managed to halt the Soviet advance on the Karelian Isthmus. In the course of the next four to five weeks some of the Russian divisions were surrounded and held in check in the immense forest regions of the east and north, and Stalin began to realise he had a problem. Of these battles, the most renowned was the Finns' defensive victory in Suomussalmi, where two Soviet divisions were fragmented and wiped out.

The Red Army was numerically superior from the start (450,000 men to the Finns' 300,000) and enlarged by continual reinforcements throughout the war. In *matériel* and firepower its superiority was utterly overwhelming, but the Arctic winter and the forests favoured the defenders, whose ski-borne troops could swiftly and effectively strike the invaders from flank and rear. The longer the war went on, the higher was the risk that the Western powers would honour their pledges to send troops to Finland's relief. Stalin therefore abandoned his original intention of occupying the country. In February 1940 the Red Army mounted an even heavier offensive on the Karelian Isthmus to push the Finnish government into a hasty peace with significant concessions, thus upholding Soviet prestige.

Finnish positions on the isthmus now began to collapse in earnest. The numbers of casualties increased drastically, reserves were declining, and at the beginning of March the Red Army reached the eastern suburbs of Vyborg. In this situation the Finnish government agreed to peace talks with

Moscow, despite the Soviet minimum demands being the transfer of the whole of Karelia and the lease of the Hanko Peninsula as a military base. Negotiations were still in progress with
the Western powers, who were planning to camouflage an
occupation of the Swedish iron fields in Norrland as military
assistance for Finland. Germany imported much of its iron ore
from Sweden, so Berlin was encouraging the Finnish government to acquiesce to Soviet terms. Germany was still the Soviet
Union's ally, but behind the scenes it let Finland know that the
lost territories would be returned with interest when Germany
had conquered and crushed the Soviet Union.

On 13 March 1940 the Finnish government signed a peace
treaty in Moscow which met the Soviet demands in all essentials. Hanko was to be leased as a Soviet naval base for thirty
years. It was no coincidence that the new frontier more or less
followed the line that had been drawn in the Peace of Nystad
in 1721. Stalin had already pointed out in 1939 that his generals considered that the security of Leningrad required Peter
the Great's frontier: it would act as an acceptable intermediate
zone. Neither party regarded the peace agreement as anything
other than a temporary solution. In his speech to parliament
immediately after the conclusion of peace, Prime Minister
Ryti emphasised that the task of reconstruction would be carried out "with sword in one hand and trowel in the other".
Mannerheim was of the same opinion, and it was his words
that proved weightiest when the decision was taken to bow to
Soviet pressure.

The barely three-month-long conflict had cost nearly 24,000
Finnish lives. The number of wounded was over 43,000. The
majority of these casualties (66,000) were front-line soldiers,
which indicated that the army had been very successful in pro-
tecting the civilian population. Enemy losses were many times
that figure. Some calculations give 131,000 Soviet soldiers dead

and 325,000 wounded in this same war. To these grim totals must be added the evacuation of nearly 400,000 civilians from Karelia and the Hanko Peninsula. Their situation was eased in the summer of 1940 by a law permitting speedy colonisation and giving the displaced farmers rights to new land.

Ryti and Mannerheim were both Anglophiles, but the Winter War had shown that neither the Western powers nor Sweden would come to the rescue militarily if it were just a question of Finnish independence. This lesson had long-term consequences for the country's foreign policy through the remainder of the World War and beyond. Laws and morality were no guarantee for the national sovereignty of a small state. Finland's geopolitical situation so near Leningrad meant that the country could not retain its independence without an alliance with one of the Baltic region's great powers. And as the German offensives broke out all over Europe in the spring and summer of 1940, the Finnish leadership began to discuss whether such support might come in some form from Germany.

There were in reality no rational alternatives. The German occupation of Denmark and Norway had made British military assistance impossible. A Finno-Swedish defence alliance had been accepted by neither Moscow nor Berlin. Nor did Finland wish to suffer the same fate as the Baltic states, which were forcibly annexed by the Soviet Union in 1940 and whose people were immediately subjected to large-scale deportations to Siberia. Moscow also increased its demands on Finland. So when the German leadership sought passage for their troops in northern Norway through Finland in August 1940, approval was promptly granted, especially as Germany in return undertook to sell Finland weapons.

During the autumn Finno-German relations grew closer, and in December 1940 they culminated in confidential soundings about possible Finnish participation in Operation Barbarossa,

Hitler's crusade against the Soviet Union. He knew that Finland felt threatened by Russia and counted on the political leadership being prepared to allow the country a military role on the northern flank. And Germany wanted to ensure the continuation of deliveries from the Finnish nickel mines up in Petsamo.

The Finnish leadership accepted the offer. The decision was influenced not only by the lessons of the Winter War, but also by information received that in November 1940 Hitler had rejected the request from the Soviet foreign minister, Molotov, that the Red Army be allowed to complete its invasion of Finland. In January 1941 Germany's chances of emerging as victor from a war against the Soviet Union looked promising, and there is also some indication that Mannerheim and Ryti, who was elected president in December 1940, took into account the possibility that things might end up as in the First World War. Germany would conquer the Soviet Union, but then the Western powers would in turn crush Germany, especially since the fighting potential of the United States was still untapped. The hope was that in any case Finland would regain its surrendered territories and be rid of its Bolshevik eastern neighbour forever. When optimism was at its height Finland's leaders dreamed of territorial gains in eastern Karelia and on the Kola Peninsula.

Ambivalent Allies

In January 1941 a plan was drawn up in complete secrecy for Finno-German co-operation in the great push to the east. The Germans would have responsibility for the offensive from the northern half of Finland. The Finnish military leadership agreed to attack both across the Karelian Isthmus and north of Lake Ladoga towards the River Svir. There the Finns would meet up with their German brothers-in-arms invading from the south, who would also take Leningrad. The entire operation was expected to be over by the autumn of 1941 at the latest. Co-ordination of the two countries' military forces took place immediately, with a general mobilisation of the Finnish field army twelve days prior to the German declaration of war on 22 June 1941. This time there was nothing wrong with the preparedness of the Finnish army. Organisation was in good shape, firepower had been doubled by huge purchases of weapons, and over half a million men were under arms. Considering the population of Finland (3.7 million), this was in fact the largest mobilisation among the belligerent countries of Europe—which reveals something crucial about the attitude of the Finns when they joined Operation Barbarossa.

All through the war, however, the Finnish government consistently refused to enter into any political concord with Germany. Firstly, it was impossible for domestic political reasons. Public opinion was clearly appreciative of the thaw in Finno-German relations in the autumn of 1940, because it was seen to reduce the risk of a Soviet invasion. But Finland's democratic institutions were already so deep-rooted that both the ordinary people and the elite felt Germany's political system and culture to be totally alien. Support for Finland's only Fascist party, for instance, was completely marginal in the parliamentary elections of 1939. Secondly, there were many aspects of foreign policy that argued against an overt political alliance with Germany. Irrespective of the progress of the war, such an alliance would have severely aggravated Finland's long-term relations with the Scandinavian countries and the Western powers, including the United States.

There was thus a constant ambivalence in the Finnish government's attitude to this war coalition with Germany, but military co-operation proceeded very effectively and systematically on that basis. By early June 1941 six German divisions (ca 90,000 soldiers) had taken up position in northern Finland.

The Luftwaffe arrived on Finnish airfields and the day before war broke out German U-boats, in consultation with the Finnish navy, laid mines round Soviet naval bases in Estonia. The war began exactly according to plan, on 22 June. The Finnish army had not yet opened its attack before the Soviet air force had started its bombing raids on southern Finland and before the government could confirm that Finland was at war again. The objective had been to present Finland's engagement in the war of aggression as a defensive measure, but when President Ryti gave his first radio broadcast after hostilities had already commenced, he spoke both of "our own defensive war" and of fighting with Greater Germany's successful forces "at our side".

When the German offensive was approaching Leningrad a few weeks later, the Finnish offensive began on several fronts. The war was seen in Finland from the outset as a follow-up to the Winter War and so was called the Continuation War. The concurrent German offensives in the Baltic states and Lapland put the Red Army this time in an extremely inferior situation. After five months of victorious fighting the Finnish army was able to dig into positions that lay several hundred kilometres to the east of the 1939 border and would hold until the early summer of 1944. Admittedly the successes had been bought at a high price: over 25,000 men had fallen, and in the winter of 1941–42 there were acute food shortages, since preparations had not been made for a protracted campaign.

Almost 60,000 Soviets were taken as prisoners of war by the Finnish Army in the first year of the Continuation War (1941–44). They were imprisoned in poorly maintained camps and almost one third of them died during the winter of 1941–42 due to undernourishment, disease, harsh treatment and a burdensome workload. After this humanitarian catastrophe had been revealed in the Western media, the treatment of prisoners improved: they were sent to the countryside as a workforce and their food rations were increased. Simultaneously, the food shortage was decisively decreased by a considerable grain import from the German-occupied Europe. The grain import continued up until the summer of 1944, and without it the Finnish military and home front would have collapsed swiftly. In fact, Finnish participation on the eastern front was so greatly valued that Finland was Germany's only ally that was allowed to buy its goods and weaponry from them on credit.

In the late autumn of 1941, the Finnish army had fulfilled what had been promised to the Germans, while the latter on the other hand had not managed to capture Leningrad, despite repeated efforts. The Germans endeavoured several times to persuade the Finns to help take the city, but Mannerheim constantly rejected the proposal, on the grounds of lack of both firepower and manpower. The real reason was that the Finnish military and political leadership had to try to avoid annoying the Soviet Union's Western allies, who were demanding via diplomatic channels that Finland break off its offensive and disengage from the war. The balancing act failed inasmuch as Britain declared war on Finland at the beginning of December 1941, since for strategic reasons the Finns could not reveal that the offensive had indeed ceased.

A day after the British declaration of war, the Japanese attacked Pearl Harbour (7 December 1941). At a stroke, that attack altered the whole course of the World War, as the Germans, in the wake of the Japanese, immediately declared war on the United States. America's entry into the war meant a decisive shift in the strengths of the various fronts. Japan turned its weapons on the Americans and south-east Asia, giving the Soviet Union the opportunity to move twenty divisions from Asia to the European front and launch a major counter-attack, which in January 1942 stepped up the pressure on the Finnish section of the front.

Finland escaped an American declaration of war because it deliberately refrained from cutting the Murmansk railway, by which a significant proportion of the Western allies' war supplies was transported to the Soviet Union. In the background too lay the goodwill that Finland had acquired in the middle of the Winter War by repaying the final instalment of a loan it had received from the United States in 1919. So Washington showed a certain amount of sympathy for the Finnish government's assertion that the country was waging a separate defensive war against the Soviet Union. There was no denying the military liaison with Germany, but Finland did all it could to convince its Scandinavian neighbours and the Western powers that the alliance had been entered under duress.

7.6: Adolf Hitler visited Finland in June 1942 to congratulate Field Marshal Mannerheim on his seventy-fifth birthday. Mannerheim on the left, president Risto Ryti on the right.

This claim was especially difficult to defend in early June 1942, when Hitler surprised the world by flying to Finland to personally congratulate Field Marshal Mannerheim on his seventy-fifth birthday. Naturally, German war propagandists capitalised on his visit by emphasising that together the two brothers-in-arms had defended Western civilization against the barbarism of the Bolsheviks, and showing news films of their meeting in cinemas all around German-occupied Europe. But contrary to what the Finns had feared, Hitler did not demand that they play a greater role in the war. Instead, he praised the Finns' courageous fight against their eternal enemy in an empathic tone. During Mannerheim's birthday lunch, part of his conversation with Hitler was secretly taped, and the recording later inspired the actor Bruno Ganz in his classic role as Hitler in the film *Der Untergang* (2004).

The attitude of front-line troops and the home front to the military coalition with Germany was more pragmatic. There was scepticism towards the official propaganda, which stressed the distinct and separate nature of the war, since it was so obvious that both the army and the civil population were very dependent on German material aid and military flank support. The long positional war in itself attracted a considerable amount of public attention, and every family would sooner or later be affected in one way or another by the horrors of conflict. It also involved a rapid mobilisation of women, over 160,000 of whom worked as "Lottas", the name given to members of the women's services (from Lotta Svärd Organisation, a female Civil Guards, named after one of Runeberg's fictional characters) in their auxiliary role, and since the men were at the front, other jobs were also performed by women. The fallen had to be transported home to be buried in their local churchyards, the wounded and invalids required nursing care and rest, and tens of thousands of children were sent over to Sweden when the lack of food and the threat of war were at their most extreme. In all, around 80,000 children were accommodated in foster homes in Sweden during the years 1939–46.

When Germany's fortunes of war had taken a definite turn for the worse in the winter of 1942–43, Finland's political leadership began to prepare for a dismantling of the coalition and for peace negotiations with the Soviet Union. But this was more easily said than done. Germany's grip on Finland and the entire Baltic region remained strong through to January 1944, when the Red Army managed to break the siege of Leningrad. Despite wartime censorship, a more Western-orientated public opinion started to make itself heard in Finland, and in the summer of 1943 hopes were being voiced that the government would intensify its efforts to get Finland out of the war between the great powers. Germany's reaction was one of anger towards such expressions of opinion, and so peace soundings were not initiated until the spring of 1944, when the situation was becoming increasingly threatening, even for Finland.

The heads of state on the Allied side had met in Tehran in December 1943 to work out the best way of bringing the World War to a close, and on the initiative of the United States the question of Finland's future was also raised. The parties agreed the country could continue as a sovereign nation if it committed to the reinstatement of the 1940 borders and an end to its ties with Germany. In addition it would have to forego either Petsamo or Hanko and pay considerable war reparations. Moscow had been making identical demands since the autumn of 1941, and to soften up the Finnish government the Russians carried out three bombing raids on Helsinki on 6, 16 and 26 February 1944.

The destruction caused by the raids was minimal, because the Soviet bombers' precision was poor and the city's air defences had been fitted out with brand new equipment from

7.7: The Finno-German Waffenbrüderschaft shifted into an open war between the former allies in autumn 1944. Scenery from the town of Rovaniemi destroyed by the retreating Wehrmacht.

Germany. But the desired effect was achieved. Exploratory peace talks began in Moscow in March 1944, but were soon broken off because the Finnish government could not see any way it could meet the Soviet demands for 600 million dollars in war reparations and a rapid expulsion of the Germans. Germany was judged still to be far too powerful. The Finnish political leadership therefore decided, jointly with Mannerheim, to await the Allies' landing in the west in the hope that that would reduce the pressure on Finland and open up possibilities for a more acceptable peace.

A few days after the landings in Normandy had commenced, all Finnish wishful thinking collapsed. Stalin had made up his mind to force Finland into a separate peace before the race for Berlin began. On 9 June a major offensive was launched on the Karelian Isthmus. It drove the Finnish troops in often chaotic retreat to new positions to the north and west of Vyborg, which was taken by the Red Army on 20 June 1944. This front line held, not only because Finnish resistance was toughening while the Red Army gathered itself for other offensives in the Baltic states and White Russia, but also because Hitler, having discontinued the supply of weapons to Finland in the spring of 1944, now gave in to Finnish pleas for assistance and immediately sent over fighter planes, troops and tanks, which substantially reinforced the Finnish defences.

The price for German aid was President Ryti's personal assurance that no one in the government he had appointed would enter peace negotiations with the Soviet Union. The undertaking was given under false pretences. When the front lines had stabilised in mid-July 1944, fresh and even more secret exploratory peace talks were set up with Moscow. When Ryti stood down from presidential office in favour of Mannerheim, the latter began by informing Hitler that he himself was not bound by Ryti's promise; after that Moscow's preliminary peace conditions were approved, and eventually a cease-fire came into operation on 4 September, preparatory to an armistice treaty two weeks later, on 19 September.

The treaty was not discernibly different from Moscow's original peace demands and in fact remained in force when the final peace agreement was signed between Finland and the Allies at the European Peace Conference in Paris in 1947. The result was a return to the 1940 frontiers and the loss of Petsamo, where the nickel mines and ice-free harbour had been of some significance for the Finnish economy. War reparations were halved to 300 million dollars, but in compensation the Porkkala Peninsula, only thirty kilometres west of Helsinki, had to be leased out as a Soviet military base. To top it all, the former coalition troops were to be disarmed or expelled from the country, and this led to a real war in Lapland in the winter of 1944–45.

The Winter War and the Continuation War, together with the Lapland War, were the young Republic's true test of maturity. Once again it was the country's proximity to Russia and its city on the Neva that sucked Finland into the conflict. A total of 94,000 Finns lost their lives (24,000 in the Winter War and 70,000 in 1941–45). In one central aspect this three-part war was different from the earlier ones. In contrast to all the other minor states involved in war in Europe, Finland was never occupied. Its political leadership was therefore able to retain the right to determine the country's future throughout the entire course of the war, despite the military coalition with Germany. The civilian population suffered severely during and after the war, but in comparison with many other war-torn lands, it escaped exceptionally lightly. This was ultimately due to the fact that the country's conscript army had succeeded in its task, in spite of losing the war. Finland was cut down and badly lacerated, but it remained independent.

8

WELFARE AND NEUTRALITY

Finland's post-war social development was defined above all by
two factors, in many respects interdependent: the establishment of the welfare state, and new policies towards the Eastern
Bloc. The construction of a modern and socially levelling welfare society required not only rapid economic growth but also
stable domestic politics and foreign policy. Such stability was
reached on the one hand by active government efforts to
reduce the mistrust between Finland and the Soviet Union,
and on the other by the eventual achievement of a domestic
consensus that facilitated both substantial investment in public
welfare and socio-political measures for income redistribution.
A key but controversial figure behind this political transformation was Urho Kekkonen, the country's president for twenty-
five years. The speed of change had an impact not only on
social structures, business life and public institutions; material
and intellectual culture was also radically altered. In a few
decades both everyday life and overall lifestyle for the Finns
was utterly metamorphosed.

In the Shadow of the Cold War

Under the terms of the Armistice Treaty of 1944 Finland was
placed under the aegis of the Allied Control Commission, to

ensure that the articles of the treaty were put into practice. The Commission was in reality directed from Moscow. Stalin's right-hand man, Brigadier-General Andrei Zhdanov, was voted in as chairman; he had been responsible for mass executions in Russia in the 1930s and had led the brutal Sovietisation of Estonia in 1940. The transition from a Finno-German coalition to a Soviet-dominated armistice was certainly abrupt. The former brothers-in-arms clashed in mid-September 1944 in the Gulf of Finland, and in the ensuing autumn months battles were engaged in Lapland with German troops who laid waste most of the buildings and infrastructure as they retreated to Norway. Another obligation that had to be complied with was the regular payment of war reparations, beginning in 1944 and continuing up to the autumn of 1952.

8.1: The war reparations to the Soviet Union were predominantly metal products.

There were big changes in Finland's political life too. Over 400 associations and organisations were dissolved on the grounds that they were Fascist and anti-Soviet. On the very same day that the paramilitary White Civil Guards was abolished (30 October 1944), the Finnish Communist Party was registered, which encouraged many people to suspect that a Sovietisation of the country was planned, especially as the conscript army was also shortly to be stood down in accordance with the Armistice Treaty. Mannerheim, now seventy-seven, remained as a figurehead in the capacity of president and active commander-in-chief, but executive power was taken over by J. K. Paasikivi, three years his junior, who was appointed prime minister in November 1944 with a broad-based coalition government and soon succeeded in creating a satisfactory working relationship with the Control Commission.

Nevertheless, the years 1945–48 were a turbulent period in domestic politics. In the spring of 1945 the extreme Left, spearheaded by the Communists, obtained nearly 25 per cent of the votes in the parliamentary elections. That gave them a place in government and a chance to set in train legal proceedings against the members of the wartime government whom the Communists regarded as primarily responsible for the Continuation War. But the chief reason such a war crimes trial was conducted in the winter of 1945–46 was that the Allied powers had agreed that the policy-makers in the vanquished countries should be held to account for the war. In Tokyo and Nuremberg these political courts handed down a great many death sentences. In Helsinki the same proceedings, necessitated by foreign policy requirements, resulted in considerably lighter sentences. Eight members of the wartime government were imprisoned, but their terms successively shortened; the former president, Risto Ryti, was the last to be freed, and that was as early as May 1949.

How was all this possible? Finland's avoidance of Sovietisation was mainly due to its not having been occupied during the war; but almost equally significant was the fact that the Finnish Communists, despite their well-established position in politics in 1945–48, did not manage to bring about regime change. The other parties, particularly the Social Democrats, successfully obstructed their efforts to take control of the police and the administration. Besides, the Soviet Union was very anxious that the country should be able to pay its war reparations, and so its delegates in the Control Commission were happy to work with the other parties in government as well. An occupation of Finland would have been much too risky and expensive. At that time the Kremlin was concentrating on transforming eastern Europe into a permanent buffer zone against the Western powers.

When the peace treaty had come fully into operation in September 1947 and the Allied Control Commission had withdrawn, Finland found itself in a completely novel situation. Europe was being divided into two distinctly opposed military camps, with a small number of neutral countries in the grey zone. Stalin did not regard neutrality as a viable alternative and urged for a treaty between Finland and the Soviet Union which would prevent Finland sliding into the Western camp and NATO. Having received sufficient guarantees that this would not lead to Finland being sucked into the Eastern Bloc, Paasikivi, elected president in 1946, agreed in April 1948 to a "Treaty of Friendship, Co-operation and Mutual Assistance" (the FCMA Treaty). The Finnish state undertook to fight off any attack aimed at Finland or at the Soviet Union by way of Finnish territory "on the part of Germany or any other state allied with it". But Finland's need of Soviet military support had to be confirmed by both sides, a clause which would prevent Moscow sending the Red Army into the country without prior consultation. The text of the agreement required Finland to strive "to remain outside any conflicts of interest of the great powers".

Yet the treaty was interpreted by many in the West as a disastrous act of appeasement. It was feared that it would tie Finland irrevocably to the Eastern Bloc. Its military clauses limited the country's ability to conduct as strict a policy of neutrality as Sweden or Switzerland, of course, but experience of the two world wars had clearly shown that relations with the East could not be stabilised in any other way than by convincing the Soviet Union that the country could never again function as a bridgehead to Leningrad. Paasikivi argued from a *realpolitik* perspective that Moscow's interest in Finland was first and foremost one of defensive security. If that could be satisfied, a constructive and stable neighbourliness was entirely feasible.

Paasikivi was proved correct, even though for historical reasons the semi-official slogans about the countries' mutual trust and bonds of friendship would always sound hollow. The treaty was renewed at regular intervals during the Cold War (1955, 1970, 1983), and it gave such stability to Finland's domestic and foreign policy that it could almost be described as a supplement to the constitution. It also provided scope for manoeuvre in domestic politics. The Communists could no longer maintain that they were the sole guarantors of good relations with the East. When their electoral coalition was heavily defeated in the parliamentary elections in the summer of 1948, a Social Democrat minority government was formed which quickly rooted out the Communist elements from the administration and built up official contacts with Scandinavia and western Europe.

The Communists went on the counter-offensive via the trade unions, but by the early 1950s they had been marginalised to such an extent that the battle for domestic political hegemony

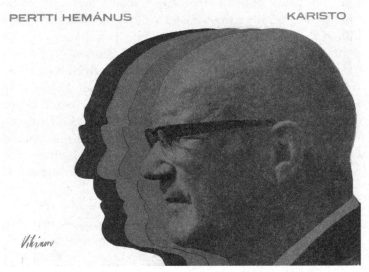

KIISTELTY KEKKONEN

PERTTI HEMÁNUS   KARISTO

8.2: Cover page of Pertti Hemánus's work *The Disputed Kekkonen*.

was waged instead between the two biggest parties, the Social
Democrats and the Agrarian Union. Both sides also relied on
foreign support in this struggle for power, which inevitably
prompts comparison with the covert games of the Hats and the
Caps with France and Russia respectively in late-eighteenth-
century Sweden-Finland. The Social Democrats received backing from their sister parties in Scandinavia and western Europe,
while the strong man of the Agrarian Party, Urho Kekkonen,
was able to persuade Moscow that he was the best guarantor
for Finland abiding by the FCMA Treaty. This rather remarkable ideological constellation came about because the Social

Democrats were regarded as class traitors both by Finnish Communists and by Moscow, which was therefore more disposed to liaise with the Agrarians, who had shown themselves flexible towards the East. For similar reasons the Right, in particular the Conservatives (Kansallinen Kokoomus, Samlingspartiet), found it easier to reach an understanding with the Western-orientated Social Democrats.

The most dramatic trial of strength took place in 1956 when Kekkonen was elected president by a margin of one vote (151:149). This immediately precipitated the country into a general strike and made constructive domestic politics much more problematical for some time to come. His opponents did their utmost to create a broad-based coalition to prevent his re-election in 1962. Kekkonen was suspected of having appeased Moscow more than was necessary in exchange for assistance in the battle for presidential office. Research has since confirmed that he did indeed forge close links with the Soviet intelligence services as early as the autumn of 1944, and that this helped him achieve his objectives.

Matters were complicated by the fact that this unconventional and often equivocal game brought considerable benefit for the country's economy and thus also for its people. In the spring of 1950 Kekkonen, when he became prime minister, had signed an extremely advantageous five-year trade agreement in Moscow; five years later his amicable relationship with the new Soviet leader Nikita Khrushchev contributed appreciably to Moscow's willingness finally to let Finland join both the United Nations and the Nordic Council. This opened up unprecedented possibilities for Finland to assert its national sovereignty and continue its efforts to stay outside great-power conflicts—provided it kept to the terms of its Treaty of Friendship.

Kekkonen's path to the presidency was somewhat eased by the Soviet Union's decision in the autumn of 1955 to relinquish its military base on the Porkkala Peninsula: nuclear missiles and jet aeroplanes with ever longer ranges had rendered it redundant for Leningrad's defence. Its closure also resulted from a number of significant agreements on international security policy. West Germany was admitted to NATO in the spring of 1955, and as a counter-move the Soviet Union formed the Warsaw Pact with its satellite states. The two military camps were able to reach accord on withdrawing their troops from Austria and making the country a neutral state, which led Khrushchev to propose that the great powers should relinquish all their foreign bases. The return of Porkkala was just one element in an international campaign, and Moscow was happy to let the shutdown of the base strengthen Kekkonen's reputation as a successful politician in his dealings with the Eastern Bloc.

But in the run-up to the presidential election in 1962 Finnish domestic politics aroused adverse Soviet reactions. In the spring of 1961 President Kekkonen's opponents united behind an alternative candidate, the Minister of Justice, Olavi Honka. In the late autumn of the same year Honka withdrew his candidacy after the Soviet Union had intervened in the presidential race with a note indirectly endorsing Kekkonen. Moscow insisted that West Germany's expanding role in NATO required military discussions as laid down in the FCMA Treaty. In the background hovered the second Berlin crisis: only a few months previously the Berlin Wall had been erected and a perilous situation had arisen in great-power politics. When the question began to be addressed, the Soviet foreign minister, Andrei Gromyko, let it be known that the note was principally intended to express concern that a political grouping had emerged in Finland which wanted to depart from the prevailing foreign policy.

Kekkonen exploited the note to the full. He dissolved parliament on the grounds that the people should be allowed to express their opinion on how relations with the Eastern Bloc were to be pursued. The ulterior motive was to create a split in the Honka coalition with another general election immediately prior to the presidential election. When Kekkonen met Khrushchev ten days later (on 24 November 1961) in the west Siberian town of Novosibirsk to discuss the consequences of the note, alarm in Finland had become so intense that Honka bowed to the inevitable. When Kekkonen then came home with the glad tidings that the Soviet Union had withdrawn its demands for military consultations, as they were content to rely on Kekkonen's ability to maintain Finland's adherence to the Treaty of Friendship, Honka's former supporters lined up timidly behind Kekkonen's candidacy instead.

Predictably, Kekkonen was re-elected president with a substantial majority, and he was re-elected another three times for the same reasons (1968, 1974, 1978) without any serious rival candidates. Everyone recognised that he had an unbeatable trump card in his hand—the support of Moscow. The advantage of this continuity was that it acted as a constraint on domestic political power games and smoothed the way for broad coalitions in government; and given stable relations with the East, Finland was in a position to pursue its active diplomacy towards the West and gradually raise its profile as a neutral state. Kekkonen, with his rhetorical brilliance, soon found an expression for this: the Finnish paradox.

But Kekkonen's primacy cast a long shadow over Finnish politics. The pressure he exerted over the formation of governments interfered with the parliamentary process and was one reason the Conservative Party remained in opposition from 1966 to 1987, irrespective of election successes. It was inevitable, too, that his oft-suspected far-reaching cosy relationship with Moscow tarnished Finland's reputation in the West. In official quarters Finland could be admired for its neutrality policy, but in the critical media the term Finlandisation was coined in the early 1960s as an admonitory example of a small country's conspiratorial political compliance.

Conspiratorial or pragmatic, the fact is that Kekkonen's diplomacy towards the East produced both economic and security dividends, and this was genuinely appreciated by his fellow countrymen, who only fifteen years earlier had been fighting for their existence as a nation. In the spring of 1961 it was thanks to Kekkonen's skilful coaxing of Moscow that Finland was able to sign a beneficial agreement with the free trade organisation EFTA, comprising western European countries which had not joined the EEC. This safeguarded the all-important export markets on the Continent and laid a solid foundation for subsequent agreements and membership of the EEC, EC and ultimately the EU.

Socio-Economic Changes

It is hardly surprising that most Finns associate Kekkonen with the country's definitive transformation from an agricultural to an industrial society. His political career more or less coincided with the rapid process of change that reshaped the country between the end of the war and the 1980s. The first post-war decade was distinguished by three issues: war reparations, new settlements and the reconstruction of destroyed homes and infrastructure. Repayment of inflation-adjusted war reparations (from 300 to 500 million dollars) began in the spring of 1945, and since the Soviet Union wanted no less than half of the compensation in the form of steel products, most of it comprised the transfer of older ships and machinery. But in order to meet the demanding delivery schedule over the longer term, the steel industry required substantial investment and restructuring. Both were achieved, and by the time the final instalment of compensation was delivered in September 1952, productivity had risen significantly, and was due not least to the ship-building industry's growing output of new vessels destined for the Soviet Union.

From 1947 the two countries also set up clearing agreements that were a modern form of commodities exchange. First, the governments mutually decided on the total value of trade to be included, then individual Finnish and Soviet firms drew up contracts. Deliveries were recorded by the respective authorities, and the firms were paid by their own national banks. The system was given a more permanent form in 1950 with a five-year clearing agreement that was renewed at regular intervals until the collapse of the Soviet economy in 1990. This trade formed a solid base for the two countries' economic co-operation and became a significant stabiliser for the Finnish export industry, which was able to even out slumps in trade in Western exports with bigger deliveries to the East.

The main import (about 80 per cent of the total) from the Soviet Union until the 1990s was unrefined oil. Steel products would continue to be a major component of Finnish eastbound exports, but in the Seventies the Finns also carried out large-scale construction projects in the Soviet Union, such as three sizeable industrial complexes in Karelia and entire satellite towns in eastern Russia and western Siberia. In the Eighties over 50 per cent by value of exports to the East was in consumer goods, but significantly, trade with the East never attained a dominant role within overall Finnish export trade during the Cold War. Forestry products continued to be easily the country's chief export throughout the whole period, and the biggest markets were as before western Europe and the United States. Around 70 per cent of all foreign trade in the years 1950–80 was conducted with EEC and EFTA countries, which meant that despite its security policy ties with the Soviet

Union, Finland remained well-anchored economically in western Europe.

The balancing act paid dividends in a fast and fairly unbroken period of economic growth up to the 1990s. The average income more than doubled from 1948 to 1979. Annual GDP rose faster than that of almost all other western European countries and by the end of the Seventies Finland had joined the richest third of European states. One reason for this upturn was of course its late industrialisation, which made it possible to adopt immediately technology which had already long been automated. In contrast to countries which had industrialised earlier, where the industrial workforce might at times have comprised over half of the population in employment, Finland would never have a predominant class of industrial workers. The majority of those freed from primary food production moved directly into the service sector.

Paradoxically, a factor in this giant leap was the great land reform of the 1940s, which had both social and political objectives. The war and the territorial losses led to some 420,000 people being evacuated, and over 230,000 of them were farming families. The authorities therefore undertook a massive land acquisition programme in 1945–47 for these farmers through clearances and statutory land transfers. The outcome was not just a marked increase in the area of land under cultivation, but also a reduction in the average size of farms in southern Finland from 14 to 11 hectares. The land reform created employment in rural areas, which in turn put a brake on immigration into the towns and prevented an already war-torn country from being hit by soaring unemployment and social unrest.

From the Fifties onwards, however, urbanisation progressed even more swiftly. The mechanisation of agriculture and forestry caused an ever-growing proportion of younger people to make their way to the towns and industrial complexes in search of jobs or further education. The number of tractors jumped in the Fifties from 14,500 to 106,000, and in the forests the chainsaw began to replace the axe. Now even smallholders could afford to buy a tractor, with a concomitant steep decline in both the number of horses and the need for hay. Together with the wider availability of concentrated feed and artificial fertiliser, this made the country self-sufficient in milk and in meat and grain products by the 1960s.

Urban building stock had suffered very badly in the war. Over 20,000 homes were destroyed by bombing and many tens of thousands lost from action on land. A vigorous rebuilding programme was launched right after the war, and when urban-isation really began to accelerate in the Fifties both capital and workforce capacity were available. From 1949 onwards the state gave substantial support in the form of loans (ARAVA loans underwritten by the Housing Fund of Finland [ARA]) and tax relief for local authorities and firms that invested in high-rise developments. The annual construction of new homes rose in the period 1950–75 from 30,000 to about 77,000. A remarkable amount of the country's housing stock was replaced in just a few decades.

Extra homes were also needed for the simple reason that Finland, like every other European country, experienced a baby boom in the immediate post-war years. The birth rate had already been creeping up in the 1930s thanks to economic growth, but as soon as the war was over annual births shot up by 25 per cent. In the most fecund years, 1948–49, the country was blessed with more than 105,000 additional inhabitants annually. These bumper years soon reversed the wartime drop in population and even resulted in an actual increase of some 330,000 persons between 1941 and 1950.

After that the birth rate began to show a steadily declining curve, and in the late Sixties the huge emigration to Sweden brought a temporary decrease in population. The general tendency, however, has been upward. Better health care and welfare provision also reduced mortality, leading to a population growth between 1944 and 1980 from 3.7 to 4.8 million, and this continued in the Eighties and Nineties for the same reasons. At the beginning of the new millennium Finland had 5.2 million inhabitants.

The shift of population from rural to urban areas depleted the villages of working-age people, required colossal investment in urban development and changed living conditions for hundreds of thousands. It was of course those born in the baby-boom years of the late 1940s who were the most mobile, reaching adulthood in the mid-Sixties; thanks to the expansion of higher and further education they had the chance to go on to university or vocational college. Internal movement was usually from central and eastern Finland to the capital and its surrounding areas. Since the vast majority of immigrants were young, they soon formed families and generated offspring, producing a population surge of nearly half a million in the county of Uusimaa (Nyland), surrounding and including the capital, in the years 1951–80. This trend persisted and by the year 2000 some 20 per cent of all Finns, or 1 million people, lived in the Helsinki area.

Geographical mobility altered the language situation as well. Finland's Swedish-speakers still lived along the south and west coasts, and since urbanisation was greatest in these same regions, the incidence of marriage across the language boundary rose and Finnish increasingly became the dominant tongue of home and workplace. In the period 1940–80 the total of registered Finland-Swedes fell from 360,000 to 300,000, which meant that in real terms their share of the population dropped from 10 per cent to about 6 per cent in forty years.

This was not all the result of Fennicisation, however. The birth rate of the Swedish-speaking population was at times much lower than that of Finnish-speakers, principally owing to the widespread emigration of younger Finland-Swedes to Sweden. Some estimates suggest that as many as 60,000 Swedish-speakers bought one-way tickets across the Gulf of Bothnia in the 1950s and 1960s. One in every five emigrants to Sweden had Swedish as their mother tongue. The reduction in numbers slowed after that, and at the end of the 2010s almost 290,000 Finns were registered as Swedish-speaking. This stabilisation was not simply because emigration to Sweden had ceased. It stemmed equally from the fact that a mounting proportion of bilingual families chose to favour Swedish and that Swedish-language educational facilities and cultural life remained intact.

Emigration to Sweden also had a broader effect on the social development of Finland. It began as soon as the Scandinavian countries had signed an agreement in 1954 on the free movement of labour. Sweden was suffering a labour shortage and since Swedish wage levels were as much as twice those of Finland, the exodus soon proliferated, especially in the late Sixties and early Seventies, when around 40,000 Finns a year emigrated to Sweden. In all, half a million Finns were registered as immigrants in Sweden in the period 1945–90; and there were many who worked there for briefer spells, giving an estimated figure for Finns who worked at some time in Sweden since 1945 of 700,000 or more.

Finns also returned to their native land in considerable numbers, and the final figure for net emigration to Sweden in those forty-five years is around 230,000. The cumulative effect of this mobility, however, was a demographic and economic integration of the two countries, the extent and structure of which bore many resemblances to the interplay prior to 1809 when they had been one kingdom. Finnish again became a living language in Stockholm and gave rise to a distinct Swedo-

Finnish culture with its own organisations and institutions. The pull of Sweden was especially strong in Ostrobothnia and northern Finland, not dissimilar to the close connections which these regions had with the Stockholm area in the days of the joint realm.

A prerequisite for all this mobility was of course a well-functioning transport network. Ferry traffic between Finland and Sweden was a profitable business with the volume of passengers rising, and the ferries themselves expanding in both number and size, the latter also dictated by the increase in the ratio of passengers travelling with their own cars. At first it was mostly Finnish emigrants to Sweden returning home for holidays and wanting to show off their hard-earned Volvos and Saabs to their relations in Finland, but as living standards there began to reach Swedish levels, more and more Finns could afford to buy their own cars anyway. In the 1950s the bus had become the preferred form of transport for shorter journeys, but by the start of the 1960s over half of all trips were by private car.

The real breakthrough was to come in the mid-Sixties, however, when the number of cars registered more than doubled in five years, from 258,000 to 602,000 vehicles. One of the obvious reasons was that the authorities deregulated car imports. In ten years the private car had become almost an essential requisite, and communications between urban centres and the rural peripheries were very much improved as a result. The oil crisis of the Seventies slowed the growth of car ownership somewhat, but the trend continued upwards through to the Nineties, when there were over 2.2 million vehicles registered in Finland. Of course the country was by and large following an international pattern.

The rampant proliferation of motor vehicles had a detrimental effect on the urban landscape and caused air pollution, provoking criticism from the ecologically or aesthetically aware. Yet most people associated the motor car with positive values, and from the late Fifties onwards immense resources were poured into modernising trunk roads and constructing motorways. The first motorway was inaugurated in the autumn of 1962, when a fifteen-kilometre stretch of four-lane highway was completed as a western exit from Helsinki.

Social and Urban Developments

Such road-building, like all the big public investment projects, was part of a wider programme, the creation of a universally accessible welfare state, levelling out distinctions of class or wealth. The redistribution of income in an agrarian society had been implemented primarily through land reform. The instrument now used for the same purpose in an industrial society was progressive income tax, which rose across the board as the state took on responsibility for various services provided for the public good and introduced new kinds of national insurance contributions. Similar developments had already begun in the United States and other western European countries in the 1930s. The first step towards modern social welfare in Finland was taken in 1939 when a law on state pensions came into force, but because of the war it was not until 1957 that the pension had any actual financial significance and was available for everyone.

The idea was not new. The political Left in western Europe had been demanding comprehensive social welfare ever since the late nineteenth century. But as long as it was seen as synonymous with a Socialist system, little was done, especially after the emergence of the Soviet Union, which had a strong deterrent effect. The turning point was the economic crisis of the 1930s, which made the decision-makers realise that a permanent form of social welfare might in practice give stability and stimulation to capitalism, since it would even out fluctuations in the economy and boost the purchasing power of the less affluent majority. The leading proponent of this economic theory in Scandinavia was the Swedish political economist Gunnar Myrdal. The Finnish sociologist Pekka Kuusi argued along similar lines, maintaining in his influential work *60-luvun sosiaalipolitiikka* (Social Policy for the Sixties) in 1961 that significant income redistribution in fact speeded up economic growth.

Kuusi avoided political and moral arguments, but precisely as in other European countries with free-market economies, Finnish welfare policy was driven by a suppressed fear that social antagonisms might lead to open social conflict, or in the worst-case scenario degenerate into revolution and Soviet-backed Communism. The looming presence of the Soviet Union on its eastern frontier gave a particular pertinence to such disquiet in Finland. Another factor was that the Finnish Communists were loyal to Moscow and had a firm grip on the far Left in Parliament, which even up to the 1970s enjoyed 20 per cent of popular support. This prompted the other parties to seek social reform and political compromise.

The most intensive phase in the creation of the Finnish welfare state was between 1950 and 1980, when three major reform packages were passed. Firstly a compulsory national insurance scheme was introduced, secondly health and social services were expanded, and thirdly the entire education system was restructured. National insurance was not simply a matter of providing a retirement pension. Over a twenty-year period from 1957 income-related pensions were brought in for all, including farmers and private businesses. When state finances were at their healthiest, in the mid-1980s, the age limits for various categories of early-retirement pension were lowered to levels (age 55–60) which later had to be revised. Significant labour-market reforms were introduced, such as the 40-hour week (1965) and improvements in unemployment benefits, which were income-related from 1985.

The extension of social and health care provision began with the construction of large hospital complexes across the country, from 1956 coming under the jurisdiction of local authorities. But public health care was still expensive, and 1964 saw the beginning of compulsory health insurance for all wage-earners. The arrangement guaranteed care for everyone and was complemented in 1972 by a national health regulation which gave local authorities the responsibility for setting up their own health clinics, a step which made a noticeable improvement in preventive medicine. Child benefit had been paid since 1948, and from the mid-Sixties a one-month maternity payment was initiated, gradually extended in the course of the next twenty years to ten months. The 1973 law on day care provision for children doubled the number of publicly financed crèche places in just a few years and had a tremendous impact on women's ability to seek gainful employment.

The education system had not undergone any substantial modification since the end of the nineteenth century, which meant that its modernisation and expansion also had significant consequences for society as a whole. The elementary school became the basic school for all children from 1946, but otherwise it was a binary system of elementary school followed by secondary school for the majority and grammar school for a select minority, up until the inception of the comprehensive school in 1968. This reform created an egalitarian system, with nine years of common schooling for all and in principle equal opportunity to continue to sixth form college, which prepared pupils for university or colleges of higher education.

The reforms were pushed through by the Left and Centre parties in Parliament, both much impressed by a corresponding school reform in Sweden in the 1950s. In many respects the change fulfilled expectations, even if the most idealistic visions of the comprehensive school as an instrument for social equality were not to be realised. Between 1960 and 1980 the proportion of pupils continuing their schooling to sixth form college rose from 20 to 50 per cent. As most of the country's private grammar schools passed into public ownership in the same period, the education ladder was unified, facilitating long-term planning and reinforcing the feeling of an egalitarian society.

The spiralling numbers of students exacerbated the pressure on the universities and colleges. Even though there was a huge expansion of higher education in the Sixties and Seventies it did not keep up with the rate of pupils coming out of the schools, and so more and more were going direct into employment. The additional places in higher education were mostly outside Helsinki: whereas in 1965 half of the country's students were taught at Helsinki University, by the start of the Nineties the proportion had dropped to 20 per cent, while the new establishments in other parts of the country accounted for some 60 per cent.

Turku (Åbo) had revived its university tradition in the late 1910s and early 1920s with the inception of the Swedish-speaking Åbo Akademi and the Finnish-speaking Turun Yliopisto (Turku University). Next in turn was Oulu (Uleåborg) University, founded in 1958, the importance of which as a centre for innovation for the whole of northern Finland would become even more accentuated in the 1990s. It was followed by the creation of a handful of new universities in cities around the country. This made Finland, together with Sweden and Norway, one of the countries with the most decentralised higher education systems in the world in comparison with relative regional population densities.

All these social reforms and investments were given additional impetus by the speed of urbanisation in the years 1940–75, a pace faster in Finland than perhaps any other European country. In thirty-five years the proportion of people employed in primary production fell from 64 per cent to 14 per cent. The figure is astonishing if one thinks of a similar change having taken about seventy years in Sweden, another country which was subject to rapid modernisation. In practice this meant that the bulk of the populace after the war had their roots in the countryside, but lived the greater part of their lives in urban surroundings.

A structural shift of that speed left its mark both on the physical environment and on everyday life. The new suburbs were built to a rather uniform plan and characterless external design. They were rushed up by contractors schooled in industrial engineering. The total concept would include municipal infrastructure and shopping centres which were expected to be ready at the same time as the domestic housing. The monotonous impression was emphasised by the relatively uniform age, work routines and consumption habits of the residents. The focus of daily life was a two- or three-room apartment, food and other necessities purchased in the local supermarket, and fairly homogeneous timetables for commuting to and from work or school.

Yet life in these suburbs represented for most people a vast improvement in living conditions. Those who came direct from rural areas frequently had running water, central heating and a reasonable distance to shops and other services for the first time. Those who moved out from cramped and decrepit blocks of flats in the inner cities were well able to appreciate the spaciousness of these functional dwellings and their proximity to nature. At the outset, people joined in activities and informal networks that were reminiscent of social life in a village, but gradually they formed different networks and routines which tended to lessen community spirit and increase the emphasis on the nuclear family and workplace.

The biggest change of all, however, was in the everyday occupations of women, owing to both advances in social provision and a rise in the general educational level of women to that of men. Between 1960 and 1980 the proportion of women in gainful employment almost doubled (from 42 per cent to 79 per cent). As women's financial dependence on men decreased, so internal family dynamics shifted and it became quite usual for it to be the woman who instigated the ending of a failed relationship. The pill and the coil also had a revolutionary impact on women's sexual emancipation by giving them their own control over contraception. One effect was that birth rates tumbled, another was that increasing numbers of people began to prefer alternative forms of cohabitation—in 1990 these constituted a fifth of all families in Finland.

Cultural Revolution

This material and structural transformation of society had its cultural counterpart. In the first few years after the war controversy raged between the political Left and the right-wing establishment. The battle ended in compromise. Hopes on the radical Left for a completely new direction in cultural life emphasising democratic values and distancing itself categorically from the White, overtly anti-Soviet Finland of the war years were not fulfilled. Most Finns did not consider it their country's fault that it had been drawn into war and become Germany's co-aggressor. There was also a distinct readiness to strip away the most nationalistic tones in literature and art in favour of a less judgemental Modernism.

Once more it was a case of "opening windows on Europe". The younger cultural elite were influenced by the French writers Sartre and Camus among others, while academics showed a mounting interest in Anglo-American theories and social projects. The major literary achievement of the epoch was Mika Waltari's historical novel *Sinuhe the Egyptian* (1945), in which the irrationality of human nature and the transience of ideologies were portrayed in such universal terms that the book became an international bestseller, translated into some thirty languages. Meanwhile, the Finnish philosopher Georg Henrik von Wright was beginning to receive international acclaim for his explorations in modern logic and concept analysis.

The real psychological break with the war years did not come until the early Fifties, when war reparations had been

8.3: The Olympic Games in Helsinki in 1952 gave a strong boost to the Finnish national pride and economy.

fulfilled, the main protagonists of the war, Mannerheim and Stalin, had gone to their graves, and Finland finally hosted the Olympic Games. Helsinki had been selected for the 1940 Summer Games, but they were cancelled because of the war. When they were eventually held in Helsinki in 1952 in exemplary fashion, it gave an enormous boost to the Finns' national self-esteem, which had taken quite a battering in the war years, especially when the Western press gave substantial coverage to the country's impressive recovery and the negligible effect of the neighbouring Soviet Union on ordinary life.

There were other clear signs of a change in the general atmosphere in society. The charm offensives of the new Soviet leadership definitely contributed to the air of optimism. By the mid-Fifties the country had a dynamic and extremely profitable popular culture, which presented a more egalitarian and urbane picture of the new Finland. The shared experience of the war years had fostered a genuinely classless sense of unity, and national icons could be treated in a more casual manner. In the autumn of 1954 Väinö Linna published his novel *Tuntematon sotilas* (*The Unknown Soldier*), in which Finland's progress through the Continuation War was depicted from the often burlesque grassroots perspective of the soldiers at the front. It immediately achieved tremendous popularity and was filmed the following year, ensuring its place as the national epic of a modern, independent Finland.

Linna was obviously inspired by Finnish comedy films, which tended to make good-natured fun of classic conservative educational ideals. They also conveyed the traditional annoyance of ordinary people at the assumption by minority elites that they had the right to dictate the tastes and consumer habits of the majority. When this attitude was transformed into popular feature films with obvious influences from American slapstick humour and cowboy romanticism, the result was a witty critique of the cultural establishment. This spirit of protest was augmented in the Sixties by an efflorescence of artistic avant-gardism, alternative grassroots movements and radical social criticism.

At first the temptation was to mock accepted icons such as Jesus or Mannerheim, but the radicalism soon took on more of a political dimension. As on so many previous occasions, the students were in the forefront, their fast-growing numbers leading to a break with university traditions and open politicisation of the previously apathetic student unions and associations. Until the autumn of 1967 public debate focused on pacifist censure of the country's military forces and conscription, which was blamed for latent warmongering and Russophobia. But then the students were swept along by the international waves of protest against the US war in Vietnam, and in the late autumn of 1968 they again followed trends in the outside world by occupying public buildings and agitating for democratisation within the universities.

Demands escalated over the next year when the movement was hijacked by a phalanx of left-wing activists who had had enough of the slow reformist politics of the Social Democrats and allied themselves to the Communist Party. The Party's radical wing of Taistoites (named after Taisto Sinisalo, a Communist loyal to Moscow) became a home for many of the most high-profile intellectuals of the time. Though they managed to attain leading positions in cultural or student affairs, all the principal demands came to nothing, and by the early Eighties their thinning ranks seemed no more than a group of harmless radicals. Yet the situation had appeared very different ten years earlier. The dalliance of student leaders with the Moscow-orientated extreme Left was seen in right-wing circles as a serious warning that the whole of society was being undermined, not least since these Taistoites paid homage both to various international revolutionary heroes such as Lenin, Che Guevara and Ho Chi Minh and, often with great enthusiasm, to the legacy of domestic revolutionaries from 1918.

Another integral part of the Sixties' cultural revolution was folk, pop and rock music and the associated youth fashions, ever more susceptible to contemporaneous change in line with international trends. The beginnings of a specific youth culture in music and consumer patterns burst onto the scene throughout the Western world in the 1950s, with Elvis Presley its shining star. The popular music business developed into a global industry that transformed the best-known rock artists into icons for an entire generation, and into multi-millionaires themselves. The influence of television guaranteed that their records sold extremely well in Finland too, and the summer of 1966 brought the unlikely spectacle of the Rolling Stones in concert on a Finnish west-coast beach. Within a few years long hair, jeans and hippie clothes of all kinds had become standard fashion for young people even in Finland.

But it would not be until the start of the Seventies that Finland acquired its own rock bands worthy of the name. The big swing and ballad singer of the Fifties, Olavi Virta, dominated the scene for a long time with his Frank Sinatra style, and in his footsteps came a sequence of female singers such as Brita Koivunen, Laila Kinnunen and Katri Helena, whose cover versions of international hits soon found a place in Finnish hearts. In the late Sixties a rich vocal tradition also arose in the student movement, but its socio-political message was often too caustic for everyday light entertainment. The main pioneers were rather the rock artist Rauli "Badding" Somerjoki and his band with the provocative name Suomen Talvisota 1939–1940 (Finnish Winter War 1939–1940), whose album *Underground* (1970) initiated a domestic rock music of homegrown lyrics and tone.

Other forerunners were Heikki "Hector" Harma and Juhani "Juice" Leskinen, whose best-known songs are still very much a living tradition for those who were young in the Seventies. The musical breakthrough was helped by the fact that Finnish Radio ended its restrictions on play time for all rock music in 1970, and the effect of that was complemented by the rise in sales of cassette players in the first half of the Seventies. Songs such as Hector's melancholy take on contemporary life "Lumi teki enkelin eteiseen" ("The Snow Made an Angel in the Porch", 1973) achieved twice the distribution that bald record sales figures might have suggested.

The influence of Finnish Radio on domestic culture and public life reached its peak in the Sixties and Seventies. The company retained its monopoly on radio broadcasting until 1985, when a privately owned radio station was granted a licence for the Helsinki area. The same company's two television channels exerted quite as much influence on the country's cultural life. They were likewise virtually the only choices on offer until the 1980s, with a mere 20 per cent of total air time leased to the commercial company Mainos-TV, which had been in at the start of television broadcasting in the late Fifties. In the latter half of the Sixties the number of TV licences doubled to 1 million and the daily programme schedule rose to ten hours.

The content of state broadcasting was determined by Finnish Radio's politically appointed Programming Board, which in the spirit of the times interpreted its educational remit as being to provide factual news reporting and informative entertainment. Some topical programmes and quizzes that improved general knowledge were also deemed suitable for the public. But the real favourites with viewers were various home-produced soap operas, comedy programmes and lotteries, whose protagonists became the celebrities of the day. Other guaranteed successes even then were international sporting events and the annual selection of Miss Finland, which gave the tabloid press ample scope to follow up with intimate personal details and gossip.

Then there were the plenteous offerings of British and American TV series, animations and feature films that occupied a significant quota of the broadcasting schedules of both the state and commercial channels and had high viewing figures from the outset. The American entertainment industry had gained a leading position on the Finnish market as early as the 1920s, so the dominance of Hollywood on TV screens was in no way revolutionary. On the contrary, it meant that many people were able to see their favourite old films repeated and simultaneously have free lessons in American English. Films are not usually dubbed in Finland and the other Scandinavian countries, but subtitled, which has not only improved viewers' linguistic competence but also maximised their receptivity to the American lifestyle.

Active Foreign Policy

A frequent face on Finnish TV screens was of course President Kekkonen. His time in office coincided with the advent of television, and he contrived to make very full use of the new medium. He had been a prolific writer ever since his youth and his ability to come across well in public had been honed through participation in the regular political debates on radio introduced after the Second World War. His schooling in the media bore fruit. He was tall and fit with a distinctive voice and could express himself concisely and intelligibly. This was seldom the case with his political rivals, who either looked altogether too ordinary or seemed to clam up whenever the TV cameras zoomed in on them for a passing comment.

WELFARE AND NEUTRALITY

Kekkonen's foreign policy initiatives really multiplied once he had been given such a convincingly renewed mandate in 1962 that he no longer needed to worry about opposition on domestic issues. The general situation was opportune for a raised profile in foreign policy as well. The Berlin and Cuba crises had tested relations between the two superpowers to the extreme in 1961–62, and raised everyone's awareness of how easily the whole of humanity might perish in the event of rivalries spilling over into a full-scale nuclear war. It brought both sides to their senses and led to a balance of terror in Europe. The superpowers' political incursions in the Third World were also increasing with the phasing out of the old colonial dominions.

The balance of terror did not, however, reduce the superpowers' build-up of their nuclear arsenals, and so the idea of nuclear-free zones began to take root in many parts of the world. Such hopes were expressed in the spring of 1963 by the heads of state of Yugoslavia and Mexico, who saw how endangered their own regions would be if nuclear war broke out. In May of the same year Kekkonen followed up their initiatives by publicly proposing that Scandinavia should be declared a nuclear-free zone. There was little enthusiasm in the other Scandinavian countries: it would not have been compatible with Denmark's and Norway's NATO membership, which required a willingness to accept support in nuclear form if war threatened; and the Swedish government's response was likewise muted, mainly because it was considered that the zone should include the Soviet Union, which had several large military bases in the Baltic states.

Kekkonen understood, of course, that Denmark and Norway could not yield on that point. Until the 1990s northern Europe's security balance was predicated on the political order of the late 1940s. Finland's treaty of friendship with the Soviet Union had to be weighed against Sweden's more strict neutrality and Danish and Norwegian membership of NATO. Any alteration to that order would inevitably have led to a disruption of the balance. Nevertheless, the Finnish government went on to air the concept of a nuclear-free Scandinavia again at subsequent stages of the Cold War. Research has not been able to uncover what really lay behind this persistence, but everything indicates that Kekkonen's stubbornness emanated from shrewd calculation. By keeping the notion alive, the Finnish government was trying to reduce the risk of the Soviet Union, if faced by any great-power crisis, demanding military consultations and the right to base nuclear weapons on Finnish soil.

Another manifestation of Kekkonen's deliberate profile-raising tactics was his assertion in the later 1960s that Finland

8.4: A lot of Soviet-produced cars were imported to Finland in the 1950s and 1960s such as this Moskvitch. The Soviet Union acquired an Opel manufacturing line from its occupation zone in Germany and produced with it a modified Opel Kadett under that name.

was pursuing an active policy of neutrality. Taking this stand was not in breach of its obligations to the East, since Finland was striving to keep out of any superpower conflicts of interest, in accordance with the FCMA Treaty. The stage for this neutrality policy was initially the United Nations headquarters in New York, where Finland could express itself constructively about crises in the Third World without much risk of antagonising the Soviet Union. But at the end of the Sixties Finland had the opportunity to show how an active neutrality policy could also benefit European security. The Warsaw Pact invasion of Czechoslovakia in 1968 had damaged the reputation of the Soviet Union in the West. As a counter-move, Moscow proposed in the spring of 1969 that a pan-European security conference be organised and an agreement drawn up to stabilise relations and confirm the political division that had emerged in Europe after the Paris Peace Treaty of 1947.

The proposal was aimed at all European states and it gave Kekkonen a chance to campaign on this matter himself without an immediate accusation of being a mouthpiece for Moscow. So he quickly set out his own proposal, that all parties should commence preparatory talks without preconditions, and since NATO was a central party in the case, that the United States and Canada should be invited to join in the negotiations as well. He offered Finland as co-ordinator and host for the summit conference itself. Both superpowers approved his proposal, since it was compatible with their own plans for multilateral negotiations on nuclear arms limitations. Preparatory discussions began immediately. Six years on Kekkonen's dream was realised when almost all European heads of state came together in Helsinki to sign the Final Act of the Conference on Security and Co-operation in Europe.

Before that juncture, however, many knotty problems of European security policy and superpower relations had been solved. The hardest nuts to crack were the Germany question and the superpowers' ongoing disarmament negotiations, which had ramifications for all other major areas of international politics. The Warsaw Pact incursion into Czechoslovakia in 1968 had been prompted by Moscow's fear that its satellites were in the process of disengaging themselves from the Soviet Bloc. To allay any suspicions that West Germany was still working for German reunification, Willy Brandt made treaties in 1970–71 with the Soviet Union, Poland and Czechoslovakia in which those countries' post-war boundaries were mutually recognised. This paved the way for a stabilising agreement between Berlin's four occupying powers in September 1971, unambiguously recognising West Berlin as part of West Germany, that being the Federal Republic of Germany. Six months after this the superpowers agreed on a limitation of nuclear warheads. This boded well for a pan-European security conference under Finland's auspices.

One factor in all the preparations was that in January 1973 Finland established diplomatic relations with both German states, enhancing its credibility as a neutral player in European security policy. That same year marked a honing of the Final Act of the conference, which featured three main points. Firstly, there should be mutual recognition of Europe's existing political borders, which meant definitive confirmation of the division of Germany. Secondly, agreements on economic cooperation, technological research and the environment were drawn up. Thirdly, all European countries undertook to promote and encourage their citizens' civil, political, social, cultural and other rights, a clause which would at a future date allow the United States to criticise the Soviet Union for human rights abuses.

The active engagement of the Finnish leadership in this process stemmed from their conviction that it would serve Finland's interests too. The country could raise its neutrality profile even while the relaxation of tension in international relations was making it easier to pursue its trade policies with the West. In the autumn of 1973, Finland concluded a beneficial free trade arrangement with the EEC which secured markets for the Finnish paper industry in western Europe and furthered the country's economic integration with the West. The EEC countries' accommodating attitudes flowed of course from a desire to tie Finland's economy more firmly to the West. But this had to be played down in view of Finland's sensitive relations with the East. Kekkonen had earlier allayed the Soviet Union's mistrust by entering a similar agreement with the Eastern Bloc, though this had much slighter economic significance.

The supreme moment in Kekkonen's fine balance of foreign policy came at the end of July and beginning of August 1975, when he hosted the Conference on Security and Co-operation in Europe and its Final Act in Helsinki. Security measures had been meticulously put in place. Never before had the heads of state of so many great powers come together simultaneously in Helsinki, which was bathed in warm sunshine in honour of the summit. The relaxed atmosphere was due in part to the fact that the leaders of both the United States and the Soviet Union saw the conference as a chance to show themselves to be world-class diplomats. President Gerald Ford wanted to win his laurels before the next year's presidential elections, and underlined the human rights aspects of the agreement. The ageing party secretary Leonid Brezhnev regarded the conference as the ultimate recognition of his own doctrine of the permanence of the Soviet Bloc.

The nub of the treaty was without doubt the mutual acceptance of Europe's political division. As chairman of the conference Kekkonen also used the occasion to stress that Finland's active neutrality policy was entirely in accord with the principles of national sovereignty and independence that the thirty-five European and North American leaders were about to sign their names to. The point was directed primarily eastwards, as Moscow had until then been rather reluctant to recognise Finland's status as a neutral country. Even towards the end of the Seventies the Soviet Union would continue to express its annoyance that Finland had so "disproportionately" emphasised its neutral status. By then it was too late to do anything about it. In his remaining six years as president, Kekkonen would on numerous occasions remind them of the mutual pledges of 1975 and gently parry Soviet approaches about military co-operation.

Western hawks were not slow to dismiss the CSCE Act as a Soviet propaganda victory, but over the next fifteen years follow-up CSCE meetings were arranged in Belgrade, Madrid and Vienna, where the Soviet Union and the other Eastern-

8.5: The Finno-Soviet relationship was stable during the Cold War and in economic terms favorable for Finland. Soviet peace propaganda from the early 1970s.

Bloc countries were criticised for infringements of the Act's stipulations on human rights. The CSCE had encouraged political dissidents in the Eastern Bloc to form "Helsinki groups" that leaked information on such violations. Some commentators even think these dissidents may have contributed to the collapse of the Soviet Union, especially after the 1981 Polish protest movement Solidarity had shown the way and inspired similar demonstrations elsewhere in the Eastern Bloc.

It was therefore something of an irony of fate that when the Norwegian Nobel Committee announced the annual winner of the Peace Prize in the autumn of 1975, Soviet dissident Andrei Sakharov beat Kekkonen by a slim majority. Kekkonen's diplomatic achievements for European stability and security could hardly be denied. The problem was that they had served Soviet interests too. He could thus never merit unreserved appreciation in the West, even though Finland's balancing act on security policy between East and West was viewed as a model for many Soviet Bloc countries and hence indirectly contributed to the dismemberment of the Soviet Union. And if Kekkonen's foreign policy is seen from a narrow national angle, the final account is absolutely positive. When he took up presidential office in 1956 Finland had very limited opportunities for independent action in the international arena. By the time he left office in 1981 the country had created for itself a certain credibility as a neutral state by small but systematic extensions of its own room for manoeuvre. Its business and trade had also derived considerable benefit from its leadership's skilful balancing act between the power blocs.

Shift of Power

An important prerequisite for this foreign policy was relative tranquillity in domestic politics. Kekkonen's unchallenged position as president from 1962 undoubtedly stabilised the situation, and in 1966, for the first time since 1959, a "Red-Earth Coalition" was formed across party lines. Seats were even found for the Communist Party in this government, which was a decisive factor in reducing social antagonisms and preparing the ground for similar broad coalitions in the Seventies. Yet the incredible speed of social change left its mark on party politics as well. In the spring of 1970 the agrarian protest party, the Finnish Rural Party (*Suomen maaseudun puolue*, *Landsbygdspartiet*) obtained nearly 10 per cent of votes in the

8.6: The Finnish textile and design industry found new markets in the 1950s and 1960s. Fashion photo from 1958 by Claire Aho.

parliamentary elections, while the old Agrarian Union (*Maal-aisliitto*, *Agrarförbundet*), in its new guise as the Centre Party (*Keskustapuolue*, *Centerpartiet*), lost votes in substantial numbers. The Finnish Rural Party was overtly critical of Kekkonen and his Machiavellian ways and would throughout the Seventies direct its scathing condemnation at the entire establishment under the slogan "The people know".

But the Finnish Rural Party's popular support soon waned, and when Kekkonen was re-elected under exceptional legislation for another four years (1974–78), it was with a safe five-sixths majority in parliament. The president came to rely more and more on the Social Democratic Party during the Seventies. Its chairman of many years' standing, Kalevi Sorsa, was prime minister in several governments, and obviously Kekkonen's intention was that he should succeed him as president in due course. Sorsa managed to tame the Communist Party into an obedient partner in government. He also eased through many key social reforms in conjunction with the Centre Party, which together with the Social Democrats formed the backbone of practically all the governments in the Seventies, irrespective of election success. The loser in this game was the conservative National Coalition (*Kansallinen kokoomus*, *Samlingspartiet*), whose capacity for government was ultimately in doubt because of Soviet mistrust. Despite its advances in nearly every one of the parliamentary elections in the Seventies, it was not able to form a government until 1987.

Soviet influence on Finnish domestic politics manifested itself in other ways as well. Ever since Paasikivi's time as president (1946–56) the political leadership had been very careful to ensure that the powerful eastern neighbour was handled tactfully by the Finnish media. This self-censorship could degenerate into distortions in the reporting of international news, which of course gave credence to the rumours of Finland's

"Finlandisation". The situation was complicated by the fact that Soviet diplomats in Helsinki built up an informal but efficient network of contacts among industrialists and politicians across almost all the parties, which tangibly facilitated communications between the decision-makers of the two countries, and right in the middle was Kekkonen himself. This network afforded Soviet diplomats and intelligence officers a superb insight into, and in some cases even influence on, Finnish domestic politics.

By the end of the Seventies Kekkonen's withdrawal from presidential office was inexorably approaching. He was re-elected for another six-year term in 1978, but his health was fragile and there were several prospective successors waiting in the wings. Opinion polls had been pointing to the Social Democrat Mauno Koivisto as the most popular candidate. His approval rating with the public climbed even higher when he became prime minister of a broad-based coalition government and began openly to defy Kekkonen's previously so invincible authority. In the autumn of 1981 Kekkonen was forced into early retirement on medical grounds. Although Koivisto's political rivals did what they could to prevent his rise to the top, he was elected president in the early spring of 1982 with a big majority.

It did not matter that Koivisto had been portrayed by his opponents as an unpopular figure in Moscow; in fact it strengthened his position in the election campaign. Many felt the cosying up to the Russians had gone too far and welcomed the idea of someone outside Kekkonen's closest circles as head of state. The wider public came to see Koivisto's twelve years as president (1982–94) as a return to Western parliamentarism and a restriction on political interference from Moscow. This view was correct in that Koivisto, in contrast to Kekkonen, did not use his constitutional powers to dissolve parliament and dismiss governments in order to get his way. All the governments were to last their full four-year terms, and in 1987 the time had become ripe for a Red-Blue coalition between the Social Democrats and the Conservatives. Such a coalition would have been impossible just a few years earlier.

Koivisto was frequently seen as taking a firmer line on Eastern policy than Kekkonen, but he was extremely anxious to maintain well-functioning relations with Moscow. No significant foreign policy advances were made in the first half of the 1980s. One reason was the power vacuum that arose in Moscow when three ageing Soviet leaders died in office in the years 1982–85: Brezhnev, Andropov and Chernenko. The absence of a strong political leadership in the Kremlin had already made itself felt in the late Seventies: Soviet actions in the international arena were motivated by narrow military considerations, resulting in several fateful errors of judgement.

One of these was the decision to replace Soviet medium-range missiles in eastern Europe, despite vociferous protests from NATO. So NATO began a corresponding replacement programme in western Europe, and both sides were sucked into an unprecedented spiral of rearmament. It became too much for the overstretched Soviet economy and was a prime reason for the total collapse of the Eastern Bloc in 1989–91. The invasion of Afghanistan in the autumn of 1979 was also ill-advised. That, together with the difficulties entailed in suppressing the Solidarity protest movement in Poland in 1981, lent credence to the picture of the Soviet Empire as a boat with neither oars nor oarsmen.

Finnish defence policy was itself to some extent affected by the harsher climate in great-power politics. The leadership's line on an active neutrality policy did not waver, for one very fundamental reason: the armed forces were duty-bound by the Treaty of Friendship to co-operate with the Soviet army if both parties agreed that the Soviet Union was threatened by invasion across Finnish territory. This obligation required the maintenance of a conscript army and ensured that military training continued despite only modest defence budgets throughout the Cold War. In the 1960s a territorial defence system was introduced that included preparations for guerrilla warfare. The country was divided into seven military zones capable of resisting an invader independently of each other. The idea arose from experience of the wars against the Soviet Union during the Second World War, and lessons had been learned from the various wars of liberation in the Third World. Territorial defence was also intended to frighten off any Soviet invasion attempts—its primary, but of course unexpressed, object.

Finland's Achilles heel was its air force, which in the Cold War years had been quite inadequate for any credible defence of its own air space. All security scenarios relied on the Soviet Union having good cause in a genuine crisis situation to insist on extending its air defences to Finland. This had been one of the reasons for Kekkonen having spoken so warmly in favour of a nuclear-free Scandinavia. It was, too, the reason for Koivisto several times expressing his concern in the years 1983–85 at the superpowers' build-up of their nuclear arsenals in Europe. Weapons technology was making it ever easier to fire nuclear missiles from the sea and from the air, which shifted the source of military tension in northern Europe to the Soviet naval bases on the Kola Peninsula. This put even Lapland and all of northern Finland in jeopardy.

The significant turning point in great-power politics came in the spring of 1985 when the dynamic Mikhail Gorbachev was elected party leader of the Soviet Union. He at once instigated economic reforms at home and resumed talks on disarmament that same year with the United States. He was well aware of the dire condition of the Soviet economy and knew the Eastern

8.7: Bore ferry.

Bloc could not compete with the NATO countries in an arms race. In the autumn of 1987 Gorbachev and the president of the United States, Ronald Reagan, signed an agreement on the dismantling of all fixed medium-range missiles in Europe. Over the ensuing three years he would witness the entire Soviet Empire being dismantled, but in the spring of 1985 Gorbachev was in no way seen as a man who could lose. On the contrary, Soviet experts in the West assumed that he was just the man who could turn developments round and lead the Soviet Union into a new golden age.

President Koivisto of Finland was one of those optimists, and his favourable opinion of Gorbachev was reinforced on their first meeting in Moscow in September 1985. The Soviet leader made no objection to Finland's wish to convert its association agreement with EFTA into full membership. The immediate need to join was as a prerequisite for Finland to be able to play an equal part in a high-technology project for all EC and EFTA countries initiated by France. But the longer-term aim was to strengthen Finland's economic and socio-political integration with western Europe. When Finland became a full member of EFTA in November 1985, a new phase of integration began which would lead, ten years on, to membership of the European Union.

9

FINLAND AND EUROPE

The break-up of the Soviet Union in 1989–91 had far-reaching consequences for all of Europe and for great-power politics as a whole. The dissolution of the Empire led to the reunification of Germany in 1990, which coincided with the birth of the next phase of economic and political integration under the new name of the European Union, expanded from twelve to twenty-eight member states over the following quarter of a century. These chain reactions decisively affected the future development of Finland and the whole Baltic Sea region. The Finno-Soviet FCMA Treaty ceased to apply, and in the spring of 1992 the Finnish government set about a rapid realignment. In just three years Finland became a member of the EU, and embarked on systematically improving co-operation with NATO at the same time that neighbouring Baltic states had regained their independence and close ties with each other— which was especially the case between Finland and Estonia.

Economically, the twenty-five years that followed encompassed three significant turning points. After a severe economic crisis in the early Nineties, Finland experienced a swift recovery up until the global financial crisis of 2008, which drew the country into a lengthy economic recession through to the latter half of the 2010s. As an EU member state, Finland shouldered its share of the burden when having to deal with the various challenges that the EU was faced with during that decade. The EU's worsened relations with Russia—due to Russia's annexation of the Crimean Peninsula—required the Finns to participate in enforcing economic sanctions against Russia, and also further heightened their military co-operation with NATO. Once again, the Finns were reminded of how much their welfare, security and whole future was dependent on driving forces that they had almost no control over—and that they needed to be flexible, adjusting their position according to circumstance as wisely as possible.

Rapid Realignment to the West

Government ministers and captains of industry and commerce used to make regular visits to the Soviet Union, and Leningrad was a popular tourist destination for the general public. So Finns were far from ignorant of the difficulties the Soviet economy was undergoing in the late 1980s. Yet the final collapse of the Soviet Union in the autumn of 1991 came as just as much of a surprise to the Finns as it did to most other Europeans. The media took a keen interest in the emancipation of the Soviet Baltic states and in the main expressed the Finns' spontaneous support for the process. But this did not mean they could foresee a peaceful dismantling of the powerful Soviet Empire. On the contrary many feared, like President Koivisto, that events might deteriorate into armed conflict, which would upset the balance of security policy in the entire Baltic region. Any assumption that the Soviet army would voluntarily withdraw from the outposts they had occupied in 1945 was seen as completely unrealistic, not to say rash.

The fall of the Berlin Wall in the autumn of 1989 was the beginning of the end for "the great and mighty Soviet Union" and its satellite states. Within a year the closure of Red Army bases in the eastern half of central Europe had commenced. The peoples of the Baltic states openly and vociferously demanded their total liberation from the Soviet yoke, now reminding the world without circumlocution that the Sovietisation of the Baltic countries in 1940 had been effected by force. In Finland it was the Estonian struggle for independence which attracted the fullest expressions of sympathy, for obvious reasons, but the Finnish leadership was extremely concerned not to damage its good relations with the Soviet Union. President Koivisto gave an interview in the spring of 1990 in which he said that the Soviet Union still had legitimate security interests in the Baltic states. This aroused criticism in both the Baltic countries themselves and in Scandinavia—Finland's official line was described as cowardly and self-centred.

Criticism of Koivisto was more subdued within Finland, and not simply because he was president. The guarded attitude had its origins in the bitter experiences of the Winter War, when the country had been turned into a pawn in great-power politics and received no substantial military assistance from anywhere, despite profuse outpourings of sympathy. When Soviet troops bloodily engaged with liberation activists in Vilnius and Riga in January 1991, Koivisto defended Finland's wait-and-see policy with two astringent arguments: firstly Finland had to remain outside any conflict that might damage its Eastern policy; and secondly it would be irresponsible to encourage the people of the Baltic countries to step up hostilities if military support could not be provided in the event of armed conflict.

The Soviet Empire was crumbling at an ever-accelerating pace. In the late summer of 1991 a conservative wing within the Soviet Communist Party failed in an attempted coup in Moscow. This had dramatic consequences. It was put down by decisive action from the liberally inclined president Boris Yeltsin, who had been defying Gorbachev's authority more and more frequently and now emerged as the hero of the moment. The power battle in Moscow favoured the Baltic states, since Yeltsin, for tactical reasons, was backing their struggle for liberation. As the coup attempt collapsed, Estonia and Latvia declared their independence. When Russia recognised the sovereignty of Estonia on 24 August 1991 and soon afterwards that of the other two countries, most Western nations and Finland did the same. With that, Gorbachev had lost all real power. In early December 1991 the presidents of Russia, Ukraine and Belarus signed a union treaty which effectively dissolved the Soviet Union and put Gorbachev out of a job.

Finland's political leadership had consistently avoided expressing an opinion on the dramatic events in Moscow. But behind the scenes continual adjustments were being made to Finnish foreign policy to take account of the simultaneous unravelling of the Soviet Empire and the increasing economic and political integration of western Europe. In the spring of 1989 negotiations on transforming the customs unions of the EC and EFTA into a common market had been intensified. The reunification of Germany in 1990 gave added impetus to the decision to develop the EC into a political union. Germany, the economic giant, had to be securely tied to its neighbours. The more apprehensive of commentators spoke of preventing a German Fourth Reich. In the spring of 1992 the EC countries concluded a treaty in Maastricht, agreeing to a comprehensive programme of integration and changing the name from European Community to European Union. The official renaming took place on 1 November 1993.

Finland's principal export markets still lay in western Europe and so it wanted active participation in the process of further integration. In the autumn of 1990 it became clear that the neutral EFTA countries Austria and Sweden were aiming at full membership of the EC, which added to the pressure on

Finland to take the same path. The situation was complicated by the fact that EC membership was incompatible with its security policy obligations to the Soviet Union under the terms of the FCMA Treaty. So the government announced the same autumn that the reunification of Germany and the European integration process had nullified the articles of the FCMA Treaty relating to Finland's obligations to repel any German attack. In view of this, the country no longer considered itself bound by the restrictions in the Paris Peace Treaty of 1947 on Finnish peacetime military strength and weapons technology.

Immediately after the failed coup in Moscow in August 1991, the Finnish government took the initiative to open negotiations for a new treaty with the Soviet Union which would not impose the obligation of military co-operation. Moscow was paralysed and willing to compromise, and negotiations soon brought accord. By the late autumn of 1991 the two sides had finalised the text of a treaty which put no obstacles in the way of Finland allying itself politically or militarily with a third party. The dissolution of the Soviet Union prevented the ratification of the treaty in December 1991, but only a month thereafter it was signed by the Finnish government and the successor state Russia with all due ceremony in Helsinki.

The FCMA Treaty had steered Finnish foreign policy for almost forty-three years and had been an important element in stabilising and improving relations with its eastern neighbour. But in the spring of 1992 there was neither time for, nor interest in, drawing attention to this. Finland's shift towards the West was advancing by leaps and bounds. On 7 February 1992—the very day the Maastricht Treaty was signed—President Koivisto announced that the time was ripe for Finland to seek membership of the EC, and some four weeks later the Finnish government's formal application was handed in to the EC Commission. The case had been prepared on several fronts. The careful disengagement from the FCMA Treaty had been accompanied by unofficial soundings of the EC Commission, which showed understanding of Finland's still very cautious attitude to integration with western Europe in security policy, and there was frenetic lobbying in parliament, where a safe majority approved the government proposal to submit an application for membership.

The government deliberately refrained from discussing the security policy motives for, and consequences of, membership of the EC/EU. The situation in Russia continued to be unstable. It was therefore best not to draw too much attention to this aspect of Finland's westward realignment, especially as EU membership was far from assured. There first had to be agreement in negotiations with the EC/EU Commission; then the Accession Treaty had to be subjected to a referendum. So public debate concentrated on the potential economic consequences. Most attention was paid to Finnish agricultural subsidies, which it was feared might be lost through membership. This suited the government admirably as it deliberately manoeuvred the discussion round to secondary questions in order not to have to express opinions on the security policy implications.

Finland was governed in 1991–95 by a non-socialist majority government with the fundamentally agrarian Centre Party predominant, and this too ensured that farm subsidies and the future of agriculture came high on the agenda. In addition a very significant defence decision was in train: the purchase of sixty-four hyper-modern F/A-18 Hornet jet aeroplanes, manufactured by one of the leading producers of military aircraft in the USA. The acquisition was justified by reference to Finland's lack of a credible air defence all through the Cold War, owing to the restrictions of the FCMA Treaty.

Compared to previous defence investments, this one was enormous, costing 2,000 million dollars even without armaments. Before the matter came up for final debate in parliament the Finnish military performed detailed technical comparisons on a number of competing models. The choice of the Hornet was made on the grounds of its superior effectiveness in battle and readily available armaments. These were weighty reasons, of course, but when a parliamentary majority approved the purchase in May 1992, it was more to do with the fact that the American vendor undertook to arrange corresponding purchases for a similar sum.

The government emphatically denied that there were any security policy considerations behind the purchase of the Hornet, but everything points to the contrary. The acquisition of modern defence technology has always had a political dimension, since the supply and maintenance of equipment necessitates continuing collaboration with a foreign manufacturer. This aircraft meant that Finland's air defences became compatible with NATO's almost immediately. It was only two months earlier that Finland had submitted its application to the EC/EU, and it was doing all it could to show that it was a country whose defence and security policy would not be a burden for the EU. Finnish pilots were sent to the USA for training, and the first jet planes were flown across the Atlantic in 1995. Co-operation increased in the period 1996–2000 as fifty-six of these jets were assembled in Finland and gradually connected to the NATO satellite system and other technical infrastructure.

By the spring of 1994 Finland and its fellow applicant countries had reached agreement with the European Union. The government would have preferred to keep its domestic agricultural subsidy, which rewarded productivity, but had to relinquish it in favour of the EU system based on land area. As some measure of compensation the EU agreed that for a transition period a substantial proportion of Finland's farmland could be classified as "set-aside", which gave a higher area subsidy. The matter received a lot of coverage in the media, but in practice the negotiations were fairly painless. The EU, and not least Germany, welcomed the rich welfare states to the union to ease the centre of gravity towards the north and help with the subvention of the poorer members in southern Europe.

Before membership could come into effect, the treaty had to be ratified by a referendum. Opinion polls had been positive from the outset, and that lead was maintained right up to the vote in October 1994. President Koivisto had been very much in favour of membership, and so was his successor Martti Ahtisaari, who took up office in March 1994 and as an experienced United Nations diplomat was an excellent advocate for the EU. He and the government stressed the economic advantages of joining, while the opponents of EU membership pointed out that the Union's political integration would entail a loss of national sovereignty and a move into the NATO camp. But a significant proportion of Finns supported membership because they expected it to strengthen the country's external security and connections with central Europe. So a majority of the popular vote was cast in favour (56.9 per cent), and the European Union membership of Finland, Sweden and Austria began on 1 January 1995.

The Swedes and the Austrians did not experience membership as any dramatic turning point in their countries' histories. In Finland, on the other hand, the mood was almost solemn. The country's existence had been seriously threatened from the east on numerous occasions in the twentieth century, and many people regarded EU membership as a guarantee of national survival and Finland's western European cultural heritage. The feeling of a fresh start was accentuated by the fact that the economy had just started to recover from severe economic recession. In the spring of 1995 a Red-Blue majority coalition government came in under the leadership of the Social

9.1: The Finnish enginer Matti Makkonen invented the SMS function for mobile phone. It changed the way we communicate.

Democrat Paavo Lipponen. In Lipponen's eight years as prime minister, he and his government eagerly supported further economic and political integration with the EU. Given that Finland shared a 1,300-kilometre-long border with Russia, a strong union was understood to be in the national interest.

Sharp Turns in the Economy

Finland was by no means the only country to be hit by an economic crisis in the early 1990s. The deregulation of the international money markets had led to a sudden and uncontrolled surge in the availability of credit in the Western world in the mid-Eighties. A drastic rise in share and house prices followed. The downturn came in the spring of 1990 and the western European economy slid into general recession. The political upheavals in Europe were a contributory factor. The reunification of Germany was beginning to eat into that country's hitherto very strong economy, which in turn multiplied the problems in many smaller economies such as Sweden and Finland, both of which had a thriving trade with the Germans.

Finland had emerged fairly unscathed from the international slump of the 1970s, and was even able to mitigate the effect of minor economic setbacks during the Eighties by repeated devaluations of the national currency and through its stable clearing-account trade with the Soviet Union. Finland had the fastest growth of all Organisation for Economic Co-operation and Development (OECD) countries during the Eighties, which steadily augmented tax revenues and provided scope for substantial additions to social services and benefits. But when this boom was combined with the banks' ever more generous provision of credit, it caused an overheating which brought on a severe deterioration in the country's economy in 1990–91.

The steep decline was exacerbated when the Soviet Union announced in the summer of 1990 that they were switching from clearing-account trade to normal currency trade. The problems in the Soviet economy had already reduced Finland's exports there; in the spring of 1991 they almost ground to a halt, since the Russians lacked currency with which to pay. This depression in eastward trade was only short-term and resumed again fully the next year, but the psychological effect was considerable, as it coincided with a wave of bankruptcies and rampant unemployment. One could say that in the spring of 1991 Finland's economy was in free fall. The banks' credit losses were increasing exponentially, unemployment figures were rising by as many as 10,000 a month, and before the year was out the Bank of Finland had been constrained to devalue the mark by 12 per cent.

The devaluation came only six months after the government had decided to tie the value of the mark to the EU's artificial currency unit, the ECU, the embryo of the present euro. Having to relinquish that link so soon represented a blow to prestige, but in practice there was no alternative. The economic downturn gave constant nourishment to rumours of devaluation. While waiting for an exchange rate adjustment, companies did not convert their export income into marks, and so the currency reserves of the Bank of Finland were swiftly depleted, especially as systematic currency speculation was taking place at the same time. Problems remained even after devaluation and in the autumn of 1992 the fixed exchange rate had to be abandoned; like many other ECU-linked countries, Finland had to let the exchange rate "float"—be determined by prevailing market forces.

The intervention had the desired effect. The sky-high interest rates immediately began to come down and by 1995 the value of the mark had climbed back to its pre-flotation level. But the road to recovery was anything but easy. The huge drop in exchange rate not only made the profligate exchange credits suddenly much more expensive; it also caused a fall in prices and yet more bankruptcies. The banks' credit losses became so immense that most of them had to rely on state support and were soon driven into mergers. In the spring of 1995 the two biggest merchant banks in the country, Kansallis-Osake-Pankki and Suomen Yhdyspankki (Föreningsbanken) were amalgamated under the name Merita, and subsequently merged with three Scandinavian banks as Nordea Bank.

Bailing out the banks was a heavy burden on state finances, but most expensive by far was unemployment, which went way up, from 3 per cent to 16 per cent, in the period 1990–94. The situation was at its worst in the winter of 1993–94, when the authorities registered over half a million jobseekers. Such a rise in unemployment had only ever been experienced before in 1930s USA. The costs of unemployment and government countermeasures escalated, on top of which came the concomitant shrinkage of tax revenue. The result was an enormous budget deficit in 1992–93, when some 15 per cent of state expenditure had to be offset by borrowing. Cuts were made in welfare provision, but the uncompromising stance of the trade unions prevented any reduction in unemployment benefit.

The economy began to recover in the autumn of 1993, and over the next five years Finland showed a growth of around 5 per cent, which was rather better than the average among OECD countries. The trend continued well into the new millennium with annual growth figures of 3 to 4 per cent, better than the EU average. Despite the austerity measures, the safety net of the welfare state had been maintained fairly intact, which kept down the level of conflict and aided a speedy economic recovery. Yet the crisis of the Nineties left a profound scar on Finnish society as a whole and business life in particular. The brisk upturn in industrial profitability was mainly due to a rationalisation of unprofitable production and workforce in a very brief space of time. Such radical cuts in costs would hardly have been likely to succeed in more equable conditions. So the crisis gave extra impetus to the adaptation of trade and industry to the market, but since this adjustment was carried out mostly through automation or outsourcing of manufacture, employment figures did not improve at the same rate. Only after six years of healthy growth, at the start of the new millennium, did unemployment drop to under ten per cent.

The Nineties were also the period of the breakthrough of modern information technology. In many respects Finland was in the van of this global trend, but as IT is characterised by constant renewal and automation, it did not create jobs at the same rate as its profitability growth. Forest industries and the traditional steel and engineering industries have accounted for some 30 per cent each of the annual industrial portion of GDP ever since the 1950s. In the Nineties the electronics industry evolved into an almost equally important branch of the economy. The flagship, Nokia, decided to concentrate on the production of mobile telephones, and the whole Finnish telecoms industry entered a unique period of expansion, doubling its share of industrial GDP from 8 per cent to 16 per cent in the years 1995–2001. Of the other OECD countries, only the Czech Republic could show a corresponding expansion in its IT industry.

The rise and fall of Nokia as a global market leader in the mobile phone business is indeed a remarkable story. The Nokia group began in 1967 with the merger of three big companies in Finnish basic industry and brought together conditions for generous investment in the electronics side of the business, which, however, did not yield any notable dividends until the late Eighties. Its main electronics market was within Finland

9.2: Martti Ahtisaari, President of Finland 1994–2000, received the Nobel Peace Prize in 2008 for his results as peace negotiator.

and in the Soviet Union. In the mid-Eighties the Nokia name acquired a foothold in the British and US mobile phone markets, and by 1990 it had captured around 10 per cent of the global market. But the real turning point did not come until 1992 when the firm was obliged to choose a different course after a number of unsuccessful investments and the decline in trade to the east—and it opted for the mobile phone market. The new head of the business, Jorma Ollila, stole a march on his competitors by a deliberate investment in brand image and product development.

The principal change in direction was the transition from analogue to digital telephone systems. The move to what was called the GSM standard (Global System for Mobile Communications) took place in just a few years all over the industrialised world and created extremely favourable conditions for the profitable sale of mobile phones. As Nokia's strength lay in precisely this sphere, the firm succeeded in capturing a third of the global market in five years. And when Nokia's dominance of the market reached its peak during the years 2005–8, its share of the global sale of mobile phones was almost 40 per cent.

But thereafter a drastic fallback occurred, which was essentially a consequence of Nokia's inability to react rapidly enough to the accelerating demand for cleverly designed and consumer-friendly touchscreen phones, such as those introduced by Apple and Samsung. After a string of astonishingly bad attempts to catch up with these forerunners, Nokia finally sold its entire mobile phone business to the American multinational tech giant Microsoft in the autumn of 2013. As a result of this rather fortunate deal, the remaining parts of Nokia could instead concentrate on successfully producing infrastructures for wireless data communication. Meanwhile, a number of innovative and globally successful digital gaming companies were taking shape in Finland.

Many other mobile phone manufacturers were also negatively affected by similar economic peaks and troughs. However, Finland's loss was especially grave, as the remarkable growth of Nokia had given birth to a whole range of smaller IT companies, which were forced to change their production and marketing methodologies significantly. These challenges were further exacerbated by a recession of the Finnish economy in the aftermath of the global financial crisis of 2008. Furthermore, when the world economy gradually began to recover, it was revealed that many of Finland's other industries that also relied on export trade had lost their competitive edge in the global marketplace. The most obvious case was the Finnish forest industry, which as a consequence of the digital revolution and shrinking consumption of paper, had to hastily rethink its strategy and focus more on the production of pulp, bioenergy and other ecologically renewable items.

The outsourcing of industrial production to low-cost-production countries and the free flow of capital were other self-evident reasons for the loss of Finland's competitive edge. But in addition to these global driving forces, Finland also struggled with a number of domestic obstacles to growth. For example, the country's wages were uncompetitive internationally, the population was ageing and the influx of productive workers continued to diminish in the 2010s when Finnish baby boomers reached retirement age. During the previous economic recession in the early 1990s, the Finns had faced much graver problems: huge unemployment numbers and considerable cuts to welfare services. Drastic measures such as these were not necessary during the 2010s—although unemployment rates remained high until 2016, when the economy finally began to regrow. However, the price for maintaining Finland's welfare services was a substantial increase of the state debts, which according to available economic forecasts will continue to grow at least up until the early 2020s.

National Deconstruction?

Considering the process of Finland's technological transformation over the last hundred years, it is clear that Finnish receptivity to new technology goes back much further than the rise of Nokia and its IT clusters in the 1990s. Finland had caught up with the technological lead of the richest industrial nations throughout the twentieth century; but the greatest strides were taken during the structural changes of the post-war years, when the majority of the younger generation were uprooted, geographically and socially, creating and inhabiting a cultural vacuum in which a rapidly rising standard of living and improved levels of educational achievement enabled both individuals and society to make full use of the latest everyday technology.

The deregulation of national telecommunications and the media exemplifies this receptivity. In the 1930s the state had allocated to itself the monopoly on long-distance telephone calls, but as the local telephone networks were still run by private companies and co-operatives there was a commercial interest in satisfying consumer demand for modern and easily installed technology. This stimulated the entire industry and guaranteed a ready capacity for substantial private investment when the state agreed in the mid-Eighties to relinquish its monopoly on the national networks. The decision was related to the Finnish government's deliberate policy of joining western European co-operation on new technology, and it was among the first to recognise the social utility of free competition.

The deregulation of the broadcast media followed a similar pattern. In the mid-Seventies a privately owned cable TV company introduced regular transmissions in Finland. Its profitability rose considerably in the early Eighties when international satellite channels brought a demand for cable programmes, and when the state relaxed its national TV monopoly, a privately financed TV channel was set up in 1985. Four years later this was merged with the established MTV, which prior to that had broadcast via the state-run channels. With that merger, all commercial TV was assigned to a separate TV channel. Another commercial TV channel began national transmission in the latter half of the Nineties.

Because of the dominance of the American entertainment industry in the audiovisual field, there has never been any clear demarcation between a national and an international television culture. When the global satellite channels made their breakthrough in the mid-Nineties, the Finnish Broadcasting Company (Suomen Yleisradio), like other public-service TV companies, had to lower its educational ambitions and increase its output of light entertainment. The transformation did not happen overnight, but with the gradual transition to digital TV broadcasting in the years 2001–7 several additional state channels were inaugurated, facilitating a distinction between factual and entertainment programmes.

Developments in radio were almost identical. Commercial radio companies came on the scene in the mid-Eighties and soon captured a significant proportion of listeners, but the Finnish Broadcasting Company managed to reinvent itself by adapting programme content and embracing digital technology. Up until the 2010s, the production of the company was financed through TV licenses, but in 2013 parliament decided to create a universal taxation for this purpose. Naturally, this stabilised the state-controlled media, but was criticised by private media companies for disturbing the free competition between establishments within the media sector.

All these sweeping technological changes appeared at the same time as the break-up of the Soviet Union and Finland's political integration with western Europe. It is therefore no exaggeration to say that the most independent phase of Finland's political and cultural history took place at the dawn of the twenty-first century. It has become ever more difficult to pursue a policy of economic or cultural protectionism. The EU and the global digital culture have also been constantly creating new interfaces and practices that have begun to change the character of a specifically Finnish identity. But there are still some conservationist forces at work, among which the country's two official languages play an absolutely vital part.

At the end of the 2010s the English language had come to dominate many sectors of international trade, and academic and cultural life in Finland. Nevertheless, in homes and schools, in civic society and in the apparatus of state, Finnish—and in some areas Swedish—were, and still are, the dominant languages. By the end of 2018, Finland had 5.5 million inhabitants; of these, 4.8 million spoke Finnish as their mother tongue and 288,000 spoke Swedish as theirs, whereas speakers of other languages collectively constituted over 390,000 inhabitants. Finland had a very restrictive immigration policy during the Cold War, but it was gradually relaxed after the war had ended. This led to an increase in the country's influx of migrants, especially from Russian- (2018: 79,000), Estonian Estonian- (2018: 49,000) and Arabic Arabic- (21,000) speaking populations.

Linguistic uniformity has facilitated the preservation of national culture, of course, and has produced excellent results in international comparisons of educational achievement in schools, but according to some studies, linguistic homogeneity is not necessarily an advantage for a small nation. It hinders the integration of immigrants into society and can even militate against the influx of skilled workers, something which a high-tech country cannot afford in the long run. But the problem will probably resolve itself without much difficulty. The educated classes in Finland already speak English fairly fluently, and within a few decades it may well be used as a lingua franca between many of the language communities in the country.

What then will remain of Finland's distinctive characteristics? Pessimists assert that continuing globalisation will inevitably bring about a gradual disintegration of the national culture and a corresponding dismantling of the welfare state. Many trends in Finnish society and in the Western world in general seem to point in that direction. Digital culture weakens any specific territorial anchorage, which in turn relativises any sense of place and home; and a global redistribution of industrial manufacturing is in progress which is very quickly transferring capital and industrial jobs to Asia and other regions with lower production costs than western Europe or the United States.

On the other hand, optimists do not see digital culture, including social media, as a threat, but as a unique chance to renew and strengthen Finland's national culture and regional traditions. Through the internet, citizens can more easily maintain contact with their local communities, and preserve the linguistic features that are unique to each one—from dialects to slang to minority tongues. Of course, there is still a question yet to be answered: does reaching out to other local inhabitants using these new types of digital technology actually strengthen community solidarity? The recent rise of populism in Western democracies has shown that the web can function as an efficient instrument that can be used to bring people together as well as divide them into oppositional groups.

European Perspectives

Finland's membership of the EU resulted in the country becoming increasingly integrated with western and central

Europe both politically and economically. And even though this integration also inevitably included a number of new responsibilities and restrictions, the overall consequences of Finland's membership were undoubtedly positive. In contrast to a country with large energy resources, like Norway for example, the Finnish industry has no protection against radical shifts in the world economy. Moreover, the Finns have been directly influenced by or dragged into geopolitical conflicts many times in history—more than other Scandinavian countries—because Finland shares a border with Russia. In both these respects, EU membership gave Finland greater stability and safety, especially when Europe was shaken by a number of economic problems and international conflicts after 2008.

The foundation for Finland's integration with the EU was already solid. The majority of Finnish exports had been directed to western Europe since the Cold War era, so Finland's EU membership only strengthened these trade relations further. During the 1990s, the leading EU countries—France and Germany—eagerly supported the implementation of the economic decisions outlined in the Maastricht Treaty of 1992. In line with this, they had decided with nine other EU member states to introduce a common currency and aim for a more centralised banking system by 1999.

Finland participated in this economic integration with enthusiasm: a safe majority of Finnish MPs voted in favour of the EU's financial reforms during the spring of 1998. However, the outcome was the opposite in Sweden, where in 2003, the decision was instead put to the people through a referendum—which resulted in a clear vote against joining the Eurozone. A similar contrast between Sweden and Finland was discernible in their respective attitudes towards political integration with the EU. While Sweden advocated the distribution of power among individual states, Finland coveted a political union held together by a supranational authority.

Finland's EU policy was boldly directed by the Social Democrat prime minister Paavo Lipponen from 1995 until 2003—he championed a politically strong and consensual union in both word and deed. Lipponen's arguments were posited on three main tenets: firstly, Finland had approved the provisions of the Maastricht Treaty; secondly, it was logical for economic integration to go hand in hand with political coordination; and thirdly, it was in Finland's national interest for the EU to have strong supranational structures and for Finland to be sitting at the table whenever the EU's future was being decided. Lipponen was supported by President Martti Ahtisaari, whose most public contribution in the European context was his successful mediation to end the Kosovo conflict in 1999.

The parliamentary election result of spring 2003 meant that the Centre Party—who were more Eurosceptical than the Social Democrats—would govern Finland for the next eight years. But this was not the only reason why sentiments towards the EU gradually became more cautious in Finland. In the first five years of membership, the Finns were genuinely enthusiastic about and satisfied with the Union, which was reflected through the Finnish media's frequent news broadcasts from Brussels and Strasbourg. For many Finns, membership was a conclusive sign that the Cold War was over. There was also widespread recognition that membership benefited the country's economy—an obvious reason why the single currency was adopted so painlessly. When membership became a feature of everyday life, public opinion turned more critical, not least when the Union faced additional challenges.

This change of attitude was hardly unexpected. In many regards it reflected views in the older EU countries and was thus a sign of the normalisation of Finnish opinion towards the EU. A further aspect of this change of mood was that Finland itself adopted a new national constitution in the spring of 2000

9.3: Finnish euro coins from 2000 and 2013.

which strengthened parliamentary democracy. The presidency lost its previous central role in the formation of governments and was henceforth allowed to lead the country's foreign policy only in co-operation with the government. Another substantial loss of the presidential power was that EU policy would from then on not be classified as foreign affairs, from which followed that it was normally the prime minister who represented Finland in the European Council, the intergovernmental organ of the EU.

The reform thus introduced a real transfer of power from president to parliament and government. The president continues to be elected by direct popular vote, however, which means the office-holder may not always have the confidence of parliament.

The constitution came into effect on 1 March 2000 when the Social Democrat Tarja Halonen began her initial term as president. As the reform happened to coincide with the incumbency of the country's first female head of state, she had the challenge of re-asserting the authority of the office in both respects. Her election victory had been narrow, but by demonstrating the scope of her remit she established gradually a stronger foundation for her leadership on foreign policy matters outside the EU. She was re-elected in the spring of 2006 and was succeeded by former chairman of the Conservative party, and Minister of Finances from 1996 to 2003, Sauli Niinistö in 2012. Niinistö was re-elected in 2018 for his second and last term.

Tarja Halonen had been foreign minister from 1995 to 2000 and so had taken part in the formulation of the new foreign policy, which included above all an end to the use of the "neutrality" concept after entry into the EU. Co-operation with NATO had burgeoned from 1994, when Finland joined the "Partnership for Peace" programme, which together with the concurrently procured sixty-four well-equipped American

9.4: Sauli Niinistö, President of Finland since 2012, in dialogue with Jens Stoltenberg, Secretary General of NATO.

F/A-18 Hornet fighter and attack air crafts provided the basis for a systematic and since then ever deepening synchronisation of Finland's and NATO's military preparedness. But the time was not yet felt to be right for full membership. In the spring of 1995 the government confirmed that its security policy objective was military non-alliance and an independent defence, but it did not exclude a reassessment if there were to be significant changes in European security mechanisms.

There were several adjustments made to these commitments in the years 1997–2016, which underlined Finland's willingness to co-operate with NATO and readiness to seek NATO membership whenever it was considered appropriate. Irrespective of this, there were no unambiguous signs in the late 2010s that Finland was in the process of applying for full membership of NATO. Their circumspect approach was not just because the majority of Finns were not in favour of membership under the prevailing circumstances. Finland's co-operation with NATO was smooth even without membership, and involved liaising closely with Sweden, which had a long history of being a "silent member" of NATO. Since Russia's annexation of the Crimean Peninsula in 2014, the synergy between Finland and Sweden has intensified. For tactical reasons, many Finnish and Swedish politicians have preferred to describe their mutual military manoeuvres and other far-reaching security plans as an alternative to co-operation with NATO. But in practice, their military partnership was directly connected to and motivated by planning their defense of the Baltic Sea region in close collaboration with NATO.

Behind these issues lay a partial unwillingness to alter the balance of defense policy too quickly in the Baltic region. The Baltic states received their NATO memberships at the same time that they joined the EU in 2004, which reinforced the security and stability of all the EU countries around the Baltic

Sea considerably. This change would often be used by the Swedish and Finnish governments as an argument for why their NATO membership was not necessary under concurrent circumstances. However, their wait-and-see policy was obviously also rooted in a silent calculation of their national interest. Neither Sweden nor Finland were enticed by the idea that as NATO members they would be burdened with the responsibility of having to play a substantial role in defending the Baltic states in a military conflict with Russia. This was especially troubling, as other European NATO members had not shown in any way that they were prepared to take on more responsibility in defense of the EU.

The history of Finland provided many examples of how shifts of power in the region had led to unforeseen chain reactions and conflicts that all had an effect on the country and its inhabitants in their various ways. However, history also showed that many of these changes in security policy had been unusually beneficial for Finland. Its development into a nation and an independent republic would not have been possible without the great European wars. Of course, the fact that these fateful events had a positive outcome cannot simply be ascribed to strategic decision-making and assertive action at a national level. Then, just as now, many turning points in Finland's history were unforeseen consequences of decisive change in great-power policy, the world economy and the political culture in Finland.

BIBLIOGRAPHY

Ahvenainen, Jorma (ed.), *Suomen taloushistoria 2. Teollistuva Suomi*, Helsinki: Tammi, 1982.

Alapuro, Risto, *State and Revolution in Finland*, Berkeley: University of California Press, 1988.

————, *Suomen älymystö Venäjän varjossa*, Helsinki: Tammi, 1997.

Alasuutari, Pertti, *Toinen tasavalta. Suomi 1946–1994*, Tampere: Vastapaino, 1996.

Åström, Sven-Erik, *Samhällsplanering och regionbildning i kejsartidens Helsingfors. Studier i stadens inre differentiering 1810–1910*, Helsingfors: Helsingfors stad, 1957.

————, *From Tar to Timber. Studies in Northeast European Forest Exploitation and Foreign Trade 1660–1860*, Helsinki: Societas scientiarum Fennica, 1988.

Bayly, C. A., *The Birth of the Modern World 1780–1914: Global Connections and Comparisons*, Malden, MA: Blackwell, 2004.

Castells, Manuel and Pekka Himanen, *The Information Society and Welfare State: The Finnish Model*, Oxford: Oxford University Press, 2002.

Charmley, John, *Churchill. The End of Glory*, London: Sceptre, 1993.

Davies, Norman, *A History of Europe*, Oxford: Oxford University Press, 1996.

Englund, Peter, *Det hotade huset. Adliga föreställningar om samhället under stormaktstiden*, Stockholm: Atlantis, 1989.

Engman, Max, *Lejonet och dubbelörnen. Finlands imperiella decennier 1830–1890*, Stockholm: Atlantis, 2000.

————, *Pietarin suomalaiset*, Helsinki: WSOY, 2004.

————, *Långt farväl: Finland mellan Sverige och Ryssland efter 1809*, Stockholm: Atlantis, 2009.

Ericson Wolke, Lars, Göran Larsson and Nils Erik Villstrand, *Trettioåriga kriget: Europa i brand 1618–1648*, Lund: Historiska media, 2005.

BIBLIOGRAPHY

Gallén, Jarl, *Finland i medeltidens Europa. Valda uppsatser*, Helsingfors: SLS, 1998.

Grünthal, Riho (ed.), *Ennen, muinoin. Miten menneisyyttämme tutkitaan*, Helsinki: SKS, 2002.

Gustafsson, Harald, *Nordens historia. En europeisk region under 1200 år*, Lund: Studentlitteratur, 2007.

Haapala, Pertti, *Tehtaan valossa. Teollistuminen ja työväestön muodostuminen Tampereella 1820–1920*, Tampere: Vastapaino, 1986.

Haapala, Pertti (ed.), *Talous, valta ja valtio. Tutkimuksia 1800-luvun Suomesta*, Tampere: Vastapaino, 1992.

Häikiö, Martti, *Globalisaatio. Telekommunikaation maailmanvalloitus 1992–2000. Nokia Oyj:n historia 3*, Helsinki: Edita, 2001.

Heikkilä, Tuomas and Maiju Lehmijoki-Gardner, *Keskiajan kirkko. Uskonelämän muotoja läntisessä kristikunnassa*, Helsinki: SKS, 2002.

Hietala, Marjatta, *Services and Urbanization at the Turn of the Century*, Helsinki: Finnish Historical Society, 1987.

Himanen, Pekka et al., *Globaali tietoyhteiskunta. Kehityssuuntia Piilaaksosta Singaporeen*, Helsinki: Tekes, 2004.

Hjerppe, Riitta, *The Finnish Economy 1860–1985. Growth and Structural Change*, Helsinki: Bank of Finland, 1989.

Hobsbawm, Eric, *Age of Extremes. The Short Twentieth Century 1914–1991*, London: Abacus, 1994.

Huldt, Bo et al. (eds), *Finnish and Swedish Security. Comparing National Policies*, Stockholm: Försvarshögskolan, 2001.

Hurri, Merja, *Kulttuuriosasto. Symboliset taistelut, sukupolvitaistelut ja sananvapaus viiden pääkaupunkilehden toimituksissa 1945–1980*, Tampere: Tampereen yliopisto, 1993.

Huurre, Matti, *9000 vuotta Suomen esihistoriaa*, Helsinki: 1995.

———, *Nokia: The Inside Story*, Helsinki: Edita, 2002.

Jalava, Marja, *J. V. Snellman. Mies ja suurmies*, Helsinki: Tammi, 2006.

Jalonen, Olli, *Kansa kulttuurien virroissa. Tuontikulttuurin suuntia ja sisältöjä Suomessa itsenäisyyden aikana*, Helsinki: Otava, 1985.

Jokisipilä, Markku, *Aseveljiä vai liittolaisia? Suomi, Saksan liittosopimusvaatimukset ja Rytin-Ribbentropin-sopimus*, Helsinki: SKS, 2004.

Jussila, Osmo, *Suomen suuriruhtinaskunta 1809–1917*, Helsinki: WSOY, 2004.

Jutikkala, Eino, Yrjö Kaukiainen and Sven-Erik Åström, *Suomen taloushistoria 1. Agraarinen Suomi*, Helsinki: Tammi, 1980.

BIBLIOGRAPHY

Jutikkala, Eino, *Kuolemalla on aina syynsä. Maailman väestöhistoria ääriviivoja*, Helsinki: WSOY, 1994.

Kallenautio, Jorma, *Suomi kylmän rauhan maailmassa. Suomen ulkopolitiikka Porkkalan palautuksesta 1955 Euroopan Unionin jäsenyyteen 1995*, Helsinki: SKS, 2005.

Karisto, Antti, Pentti Takala and Ilkka Haapola, *Matkalla nykyaikaan. Elintason elämäntavan ja sosiaalipolitiikan muutos Suomessa*, Helsinki: WSOY, 1998.

Karonen, Petri, *Pohjoinen suurvalta. Ruotsi ja Suomi 1521–1809*, Helsinki: WSOY, 2008.

Karonen, Petri (ed.), *Hopes and Fears for the Future in Early Modern Sweden 1500–1850*, Helsinki: SKS, 2009.

Kaukiainen, Yrjö, *A History of Finnish Shipping*, London: Routledge, 1993.

Kervanto-Nevanlinna, Anja and Laura Kolbe (eds), *Suomen kulttuurihistoria 3. Oma maa ja maailma*, Helsinki: Tammi, 2003.

Kettunen, Pauli, *Poliittinen liike ja sosiaalinen kollektiivisuus. Tutkimus sosialidemokratiasta ja ammattiyhdistysliikkeestä Suomessa 1918–1930*, Helsinki: SHS,1986.

Kiander, Jaakko and Pentti Vartia, *Suuri lama. Suomen 1990-luvun kriisi ja talouspoliittinen keskustelu*, Helsinki: Taloustieto, 1998.

Kirby, David and Merja-Liisa Hinkkanen, *The Baltic and North Seas*, London: Routledge, 2000.

Kirby, David, *Northern Europe in the Early Modern Period. The Baltic World 1492–1772*, London: Longman, 1990.

Klinge, Matti et al., *Kungliga akademien i Åbo 1640–1808. Helsingfors universitet 1640–1990, 1. delen*, Helsingfors: Otava, 1988.

Klinge, Matti, *Let us be Finns: Essays on History*, Helsinki: Otava, 1990.

Knapas, Rainer and Nils Erik Forsgård (eds), *Suomen kulttuurihistoria 2. Tunne ja tieto*, Helsinki: Tammi, 2002.

Konttinen, Riitta, *Sammon takojat. Nuoren Suomen taiteilijat ja suomalaisuuden kuvat*, Helsinki: Otava, 2001.

Kuisma, Markku, *Metsäteollisuuden maa. Suomi, metsät ja kansainvälinen järjestelmä 1620–1920*, Helsinki: SHS, 1993.

Kuisma, Markku (ed.), *Metsäteollisuuden maa. 5. Kriisi ja kumous: Metsäteollisuus ja maailmantalouden murros 1973–2008*, Helsinki: SKS, 2008.

BIBLIOGRAPHY

Kujala, Antti, *Venäjän hallitus ja Suomen työväenliike 1899–1905*, Helsinki: SHS, 1996.

———, *Miekka ei laske leikkiä. Suomi suuressa Pohjan sodassa 1700–1714*, Helsinki: SKS, 2001.

———, *The Crown, the Nobility and the Peasants 1630–1713: Tax, Rent and Relations of Power*, Helsinki: SKS, 2003.

Kuvaja, Christer, *Försörjning av en ockupationsarmé. Den ryska arméns underhållssystem i Finland 1713–1721*, Åbo: Åbo Akademi, 1999.

Lackman, Matti, *Suomen vai Saksan puolesta? Jääkäriliikkeen ja jääkäripataljoonan 27:n (1915–1918) synty, luonne, mielialojen vaihteluita ja sisäisiä kriisejä*, Helsinki: Otava, 2000.

Lähteenmäki, Maria (ed.), *The Flexible Frontier. Change and Continuity in Finnish-Russian Relations*, Helsinki: Aleksanteri-instituutti, 2007.

Larsson, Lars-Olof, *Gustav Vasa—landsfader eller tyrann?*, Stockholm: Prisma, 2002.

Lehtonen, Tuomas M. S. and Timo Joutsivo (eds), *Suomen kulttuurihistoria 1. Taivas ja maa*, Helsinki: Tammi, 2002.

Liikanen, Erkki, *Brysselin päiväkirjat 1990–1994*, Helsinki: Otava, 1995.

Liikanen, Ilkka, *Fennomania ja kansa. Joukkojärjestäytymisen läpimurto ja Suomalaisen puolueen synty*, Helsinki: SHS, 1995.

Lipponen, Paavo, *Kohti Eurooppaa*, Helsinki: Tammi, 2001.

Luntinen, Pertti, *The Imperial Russian Army and Navy in Finland 1808–1918*, Helsinki: Finnish Historical Society, 1997.

Manninen, Ohto (ed.), *Itsenäistymisen vuodet I–III*, Helsinki: VAPK-Kustannus, 1992–1993.

Meinander, Henrik, *Tasavallan tiellä. Suomi kansalaissodasta 2000-luvulle*, Espoo: Schildt, 1999.

———, *Den nödvändiga grannen. Studier och inlägg*, Esbo: Schildt, 2001.

Myllyntaus, Timo, *Electrifying Finland: The Transfer of a New Technology into a Late Industrializing Society*, London: Macmillan, 1991.

Odelberg, Wilhelm, *Viceadmiral Carl Olof Cronstedt. Levnadsteckning och tidsskildring*, Stockholm: Folk och Försvar, 1954.

Ojala, Jari, Jari Eloranta and Jukka Jalava (eds), *The Road to Prosperity: An Economic History of Finland*, Helsinki: SKS, 2006.

Ollila, Anne, *Jalo velvollisuus. Virkanaisena 1800-luvun lopun Suomessa*, Helsinki: SKS, 1998.

Peltonen, Matti (ed.), *Rillumarei ja valistus. Kulttuurikahakoita 1950-luvun Suomessa*, Helsinki: SHS, 1996.

BIBLIOGRAPHY

Polvinen, Tuomo, *Imperial Borderland: Bobrikov and the attempted Russification of Finland 1898–1904*, London: Hurst, 1995.

Rasila, Viljo, Eino Jutikkala and Anneli Mäkelä-Alitalo, *Suomen maatalouden historia 1. Perinteisen maatalouden aika: Esihistoriasta 1870-luvulle*, Helsinki: SKS, 2003.

Rentola, Kimmo, *Niin kylmää että polttaa. Kommunistit, Kekkonen ja Kreml 1947–1958*, Helsinki: Otava, 1997.

Saarikangas, Kirsi, Pasi Mäenpää and Minna Sarantola-Weiss (eds), *Suomen kulttuurihistoria 4. Koti, kylä, kaupunki*, Helsinki: Tammi, 2004.

Salokangas, Raimo, *Aikansa oloinen. Yleisradion historia 2: 1949–1996*, Helsinki: YLE, 1996.

Savolainen, Raimo (ed.), *Suomen keskushallinnon historia 1809–1996*, Helsinki: Edita, 1996.

Schauman, August, *Från sex årtionden i Finland. Förra delen*, Helsingfors: Schildt, 1922.

Screen, J. E. O., *Mannerheim: The Years of Preparation*, London: Hurst, 1970.

——— *Mannerheim: The Finnish Years*, London: Hurst, 2000.

Skuncke, Marie-Christine and Henrika Tandefelt (eds), *Riksdag, kaffehus och predikstol. Frihetstidens politiska kultur 1766–1772*, Stockholm: Atlantis, 2003.

Suolahti, Gunnar, *Elämää Suomessa 1700-luvulla*, Helsinki: SKS, 1991.

Suomi, Juhani, *Liennytyksen akanvirrassa. Urho Kekkonen 1972–1976*, Helsinki: Otava, 1998.

Turtola, Martti, *Erik Heinrichs, Mannerheimin ja Paasikiven kenraali*, Helsinki: Otava, 1988.

Vihavainen, Timo, *Kansakunta rähmällään. Suomettumisen lyhyt historia*, Helsinki: Otava, 1991.

Vilkuna, Kustaa J. H., *Viha. Perikato, katkeruus ja kertomus isostavihasta*, Helsinki: SKS, 2005.

Wolff, Charlotta, *Vänskap och makt. Den svenska politiska eliten och upplysningstidens Frankrike*, Stockholm: Atlantis, 2005.

Wrede, Johan, *Världen enligt Runeberg. En biografisk och idéhistorisk studie*, Helsingfors: SLS, 2005.

INDEX

INDEX

INDEX

INDEX

INDEX

INDEX